SQL Server™
Essential
Reference

New
Riders

Other Books by New Riders Publishing

Windows NT Power Toolkit
Stu Sjouwerman and Ed Tittel,
0-7357-0922-x

Planning for Windows 2000
Eric K. Cone, Jon Boggs, and Sergio
Perez, 0-7357-0048-6

Windows NT DNS
Michael Masterson, Herman Knief,
Scott Vinick, and Eric Roul,
1-56205-943-2

Windows NT Network
Management: Reducing Total Cost
of Ownership
Anil Desai, 1-56205-946-7

Windows NT Performance
Monitoring, Benchmarking and
Tuning
Mark T. Edmead and Paul Hinsburg,
1-56205-942-4

Windows NT Registry: A Settings
Reference
Sandra Osborne, 1-56205-941-6

Windows NT TCP/IP
Karanjit Siyan, 1-56205-887-8

Windows NT Terminal Server and
Citrix MetaFrame
Ted Harwood, 1-56205-944-0

Cisco Router Configuration and
Troubleshooting, 2nd Edition
Mark Tripod, 0-7357-0999-8

Exchange System Administration
Janice Rice Howd, 0-7357-0081-8

Implementing Exchange Server
Doug Hauger, Marywynne Leon,
and William C. Wade III,
1-56205-931-9

Network Intrusion Detection:
An Analyst's Handbook
Stephen Northcutt, 0-7357-0868-1

Understanding Data
Communications, Sixth Ed.
Gilbert Held, 0-7357-0036-2

SQL Server System Administration
Sean Baird, Chris Miller, et al.,
1-56205-955-6

Domino System Administration
Rob Kirkland, 1-56205-948-3

Understanding Directory Services
Doug & Beth Sheresh, 0-7357-0910-6

Understanding the Network: A
Practical Guide to Internetworking
Michael J. Martin, 0-7357-0977-7

Internet Information Services
Administration
Kelli Adam, 0-7357-0022-2

Inside Windows 2000 Server
William Boswell, 1-56205-929-7

Windows 2000 Active Directory
Edgar Brovick, Doug Hauger, William C.
Wade III, 0-7357-0870-3

SMS 2 Administration
Darshan Doshi and Michael Lubanski,
0-7357-0082-6

Windows 2000 User Management
Lori M. Sanders
1-56205-886-X

Windows 2000 Deployment and
Desktop Management
Jeffrey Ferris, 0-7357-0975-0

Windows 2000 Routing and
Remote Access Service
Kackie Charles, 0-7357-0951-3

Windows 2000 Professional
Jerry Honeycutt, 0-7357-0950-5

SQL Server™
Essential
Reference

Sharon Dooley

New Riders

201 West 103rd Street, Indianapolis, Indiana 46290

SQL Server™ Essential Reference

Copyright © 2000 by New Riders Publishing

International Standard Book Number: 0-7357-0864-9

Library of Congress Catalog Card Number: 99-068977

04 03 02 01 00   7 6 5 4 3 2 1

Interpretation of the printing code: The rightmost double-digit number is the year of the book's printing; the rightmost single-digit number is the number of the book's printing. For example, the printing code 00-1 shows that the first printing of the book occurred in 2000.

Composed in Quark and MCPdigital by New Riders Publishing

Printed in the United States of America

FIRST EDITION: *July, 2000*

Trademarks

Warning and Disclaimer

Publisher
David Dwyer

Executive Editor
Al Valvano

Acquisitions Editor
Theresa Gheen

Development Editor
Ginny Bess

Managing Editor
Gina Brown

Product Marketing Manager
Stephanie Layton

Manager of Publicity
Susan Petro

Project Editor
Elise Walter

Copy Editor
Keith Cline

Indexer
Lisa Stumpf

Technical Reviewers
Wayne Snyder
Neil Pike

Proofreader
Debbie Williams

Compositor
Amy Parker

Contents

About the Author

Sharon Dooley's love affair with computers began 35 years ago when she learned to write FORTRAN for the IBM 7094. Since then she has worked with a variety of mainframe, minicomputer, and PC database management systems including SQL Server, Sybase, IMS, Oracle, and IDMS (not to mention the venerable dBase). A true veteran of Microsoft's SQL Server, Sharon has been working with the product since the OS/2-based Version 1.0. Since then, she has maintained an active consulting practice specializing in Microsoft SQL Server. She works as a database designer, database administrator, and as a mentor for application developers who are writing front ends in Visual Basic and ASP. For 12 years, Sharon has been writing Transact-SQL code for stored procedures, triggers and views that implement complex security schemes for applications, such as document image management, telephony market research, sales force automation, and marketing communications tracking. She is skilled at analyzing and solving performance problems.

Well-known as an instructor and author, Sharon continues to share her knowledge with the IT community. Currently an instructor for Learning Tree International, Sharon has also authored many of their training seminars, including *SQL Server 7 Administration, SQL Server 6 System Administration, Optimizing SQL Server Database and Application Performance*, and *Sybase System 10 Hands-On Introduction*. She is the technical editor of Learning Tree's *SQL Server 6 Introduction* and *Developing SQL Server Applications with Visual Basic* courses. In addition, Sharon frequently presents at professional conferences and contributes articles to www.swynk.com. She faithfully follows SWYNK's SQL Server list servers where her explanations and answers to questions have lead to her being referred to as a "SQL Server goddess." She is also the lead author of *Professional SQL Server 6.5 Administration* published by Wrox Press, and served as technical reviewer for Joe Celko's *Instant SQL Programming* (Wrox Press).

Among her other positions and achievements, Sharon is a member of the Professional Association for SQL Server (PASS) Web Services Committee, which is responsible for (among other things) developing a SQL Server-based Knowledge Portal that provides a repository of SQL Server information. Ms. Dooley also holds a bachelor's degree in Computer and Information Sciences (Magna cum Laude) from the University of Pennsylvania.

When Sharon can tear herself away from SQL Server, she is an avid vegetable gardener and entertains her three feline housemates.

About the Reviewers

These reviewers contributed their considerable hands-on expertise to the entire development process for *SQL Server Essential Reference*. As this book was being written, these dedicated professionals reviewed all the material for technical content, organization, and flow. Their feedback was critical to ensuring that the content of this book fits our reader's need for the highest-quality technical information.

Neil Pike is an independent consultant living near Cambridge in the United Kingdom. He has been working in IT since 1985. Between 1985 and 1992, he worked as an MVS/CICS/VTAM Systems Programmer, a DB2/Oracle/SUPRA dba, and he did mainframe and PC development work in Assembler, C, COBOL, and PL/1. In 1992 he switched to working full-time on client/server infrastructure using Windows 3.x, DOS, OS/2 1.x, LAN Manager, and SQL Server 1.1. Since then he has worked with all beta and release versions of Windows NT and SQL Server together with the rest of the BackOffice suite. He specializes in infrastructure, architecture, performance, and diagnosis of PCs, LANs, WANs, firewalls, routers, network protocols, server hardware, Citrix/NTTE, mainframe connectivity, Windows NT, and SQL Server. He is an MCSE and MVP.

Wayne Snyder has been a Database Administrator and Project Lead for development, production, and support environments since 1981. As an instructor/consultant for IKON Education Services, in Charlotte, North Carolina, he has been teaching since 1995. He is one of approximately half a dozen people certified to teach internal SQL classes to Microsoft employees. During Wayne's tenure at IKON, he has participated in newsgroups and online chats on the Internet, eventually winning Microsoft's prized award for Most Valued Professional (MVP). (You may receive no-charge assistance from Wayne and the other SQL Server MVPs at msnews.microsoft.com).

Wayne also writes for *SQL Server Magazine*, writes technical reviews of SQL Server books for several publishers, and is working on his own book about English Query. Learnkey International has recently produced a video and CD-ROM to assist those who would seek additional help in passing the Microsoft SQL Server exams (www.learnkey.com). Wayne authored the original material, and appears on the videos and CDs.

He has been using SQL Server since its first release. Mr. Snyder is also an MCT, MCSE, and has received several technical awards from Unisys for database strategies and techniques developed during his tenure at Unisys Healthcare Systems as well as the IKON Top Performer Award for SouthEast District in 1999. Wayne can be contacted at wssnyder@ikon.com.

Dedication

To my three faithful feline companions (who have contributed to this book largely by walking on my keyboard): Tiny Zebra, the ever-skittish mackerel tabby who's been with me since she was five weeks old; Tigger, 14 pounds of ginger tabby with the vocabulary of a sailor; and Patchwork, the "baby" who looks like a badly pieced quilt and whose life revolves around making Zebra miserable.

Finally, in loving memory of Tank, Maine Coon cat *extraordinaire*, 1987–2000.

Acknowledgements

A lot of people have helped me on the way to seeing this book (the one I swore I would never write) into print. First, I want to thank my peer reviewers, Neil Pike and Wayne Snyder, for their comments, criticisms, corrections, questions, and suggestions. The book is far better because of them. And special thanks must go to Andrew Zanevsky, whose final review of the book caught all sorts of things that I had missed.

I've benefited from the challenging and thoughtful questions of my many students.

I've learned a lot from the folks on the MSSQL7 list at www.swynk.com and a lot of that knowledge flowed into this book.

I'm particularly grateful for the continual support and discovery sharing of Learning Tree's SQL Server curriculum team—Geoff Ballard, Jamie Beidleman, Charles Kangai, Efrem Perry, and Bobbie Townsend—love and thanks to all of you.

This book has been a long time in the "birthing," and I really appreciate the help I have received from people at New Riders: Amy Michaels, who initially asked me to write the book, and with whom I had amusing email discussions about who owned the rights to the "SQL Server action figures"; Al Valavano, who shepherded this book through its early stages; Theresa Gheen, who beat me up and made me get it done; and Ginny Bess, whose eye for detail and structure turned the book from a somewhat formless mass into a clear shape.

Many of the figures in this book are taken from Learning Tree International's SQL Server Database Administration course. I appreciate being given permission to use them, and want to thank John Opiola, Product Manager for Learning Tree's SQL Server curriculum, for granting this permission as well as for being a great Product Manager.

Your Feedback Is Valuable

As the reader of this book, *you* are our most important critic and commentator. We value your opinion and want to know what we're doing right, what we could do better, what areas you would like to see us publish in, and any other words of wisdom you're willing to pass our way.

As the Executive Editor for the Networking team at New Riders Publishing, I welcome your comments. You can fax, email, or write me directly to let me know what you did or didn't like about this book—as well as what we can do to make our books stronger.

Please note that I cannot help you with technical problems related to the topic of this book, and that due to the high volume of mail I receive, I might not be able to reply to every message.

When you write, please be sure to include this book's title and author, as well as your name and phone or fax number. I will carefully review your comments and share them with the author and editors who worked on the book.

Fax: 317-581-4663

Email: nrfeedback@newriders.com

Mail: Al Valvano
        Executive Editor
        New Riders Publishing
        201 West 103rd Street
        Indianapolis, IN 46290 USA

Introduction

Welcome to *SQL Server Essential Reference*. It's important to understand what this book is, as well as what it is not. My goal in writing this book is to provide information that helps SQL Server Administrators do their jobs. This is not a tutorial, though I do try to explain topics clearly. I think it is very important that you understand the *why* and not just the *how*. Thus, I don't walk you through every SQL Server Wizard (in fact, you'll find very few discussions of wizards in this book). If you need to be told to "Click Next," then this book is definitely not for you!

I'm also not going to take you through every screen in Enterprise Manager. Instead, I am going to show you important aspects of the GUI that you might otherwise miss. I will show you how to perform specific tasks with Transact-SQL, the language you use to manipulate SQL Server. In addition, I tie the Transact-SQL commands to the GUI, and show you what you can do with SQL that can't be accomplished with the GUI. I also tie the Transact-SQL tasks to SQL DMO, the object model that can be used by programmers to build tools. Some of this information is presented in chart format, so if you're allergic to VB (or Visual C++, Java, and so on), you can simply ignore the DMO sections. I'm not going to teach you how to program for this object model, but if you already know how to program against an object model, you should find enough information in this book to get you started with SQL DMO.

This book focuses on SQL Server for Windows NT Server. I point out those instances that don't apply to the desktop version; however, this book isn't limited by a concentration on the desktop version.

What You Should Know Before Reading This Book

I've made some assumptions about what you, the reader, already know about SQL Server. To gain optimal value from this book, you should already:

- Have a basic understanding of relational database concepts (tables, rows, columns, relationships, and so on).
- Know how to create logins with User Manager for Domains.
- Have a basic understanding of Windows NT security architecture.
- Know how to issue basic Transact-SQL statements, including how to execute stored procedures.
- Have familiarity with the syntax notation used in Books OnLine.
- Know how to move around at the command line (DOS prompt) in Query Analyzer and in Enterprise Manager.

What Is a SQL Server Administrator?

The term *Database Administrator* covers a variety of job functions. These include managing resources, designing databases, managing login security, managing database security, ensuring that backups are performed on a regular basis, monitoring and troubleshooting, writing stored procedures, optimizing queries, and, I sometimes think, carrying out the trash! In this book, I am going to focus on the administrative aspects of SQL Server, including the following:

- Managing resources
- Managing security at all levels
- Backup and recovery
- Troubleshooting & monitoring

I'm not going to cover designing databases; there are plenty of books out there on that topic. Likewise, I'm not going to teach you Transact-SQL programming. You won't get to be a whiz at writing stored procedures from this book. I will show you some tools for monitoring query performance, but I will not cover the process of tuning SQL statements (or writing them correctly to begin with)! If I survive this book, I'll consider approaching that topic in a new book.

You might have heard that Microsoft considers SQL Server 7 to be "self-administering." They have indeed made it much easier—many things you had to do in previous versions are no longer absolutely necessary in 7.0. But the environment is much more complex, and there is still a need for DBAs and the skills they bring to administering SQL. The automatic administration makes it easy for a small shop, perhaps a shop with one database on Windows 95. But most of us don't work in those shops, and we need to learn how we can do things that will make SQL Server "purr like a kitten." I see this book as a tool to help you tame your SQL Server environment.

Important Resources

As people use SQL Server, they encounter bugs and areas where the documentation is not clear. Microsoft maintains a Knowledge Base that contains descriptions of bugs and their workarounds and articles that expand on the documentation. This Knowledge Base is available on the Web. It's also included with the TechNet and Microsoft Developer Network subscriptions. As an administrator you should subscribe to TechNet if you haven't already. It's a great resource for all Back Office Administrators. See Appendix A of this book for information on how to subscribe to TechNet.

How to Use This Book

This book is organized in terms of administrative tasks—those things that you must perform correctly to ensure that your SQL Server functions smoothly. After an initial chapter laying out some fundamental concepts (it will be easier if we have a common vocabulary), each chapter focuses on a specific task. The opening page of each chapter shows you the tasks that are covered for that chapter.

General Tip

If you are an experienced SQL Server user, you may want to skim, or skip over, Chapter 1.

The following are stylistic conventions and typographical features used to maximize the design and the functionality of the book:

- **Cross-references** are used throughout the book to refer you to related discussions or to point you to additional information on a subject or task.
- *Italic* is used to emphasize key terms.
- `Monospace text` is used to designate code and code listings in the text.
- **Code continuation characters (➡)** are inserted into the code when a line should not be broken, but there is no space on the page to fit it.
- **Menu selections** appear as either **Menu | Command** or **Menu, Command.**

In addition, the following are used to designate special conventions including tips, warnings, and so on:

General Tip

This designates a general tip.

Danger

This designates that there is danger in performing a specific task or in skipping one.

Performance Tip

This designates a performance tip. These tips tell you how to improve or enhance performance.

Warning

This designates a warning. I warn you or caution you about items that might affect a task you are performing. The tips are meant to prevent you from doing something that might eventually result in danger.

> **IMO**
>
> This is where I give you my opinion (IMO stands for In My Opinion) on what the best practices are. Realize that this is an area where there may be disagreement. Obviously, there are often many ways to accomplish the same task. IMOs are my opinion on what the best methods are for accomplishing a task, and in some cases, they are just my opinion about a particular subject, tool, or aspect of SQL Server.

1

Fundamental Concepts

The purpose of this chapter is to help people who are new to SQL Server by outlining some fundamental elements. I'll talk about some of the important concepts and provide definitions. If you're already familiar with SQL Server, you can skip this chapter.

What Is SQL Server 7.0?

Everybody knows the answer to the question of what is SQL Server: It's Microsoft's hot new version of its relational database management system. The product was rebuilt from the inside out with several very ambitious goals, including the following:

- **Scalability.** The same code runs on platforms from Windows 95 to the Windows NT Enterprise Edition.
- **Performance.** High-performance storage and query engines to support enterprise-wide applications.
- **Ease of use.** Automate many administrative tasks, freeing the *Database Administrator* (DBA) for other important pursuits.

SQL Server has also been designed to integrate well with other BackOffice products, such as Microsoft Exchange, Internet Information Server, Site Server, and so on.

But let's look a bit more deeply into what comprises this product.

Editions

Edition is one of the most confusing marketing terms that Microsoft has come up with. Microsoft describes three editions in *Books OnLine* (BOL), as noted in the following list:

- Enterprise (for Windows NT Enterprise Edition)
- Standard (for Windows NT Server and Enterprise editions)
- Small Business Server (for Small Business Server)

SQL Server also comes in two other versions: the Desktop Edition—which runs on Windows 95, Windows 98, and Windows NT Workstation—is included with the Enterprise, Standard, and Small Business Server editions; and there is the exciting new *Microsoft Data Engine* (MSDE), which is available for independent software vendors (and others) who want to embed SQL Server 7.0 in their products. Starting with Office 2000, you can use this engine with Microsoft Access rather than the JET engine. MSDE is also shipped with MSDN and with Visual Studio. In general, features are only constrained by the operating system, as shown in the following table.

Feature	Desktop/ MSDE	SBS	Standard	Enterprise
Maximum database size	Unlimited	10GB	Unlimited	Unlimited
Number of CPUs	2	4	4	32
Extended memory support	No	No	No	Yes
Microsoft Search Service (full-text indexing)	No	Yes	Yes	Yes
OLAP Services	Yes (on Windows NT only)	No	Yes (except user-defined cube partitions)	Yes
Replication	Merge only	Full	Full	Full
Performance	Limited only by hardware and operating system	Limited to throughput and operating system	Limited only by hardware typical of 50 concurrent users	Limited only by hardware and operating system

SQL Server on Windows 9x has a few limitations beyond those of the Desktop Edition. SQL Server running on that platform supports only one *central processing unit* (CPU), has no support for asynchronous *input/output* (I/O), and doesn't support named pipes.

Components

A lot of components come with SQL Server 7.0. Some are servers, and some are clients.

Servers

SQL Server includes the following five servers:

- **SQL Server.** This is the heart of SQL Server. It includes the query engine that retrieves data and the storage engine that puts data into SQL Server. It manages security and concurrent use of resources.

- **SQL Server Agent.** This server manages scheduled jobs, replication, and notifications. Chapter 8, "Jobs and Alerts," shows you how you can use the SQL Server Agent to automate routine tasks. In SQL Server 6.x, this service was called SQL Executive.

- **Microsoft Distributed Transaction Coordinator (MS DTC).** This server is responsible for handling logical units of work that occur on multiple servers. It is also a fundamental component of Microsoft Transaction Server.

- **Microsoft Search.** This server, similar in concept to Microsoft's Index Server, is used to provide searching of full-text indexes. These indexes can be created from data residing in SQL Server databases.

- **OLAP.** This server is the engine for Microsoft Decision Support Services. This product supports data warehousing and enables the user to build data cubes for analysis. Microsoft Decision Support Services is a separate product from SQL Server, although it is currently bundled with the core product.

All these servers run as services on Windows NT. SQL Server, SQL Server Agent, and MS DTC run as background executables on Windows 9x. The Microsoft Search and OLAP products aren't available for Windows 9x.

Clients

Everything else in the SQL Server product, except the documentation, is a client, whether it is running on the same machine as SQL Server or on a different machine. Client components include the following:

- Command-line utilities
- Query Analyzer
- Enterprise Manager
- SQL Profiler
- Data Transformation Services
- Client Network utility
- MSDTC Administrative Console
- Microsoft English Query
- SQL Service Manager
- SQL Performance Monitor
- Server Network utility

Command-Line Utilities

The following three utilities run in the command shell:

- **bcp.** This is the bulk copy program used for transferring data to and from SQL Server.

- **osql.** This tool allows Transact-SQL commands to be issued from the command line. It is often used to set up batch processes because it can read input text files (usually called *scripts*) and log results to a file. *osql* replaces an earlier tool called *isql*.

- **isql.** This tool is still available, but it does not support new SQL Server 7.0 features.

Query Analyzer

Query Analyzer replaces the tool called ISQL/W and Query Tool from previous versions. It is much more powerful, but it is still just a vehicle for editing and issuing Transact-SQL statements. (Personally, I spend far more time using this tool than I do using the Enterprise Manager.)

SQL Enterprise Manager

This tool is a snap-in for the Microsoft Management Console. Other Microsoft products (such as Internet Information Server and Transaction Server) can also be managed from this console, which is becoming a Microsoft standard. Enterprise Manager enables you to carry out about 95% of your administrative tasks through a graphical interface. For the remainder, you must use Transact-SQL.

SQL Profiler

This is high on my list of most-loved new features (and it's a very long list, believe me). SQL Profiler is a tool that enables you to monitor statements and remote procedure calls sent to the SQL Server. It enables you to see inside stored procedures as well. It collects a great deal of data and responds to numerous events. (Chapter 10, "Performance Tuning," discusses this tool in more detail.)

Data Transformation Services

Data Transformation Services is another feature high on my list. It enables you to do complex conversion and migration of data from diverse sources. You can take data from Oracle, for example, join it with some data in Access, and pop the whole result into SQL Server. You can script transforms in JScript, Perl, and VBScript.

Microsoft English Query

Microsoft English Query is a developer's tool that helps create applications that respond to English-language queries. It is quite powerful, but does nothing right "out of the box" unless you want to issue English-language queries against Northwind and pubs. (Northwind and pubs are discussed in the section, "SQL Server Databases" later in this chapter.) To make use of it, you need to define the terms on which you want to query and specify how these relate to the database. In a book's database, I would want to issue queries such as, "Which books did Mark Twain write?" I would have to tell English Query that Authors, located in the Authors table, write Books, located in the Titles table, and how the two are related.

Client Network Utility

The Client Network is a little application that is invaluable for troubleshooting connectivity problems. (Chapter 3, "Managing Client Connectivity," discusses this utility in more detail.)

MSDTC Administrative Console

The MSDTC Administrative Console is used to administer and troubleshoot distributed transactions.

SQL Performance Monitor

The SQL Performance Monitor is actually a set of objects and counters for SQL Server integrated with NT's Performance Monitor. This application is not available on Windows 9x.

SQL Service Manager

The SQL Service Manager is a nice, lightweight (that is, quick to start up) application that can be used for starting and stopping the SQL Server, SQL Server Agent, MSDTC, and Search Services. It can only run on the machine where the services are running.

Server Network Utility

Analogous to the Client Network utility, the Server Network application is used to troubleshoot connectivity problems. It can only be run on the machine where the SQL Server is running.

Books OnLine

One other important tool ships with SQL Server: Books OnLine (BOL). It is a complete documentation set with a powerful search engine. A great deal of effort has gone into the documentation, and it will serve you well to read the manual. Personally, I wish it were more linear and less hypertext. Printed documentation (an exact copy of BOL) is also available from bookstores. I find it useful to have both the online and paper versions. The online version gives me a powerful search capability. But it's easy to carry the paper manual on the bus and catch up on my reading.

" IMO

Books OnLine should be on every administrator and developer desktop.

SQL Server Databases

SQL Server stores data in *databases*. Although this may seem obvious, it's important to know that there can be many databases (a maximum of 32,767) on any given SQL Server. Some systems have a single database, which may be spread across many physical drives; and all tables, regardless of the applications they support, are in that database. In SQL Server, databases are named objects. Tables and other objects can be created in several databases. Often, a database is used for a specific application or a particular set of business functions. Users see the data as logical components: tables and relationships. Only the DBA has to worry about physical implementation. It's SQL Server's job to manage storing the data in the database and to retrieve it when necessary.

SQL Server databases fall into two classes: system and application. System databases come with SQL Server and are used by SQL Server to manage itself. SQL Server comes with the following four system databases:

- **master.** The master database contains tables that describe all other databases on the server, logons, running processes, and configuration settings. It is the most important database; SQL Server will not start if master is damaged or destroyed.

- **model.** This acts as a source for all new databases that are created. It contains tables common to every database.

 General Tip

If you have an object that you want to appear in all databases (including tempdb), create it in model and it will appear in all databases subsequently created. If you use user-defined datatypes, this is an easy way to make sure that they are available in all databases.

- **msdb.** The SQL Server Agent uses this database. It contains tables describing scheduled jobs, alerts, notifications, and replication setups. Backup and job histories are also stored here. If you store *Data Transformation Services* (DTS) packages in SQL Server, they are also stored in msdb.

- **tempdb.** This is a scratch pad database used by everyone. For example, tempdb provides workspace for sorting data. Objects created in tempdb are transient; they die when the user who created them disconnects from SQL Server. However, there are two exceptions:

1. Objects created in tempdb without the # prefix persist until SQL Server is stopped and restarted.
2. Objects created with the ## prefix are global, and persist until the creator and all users accessing them have disconnected.

Two application databases ship with SQL Server: Northwind and pubs. These are used for examples in the documentation.

 General Tip

Both Northwind and pubs can easily be rebuilt with the scripts instnwnd.sql and instpubs.sql. These are stored in your \mssql7\install folder.

 IMO

I'd advise you to get a bit familiar with the Northwind and pubs databases because everybody tends to use them for reference.

Inside a SQL Server Database

A SQL Server database contains many *objects*. The term object doesn't have anything to do with object-oriented databases. Instead, it just means "stuff" in the database. You will find a variety of objects in most SQL Server databases. The following sections contain a brief discussion of each of them.

Tables

A *table* is a named set of rows and columns. Each column has, at a minimum, a name, a datatype, and nullability.

Nullability says whether the column allows "null" values. Null is a special database value that means missing or not known. It's not the same as an empty string, a blank, or a zero.

 General Tip

By default, SQL Server deviates from the ANSI standard with respect to nulls. ANSI says that if you don't declare the nullability for a column, the column permits null values. SQL Server assumes that the column does *not* allow nulls. You can set some options to change this behavior, but it is wise to explicitly state whether you want to allow nulls for every column.

SQL Server has two types of tables: system tables and user tables. *User tables* are the ones that support applications, such as an Employee table. *System tables* are used by SQL Server to manage its operations. Some system tables exist in all databases, some exist only in master, and some exist only in msdb. Sometimes it is useful to write queries against these tables. (I explain some of them in the "Under the Covers" sections of this book.) In many cases, similar information can be obtained by querying the ANSI Information Schema views that are part of SQL Server 7.0, so I will use those where they exist.

General Tip

You should always treat the system tables as Microsoft's private property. If you query them directly, you should be aware that they may change in future releases. Where possible, use the ANSI Information Schema views. These will insulate you from any changes Microsoft may make.

Danger

It is possible to modify system tables. If you are going to modify system tables, you must have a thorough understanding of how they work. Incorrect or incomplete changes to the system tables can make your SQL Server unusable.

IMO

Modifying system tables is one of those things that I do only when my back is to the wall or when directed to by Microsoft Product Support.

Datatypes

A *datatype* defines the type of values that can be placed in a column. Columns of datatype char can hold character strings, for example, and columns of datatype int (integer) can only hold whole numbers. SQL Server includes a rich set of datatypes, including some that support Unicode data.

Each ASCII character is stored in 1 byte, which means there are 255 possible characters. The characters of some languages cannot be represented in a single byte. Unicode stores each character in 2 bytes, which allows for 65,536 possible characters.

SQL Server also allows user-defined datatypes. These are just additional names for the existing datatypes. It is not possible, for example, to create an enumerated type (Color = Red, Green, or Blue) or anything fancy with user-defined datatypes. You can't modify a user-defined datatype after it has been used in a table; you must first get rid of the table, so these don't insulate you from changes, either.

Views

A *view* is a stored SQL SELECT statement that serves as a virtual table. It can be used just about anywhere that a table can be used. It is possible to update data through some views as well. Only the definition of a view is stored in a database. The data is retrieved only when someone uses the view.

Constraints

Constraints are used to make sure that data in a database is correct. The various types of constraints include the following:

- **Primary key constraints.** These define a column or set of columns that uniquely identify each row of a table. None of the columns of a primary key may allow nulls. A table can have only one primary key constraint.
- **Unique constraints.** These require that all the values in a column or set of columns be unique. There can be many unique constraints on a table.
- **Default constraints.** These specify a value that will be used if the value isn't provided when the row is added to the database.
- **Check constraints.** These are used to limit the values in a column to a specific set of values.
- **Foreign key constraints.** These are used to enforce relationships between tables. Assume, for example, that we have a Department table and an Employee table. The Employee table contains the department number for each employee. A foreign key constraint would require that every department number in the Employee table match a department number in the Department table. SQL Server implements only a subset of the ANSI standard for foreign key constraints. It supports a Restrict rule for delete and update, but does not support Cascade or Nullify.

Constraints (also called *declarative referential integrity*, or DRI) were introduced in SQL Server 6.0.

 General Tip

Remember DRI! Enterprise Manager uses this abbreviation in several screens.

Rules and Defaults

Prior versions of SQL Server provided another way of enforcing integrity: rules and defaults. These are still supported for backward compatibility. *Rules* limit the values in a column (similar to check constraints), and *defaults* provide an initial value for a column (identical to default constraints).

> **" IMO**
>
> You will see rules and defaults used in legacy systems. New systems should always use the constraints. They conform to the ANSI standard. Before the introduction of foreign key constraints, it was necessary to write programs to ensure that the relationships between tables were correct. The foreign key constraints do this automatically unless your business rules dictate Cascade or Nullify rules.

Stored Procedures

A *stored procedure* is a program written in Transact-SQL. *Procedures* are reusable objects stored in SQL Server databases and executed on the server. They are a very important part of getting a high-performance system, and also have a part to play in security. (See Chapter 9, "Security," for more information on security.) Extended stored procedures are *dynamic link libraries* (DLLs) that act like stored procedures and can be executed in the same way that stored procedures are. These generally enable you to do things that can't be done with SQL, such as interact with the Registry or the file system. Many stored procedures come with SQL Server. Commands that start with **sp_** are usually Transact-SQL system stored procedures, although a few extended stored procedures have names that start with **sp_**. All procedures with names that start with **xp_** are extended stored procedures.

> **" IMO**
>
> Many people think that because Microsoft names its stored procedures with sp_, they should too. However, sp_ implies that the procedure can be invoked from any database and will still function. I don't think you should name them sp_ unless they actually conform to this rule. And even if you don't agree with that, imagine calling Microsoft Product Support and saying that sp_MonthReport doesn't work and having them tell you that they never heard of such a procedure!

Triggers

Triggers are a special kind of stored procedure. Triggers are tied to insert, update, and delete operations on tables. They happen as part of the operation without requiring the user to take any special action, or even be aware of their existence.

Triggers are often used to create audit trails, for example. Before constraints were available, triggers were used to make sure that the relationships between tables were being maintained. You may find current applications still need to do this in triggers when cascaded deletion is required, because constraints don't support that. You may also need to use triggers if you have complex validation logic that can't be expressed in a check constraint.

Indexes

Indexes are used to enforce uniqueness. (Both primary key and unique constraints automatically create indexes.) But the major purpose for indexes is to allow data to be retrieved quickly. SQL Server has two types of indexes: clustered and non-clustered. *Clustered* indexes sort the data in order on the clustering key. *Non-clustered* indexes sort the keys in order on the key, but the data is not in the same order as the index. A table may have only one clustered index; it can have many non-clustered indexes (Non-unique indexes are used for transaction performance.)

Performance Tip

Many people think that the primary key has to be the clustered index. A primary key can be implemented with a clustered index, but it doesn't have to be. Because clustered indexes are best for range queries or queries that will return a high percentage of duplicates, they may be better used for other fields in the table. Primary key searches usually return a single value.

2

Installation and Upgrade

As an administrator, the first thing you'll want to do is install SQL Server 7.0. If you have used previous versions of SQL Server, you must upgrade your databases.

This chapter covers the SQL Server 7.0 installation process, and the process of upgrading databases.

Installing SQL Server 7.0

When you install SQL Server 7.0, it does not replace an earlier version of the product. The first thing you have to do, whether you are starting from scratch or upgrading an existing SQL Server installation, is install it. SQL Server 7.0 can be installed on a machine that has 6.x installed on it. The two versions can coexist; however, only one version can be running at a time.

Planning the Installation

Before you install SQL Server 7.0, you should ensure that you have everything you need. In addition, you need to answer some questions. This section outlines the requirements for installation and explains the answers to relevant questions. Then, you can determine which solutions best fit your organization.

Operating System Requirements

As discussed in Chapter 1, "Fundamental Concepts," SQL Server comes in several versions. Each of these runs on certain operating systems. The following table shows a list of SQL Server versions and the operating systems that they can run on.

Operating System	Desktop Version	Small Business	Standard	Enterprise Standard
Windows 95/ 98	OK	No	No	No
NT 4.0 Workstation★	OK	No	No	No
NT 4.0 Server★	OK	No	OK	No
NT 4.0 Server, Enterprise★	OK	No	OK	OK
BackOffice Small Business Server	No	OK	OK	No

★ *Requires Service Pack 4 or later*

Processor Requirements

SQL Server 7.0 can run on an Intel or compatible, Pentium 133MHz or higher, Pentium Pro, Pentium II, and DEC Alpha AXP or compatible. Because Microsoft has abandoned development of Windows NT/Windows 2000 for the Alpha platform, you probably don't want to buy a new Alpha box at this point; if you have one, however, SQL Server will run on it. SQL Server performance is greatly enhanced if you have multiple processors.

Memory Requirements

SQL Server 7.0 requires a minimum of 32MB of memory. You should have at least 64MB for on any machine that will be a distributor of replicated data. You want to get as much memory as you can afford, because memory has a substantial influence on performance.

CD-ROM

SQL Server 7.0 ships on a CD, so you need a CD-ROM. You can install SQL Server from a copy of this CD on a network drive. You can also use remote install to another server or workstation, in which case you don't need a CD-ROM on the target server, but you need access to the CD-ROM on the computer you use to start installation.

Disk Space Requirements

The following table outlines the disk space requirements for various installations of SQL Server and other components. These requirements don't include the disk space you need for your databases. Chapter 4, "Storage Management," tells you how to figure out how much space a database requires.

Component	Installation	Disk Space Required
SQL Server	Full	210MB
	Typical	185MB
	Minimum	80MB
OLAP		56MB
English Query		20MB
Books OnLine		15MB

Other Requirements

Other SQL Server requirements include the following:

- Internet Explorer 4.01 with Service Pack 1 or later (this is included on the SQL Server CD)
- Any required software for Banyan VINES or AppleTalk ASDP
- ODBC drivers for Macintosh, UNIX, and OS/2 clients

Installation Options

SQL Server 7.0 has three separate installation choices: Typical, Custom, and Minimal. You should only use Minimal when you do not have enough disk space to use Typical or Custom. Choose Typical if you are satisfied with the default installation options. (See the following table to view the options.) If you want to change any of the options, or if you want to install full-text indexing, choose Custom. You must also choose Custom if you want to install only client tools on a workstation. Client tools are automatically installed on the server unless you choose not to do so in a custom install.

 General Tip

If you choose a Typical install, and you are installing on a machine on which SQL Server 6.x is installed, the options are set to those chosen for your 6.x installation. They may differ from the options shown in the following table.

 General Tip

If you are planning to upgrade your SQL Server 6.x databases, you can choose different options from those of your 6.x installation.

Install Option	Typical	Custom	Minimal
Server	Yes	Yes	Yes
Upgrade tools	Yes	Yes	No
Replication support	Yes	Yes	Yes
Full-text search	No	No (default)	No
Client management tools	All	All (default)	None
Client connectivity	Yes	Yes	Yes
Online documentation	Yes	Yes	No
Development tools	None	None (default)	None
Character set	1252-ISO	1252-ISO (default)	1252-ISO

Install Option	Typical	Custom	Minimal
Sort order	Dictionary, not case-sensitive	Dictionary, not case-sensitive	Dictionary not case-sensitive
Unicode collation	General	General (default)	General
NT network	Named pipes, TCP/IP, and multiprotocol	Named pipes, TCP/IP, and multiprotocol	Named pipes TCP/IP, and multi-protocol
Windows 9x	TCP/IP and multiprotocol	TCP/IP and multiprotocol	TCP/IP and multi-protocol

 General Tip

You will need a Custom install if you want to install full-text indexing.

Which Components Should I Install?

The first thing you need to do (after you install the prerequisites) is to install SQL Server itself. After that, you can install the OLAP (Decision Support Services) and Microsoft English Query if you want those features.

Where Should I Install SQL Server?

SQL Server performs best if installed on a machine of its own. If possible, dedicate a machine to it. Although SQL Server will function if installed on your PDC, BDC, Exchange Server, Internet Information Server, and so on, the performance of *everything*, including SQL Server, on that machine will be impaired.

By default, the SQL Server code and sample databases are installed on the server's C: drive in a folder named MSSQL7. You can modify this when you install if you want to put it somewhere else. If you already have a previous version of SQL Server installed, you should not use this folder; many of the DLLs have the same name and you will break SQL Server 6.x if you install 7.0 to the same directory.

Choosing a Character Set, Sort Order, and Unicode Collation

When choosing a character set, sort order, and Unicode collation, you need to make decisions carefully. You should use the same character set, sort order, and Unicode collation for all servers that may share applications. This may include all the servers in your organization or just those within a given department or workgroup. Applications may not produce the same results, or may not work at all if any of these differ.

It is not possible to restore a database backup made on one server to another server when the character set, sort order, or Unicode collation differs.

After you have installed SQL Server, you cannot change the character set without unloading all the data to a text format, rebuilding the master database (or reinstalling SQL Server), and loading all the data from the text files.

 General Tip

You can find out what sort order is in use by looking at the Error log. SQL Server lists the sort order when it starts up. You can also issue the command **sp_helpsort**, which shows you the character set, sort order, and Unicode collation.

Character Sets

A *character set*, also called a code page, specifies the internal encoding of all characters. In most cases, the default (1252, ISO character set) will be the one you want. It is also known as the ISO 8859-1, Latin 1, or ANSI character set. It is compatible with the ANSI characters used by the Microsoft Windows NT and Microsoft Windows operating systems. This code page is appropriate if you intend to use clients running Windows NT or Windows 95/98 exclusively, or if you need to maintain exact compatibility with a Sybase environment on UNIX or VMS.

Code page 850 is a multilingual character set that includes all the characters used by most of the languages of European, North American, and South American countries.

Code page 437 is the most commonly used character set in the United States. Use this character set if you have character-based applications that depend on extended characters for graphics. Otherwise, use code page ISO 8859-1, which provides more compatibility with languages other than U.S. English. The following table describes each of the code pages.

Code Page	Description
1252	ISO character set
850	Multilingual
437	U.S. English
874	Thai
932	Japanese
936	Chinese (simplified)
949	Korean
950	Chinese (traditional)
1250	Central European
1251	Cyrillic
1253	Greek
1254	Turkish
1255	Hebrew
1256	Arabic
1257	Baltic

Sort Order

The *sort order* determines how data is sorted when you issue a SELECT statement that contains an Order By clause. It also determines how data is compared when searching for character strings. The default sort order is dictionary order, not case sensitive. The following table describes the available sort orders.

Sort Order	Description
Dictionary order, not casesensitive	Upper- and lowercase letters are considered the same: A = a. Letters with accents or other diacritical marks are considered different: a − å. Characters with diacritical marks are sorted after characters without them, and are sorted in the order they appear in the code page.
Dictionary order, case sensitive	Upper- and lowercase letters differ: A ≠ a. Uppercase letters are sorted before lowercase letters. Letters with diacritical marks are sorted in the order in which they appear in the code page: A, a, à, á, â, Ä, ä, Å, å. Note that the names of objects are case sensitive as well: SELECT * FROM Customer is not the same as SELECT * FROM CUSTOMER.
Binary	Upper and lowercase letters differ. Characters are sorted in order on the numeric value (0–255) of the character. In this sort order, the data is not in dictionary order; for example, ZYXWV sorts before abcde.

continues ▶

Sort Order	Description
Dictionary order, not case sensitive, uppercase preference	Like dictionary order, not case sensitive except that uppercase letters sort before lowercase letters. Letters without diacritical marks sort before those with diacritical marks.
Dictionary order, not case sensitive, not accent sensitive	Upper and lowercase letters, with or without diacritical marks, are considered the same: A = a = å = á = â = Ä = ä = Å = å.

Additional sort orders that support other languages are available. Most of these provide case-sensitive and non-case-sensitive sort orders.

Performance Tip

Binary is the fastest sort order. However, that may be outweighed by the fact that the results are not in dictionary order. Choosing uppercase preference may require sorting that would otherwise have been skipped.

Unicode Collation

Unicode is standard in SQL Server 7.0. This is a method of encoding character data that allows for 65,536 possible characters as opposed to ASCII's 256. Two bytes are used for each character rather than one. The Unicode collation is similar to the character set and sort order. The SQL Server installation program proposes the Unicode collation that goes with the character set and sort order chosen. You should accept this default. The program also proposes the general locale. This determines how Unicode data is sorted. You should use the general locale for any of these languages:

Afrikaans	Faeroese	Malay
Albanian	Farsi	Russian
Arabic	Georgian	Serbian
Basque	Greek	Swahili
Bulgarian	Hebrew	Urdu
Belarusian	Hindi	
English	Indonesian	

For other languages, see the documentation in *Books OnLine* (BOL).

You will also see four comparison style options. The case-sensitive and non-case-sensitive options have the same meaning as they do for sort order. Non-width-sensitive and non-Kana-sensitive styles have meaning only for certain East Asian languages.

Danger

You must accept the default if you are planning to upgrade 6.x databases to 7.0.

Determining Necessary Network Libraries

It is important not to confuse network libraries with the Windows NT network protocols. These network libraries sit on top of whatever network transports Windows NT is using, and specify how SQL Server sends and receives data (see Figure 2.1). For example, named pipes and multiprotocol can both be used with a TCP/IP network.

Figure 2.1   SQL Server network library architecture.

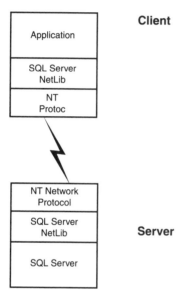

Performance Tip

Don't install network libraries that you don't need. If there will not be any Banyan traffic, for example, it wastes SQL Server's time to listen for it.

Named Pipes

The named pipes network library is required on NT. This network library can be used with NT network protocols NetBIOS and TCP/IP. It is not available on Windows 9x. SQL Server listens on the standard pipe, \\.\pipe\sql\query, for named pipes network library connections. After SQL Server is installed, you can add additional named pipes to improve performance. You can also drop named-pipe support and set SQL Server to listen only on other network libraries.

IMO
You should *not* remove named pipes. SQL Server seems to depend on having it around for some activities. You can have all your client systems use TCP/IP, however.

 Warning
Don't drop named pipes if you are planning to upgrade 6.x databases.

TCP/IP Sockets

The TCP/IP Sockets network library allows SQL Server to communicate with the Windows Sockets *Inter-Process Communication* (IPC) method over TCP/IP. This is the default library for Windows 9x. SQL Server's default port number, assigned by the Internet Assigned Number Authority, is 1433. You can change this, however. If you want SQL Server to listen on Microsoft Proxy Server, provide the proxy server address in the proxy address box when you set up this network library.

 General Tip
Because SQL Server's default number is a widely known port number, you might want to choose a different one if your SQL Server is accessible to the Internet, so that you will be less subject to hackers.

Multiprotocol

The multiprotocol network library uses the Windows *Remote Procedure Call* (RPC) facility. It can communicate over most network protocols, although only named pipes, TCP/IP, and NWLink IPX/SPX have been tested. When you use multiprotocol, network traffic can be encrypted.

 Warning
Books OnLine is contradictory. In one place it says that you must use named pipes or multiprotocol to use NT Authentication. Yet in another place it says you do not need it. I have tested TCP/IP and found that I can connect with NT Authentication perfectly well without using multiprotocol.

NWLINK IPX/SPX

NWLINK IPX/SPX allows SQL Server to communicate with Novell clients. You need to supply the Novell Bindery name when you choose this network library.

AppleTalk ADSP

The ADSP network library allows Apple Macintosh clients to connect to SQL Server by using native AppleTalk (as opposed to TCP/IP Sockets). When you set up SQL Server to listen on AppleTalk, you need to provide the AppleTalk service object name. It is not necessary to enter an AppleTalk zone because the local zone is used when registering the service. Windows 95/98 does not support this network library.

Banyan VINES

The Banyan VINES network library allows Banyan VINES *Sequenced Packet Protocol* (SPP) to be used as the IPC method across the Banyan VINES IP network protocol. Banyan VINES support for clients and servers running Windows NT is available for SQL Server on the Intel platform only; it is not currently available on Windows 95/98 or the Alpha AXP platform. When you choose this network library, you need to provide a StreetTalk service name. You need to create this service name by using the MSERVICE program included with your VINES software before you can refer to it.

SQL Server and SQL Server Agent Logon Accounts

Both SQL Server and SQL Server Agent log on to Windows NT as *services*. If you do not plan to do any cross-server activities (running jobs on other servers, replication, and so on), they can both log on with the Local System account. In most cases, however, you will want them to have a special NT Logon account. This account should be a domain user, and must have the advanced right, *Log On as a Service*. I personally think this should be a domain administrator account, but this is not required, and some organizations have security policies that prohibit this. If the account is not a domain administrator, you will probably want to add it to the local administrators group on each machine that will run SQL Server, because it makes things easier. It is best if all SQL Servers interacting with each other log on to NT with the same account.

Determining Whether to Upgrade 6.x Databases

You get an opportunity to upgrade databases when you install SQL Server 7.0. I don't recommend upgrading during installation. First of all, the upgrade takes planning (see the second part of this chapter). Second, you want to make sure that the SQL Server 7.0 installation is okay before you begin upgrading.

Licensing Modes

You should discuss licensing mode, as well as the number of licenses you need, with your Microsoft representative to determine whether your needs are best suited by Per Server or Per Seat licensing. If you are unsure of which is best, choose Per Server. You can change from Per Server to Per Seat, but not the reverse.

Installing SQL Server

After all the decisions have been made regarding network libraries, components, licensing mode, and so on, the actual installation is easy. Just run the Setup program and follow the bouncing ball. You need the CD key from the SQL Server Install CD. When you get to the licensing section, you must agree twice! This bug has carried forward from 6.x. After you have finished installing, you should reboot. Then you can install Decision Support Services and Microsoft English Query if you want.

 Danger

Don't rename the computer after you install SQL Server 7.0. If you do, an error message tells you that your SQL Server installation is corrupt or has been tampered with. Microsoft says this problem can be corrected by rerunning the Setup program. However, it is my experience (and the experience of others) that this does not always fix everything. In particular, the graphical tools may fail to work.

Version Switch Utility

If you have installed SQL Server 7.0 on a machine that is running 6.x, you will find a handy version switch utility that enables you to switch from one version to another. It's in your Start menu under the Microsoft SQL SERVER–SWITCH folder. Make sure to exit from the SQL Server Service Manager by right-clicking the icon that's in your System Tray (at the right side of your taskbar) and choosing Exit before you run the switch. After the switch, your Start menu might be messed up. If this happens, log off and log back on again.

If you have trouble using the graphical switch utility, you can run VSWITCH.EXE at the command prompt. It's in the \MSSQL7\BINN folder. It has three switches that you can put on the command line:

- **-SwitchTo <60¦65¦70>**   Version to switch to.
- **-Silent <0 ¦ 1>**   If 1, there will be no UI or messages (default 0).
- **-NoCheck <0 ¦ 1>**   If 1, there will be no check for running applications (default 0).

For example:

```
vswitch -SwitchTo 65
```

Upgrading SQL Server 6.x Databases

Microsoft has provided a convenient Upgrade Wizard. If you have installed 7.0 on a machine running 6.x, you will find the wizard in the Microsoft SQL SERVER–SWITCH folder in your Start menu. If this choice is not there, you will find the wizard in the \MSSQL7\UPGRADE folder. It is named UPGRADE.EXE.

Like your SQL Server installation, an upgrade also requires a good deal of planning. In most cases, you should upgrade databases onto a test box and thoroughly test your applications before moving them to production on SQL Server 7.0.

You can only upgrade 6.x databases. If you have databases on a 4.x SQL Server, you must upgrade that server to 6.0 or 6.5 before you can upgrade to 7.0.

This is not an "in-place" upgrade. When you complete the upgrade, your SQL Server 6.x installation will still be intact, unless you do a single machine pipe upgrade and choose the Delete 6.5 Databases option. You can remove it when you feel comfortable with the results of the upgrade.

You can upgrade on a single computer that has both SQL Server 6.x and SQL Server 7.0 installed, or you can upgrade with 6.x on one computer and 7.0 on another.

During the upgrade process, both the 6.x and 7.0 servers are stopped and restarted several times. Users can't be active while the upgrade is in progress.

 General Tip

You can't use the upgrade process to consolidate databases from multiple 6.x servers. It will only upgrade databases from one server. Any consolidation will need to be done with manual techniques, such as bulk copy or Data Transformation Services.

Planning the Upgrade

Before you start, you must make some decisions about the mechanics of the upgrade. This section outlines the requirements and explains the decisions that you must make so that you are prepared when you start the upgrade.

Requirements

In addition to the requirements for SQL Server 7.0, you need approximately 1.5 times the amount of disk space you needed for your SQL Server 6.x databases. Some of this space is given back at the conclusion of the upgrade.

If you are running 6.0, you must be running with Service Pack 3. For 6.5, you must be running with Service Pack 3 or later. (The latest service pack, as of this writing, is 5a.) Service packs are part of the TechNET subscription. You can also download them from Microsoft's Web site.

If you are performing a one-computer upgrade, you must be running NT 4 with Service Pack 4 or later.

General Tip

Although Microsoft does not support SQL Server 6.0 on NT 4, they have agreed that they will provide necessary support for 6.0 if SQL Server 7.0 is also installed on the machine.

You must have the named pipes network library on both SQL Server 6.x and 7.0. In addition, the 7.0 SQL Server must be listening on the default pipe: \\.\pipe\sql\query. This is required even if you are performing a tape upgrade.

Your 6.x tempdb must be at least 10MB.

It is possible for a SQL Server 6.x installation to have a server name in sysservers that is not the same as the computer name. You cannot upgrade when this is the case. You will need to drop the entry in sysservers with sp_dropserver, and then add a new one with sp_addserver before you can upgrade.

If you are planning a two-computer upgrade, both SQL Servers must log on with an account that is a member of the domain administrators group. If you are planning a two-computer upgrade, you must run the Upgrade program on the target (7.0) computer.

Upgrading Servers Involved in Replication

Although the upgrade will handle servers that are using replication, you should disable replication and start over with its configuration after the upgrade. The architecture of SQL Server 7.0 replication differs substantially from that of previous versions and you will most likely want to rethink the setup. If you choose not to do this, you must stop replication before you can do the upgrade. You must upgrade the distribution server (or publisher/distributor server) first, and you can only do a single-machine upgrade. You can't upgrade 6.0 replication to 7.0; you must upgrade to 6.5 first.

Cross-Database Dependencies

The upgrade enables you to upgrade databases separately. If you choose this option, however, you must be very careful. You need to watch out for cross-database dependencies. There are two different types of dependencies: code dependencies and logon dependencies.

Code Dependencies

Code dependencies exist when applications (particularly stored procedures) refer to more than one database. Assume, for example, that there are two databases: Sales and SalesHistory. When a new order is taken, it is recorded in the Orders table in the Sales database, and the OrderHistory table in the SalesHistory database is updated with the new order value. The stored procedure that does this was created in the Sales database. If Sales is upgraded and SalesHistory is not, that stored procedure will fail when someone tries to run it because the SalesHistory database does not exist on SQL Server 7.0.

Logon Dependencies

The logon dependency is subtler. The upgrade process creates logons based on a logon's *default* database. If a logon's default database is not one being upgraded, the logon will not be created. If that logon owns objects in a database being upgraded, those objects will not be created because there is no logon to own them (see Figure 2.2).

Figure 2.2   Result of upgrading a database with logon dependencies.

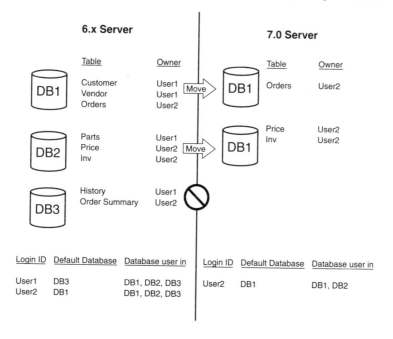

In many cases, you will not encounter this situation because all objects are owned by dbo. You do need to make sure that all your logons have a default database other than master or pubs, however, because those databases will not be upgraded.

Upgrade "Gotchas"

You might find some situations in your databases that will cause the upgrade to fail or to be incomplete.

Missing Text in syscomments

The syscomments table contains the text of all stored procedures, views, triggers, and old-style rules and defaults. If a stored procedure exists in sysprocedures, but there is no corresponding text in syscomments, that stored procedure cannot be created in your 7.0 database. This situation can exist for a couple of reasons. First, using sp_rename does not modify the text in syscomments. Second, before it was possible to encrypt stored procedures, third-party application vendors sometimes deleted this text to protect their proprietary software.

The upgrade won't fail because of missing text, but you will not have the stored procedure. Hopefully, if this situation occurs, the text will exist in an external source because it won't be possible to script the procedure in Enterprise Manager or with DMO.

❝❝   IMO

In general, you should avoid the use of **sp_rename**, even in SQL Server 7.0. It causes more problems than it solves. The only time you should use it is when you are planning to delete the renamed object. If you want to change a table structure, for example, you might rename the table to table_old, create the new table, and insert data into the new table by selecting it from the old table and dropping table_old. This is what the graphical tools in SQL Server 7.0 and in Visual Interdev do.

↑   Performance Tip

In SQL Server 7.0, you can modify table structures in many ways with the **Alter Table** statement. This does not do a copy, and, when you're working with large tables, will be much faster than the same operation done through the graphical tools.

Stored Procedures that Update System Tables

It has always been considered unwise to update system tables. However, people on occasion have developed stored procedures that do this. These procedures will not be upgraded. The upgrade proceeds in this situation, but does not move the offending procedure to 7.0. You need to determine why these procedures exist and whether they are appropriate for your 7.0 environment. Keep in mind that there are many changes to the system tables in 7.0, and the procedures may no longer work.

Corrupt Databases

Corrupt databases cannot be upgraded. You should run DBCC to check for corruption and, if found, restore from a non-corrupt backup before you begin the upgrade.

Choosing an Upgrade Method

Two upgrade methods are available: tape and named pipe. You should choose tape only if you are doing a single-machine upgrade and do not have sufficient disk space for both the 6.5 and 7.0 databases. Otherwise, choose named pipe; it is much faster. Note that you must have the named pipes network library installed, and SQL Server must be listening on the default pipe even if you are doing a tape upgrade.

 General Tip

If you do choose tape because you don't have enough disk space, the upgrade can automatically delete the SQL Server 6.x device files for you. It can also back up the SQL Server 6.x databases. Be careful here. If there are multiple databases sharing the same device, it will be deleted even if you didn't upgrade that database.

Validation Selection

There are two levels of validation: successful object transfer validation and exhaustive data integrity validation. In the first level, a list of objects and row counts is made on the 6.x installation. Then, these are compared with the list of objects and row counts on the 7.0 server after the upgrade. I recommend choosing at least this validation. If you want more certainty, you can choose exhaustive validation. This computes a checksum for each column of each table and compares the before-and-after checksums to be certain that they are identical. This slows down the upgrade, but ensures that not a single bit has been lost.

Startup Parameters

Because the SQL Servers are stopped and restarted several times during the upgrade, you must specify any trace flags or other startup arguments that you normally use for the SQL Servers. You must also disable any system startup stored procedures in the 6.x and 7.0 servers.

Code Page Selection

The Upgrade Wizard proposes a code page for you. In most cases, the default (ISO) is appropriate. International users who require a different code page may need to change this. If you're not familiar with code pages, see the section titled "Choosing Character Sets, Sort Orders, and Unicode Collation" earlier in this chapter.

Selecting Which Database to Upgrade

In most cases, it is best to upgrade all the databases on the 6.x server simultaneously. If you are certain that no dependencies exist, however, you can upgrade them at different times.

You cannot upgrade master, msdb, or pubs. You can transfer your tasks, operators, and alerts to SQL Server 7.0; however, this is not done by upgrading msdb, but by choosing an option.

After you have upgraded a database, you can't upgrade it again. If you do want to redo the upgrade, you must drop the SQL Server 7.0 database before you can upgrade.

Methods for Creating SQL Server 7.0 Databases

The Upgrade program proposes a SQL Server 7.0 database layout based on the devices you have used in your 6.x installation. If a database uses multiple devices, a file corresponding to each device is created by default. You can edit this configuration to place files in the locations where you want them. You can also remove files that you don't want to use. If you do keep multiple files, the upgrade process distributes data across all the files.

You can also create the database yourself before doing the upgrade (see Chapter 4 for details on this process). The database must have the same name as the 6.x database. You can also supply a script that creates the database (using SQL Server 7.0 syntax). The Upgrade Wizard tells you that you don't know what you're doing if you choose either of these options, but you can ignore it.

---

66   IMO

I think the wizard is over-protective when you try to create databases yourself instead of letting it do it.

Moving Configuration Options, Executive Settings, and Replication Settings

You will be given a choice as to whether you want to move SQL Server configuration options, SQL Executive settings, and replication settings.

---

66   IMO

I recommend that you move the SQL Executive settings only. Moving configuration options changes things around in SQL Server 7.0. You should deal with SQL Server 7.0 configuration using SQL Server 7.0 facilities. Contrary to the documentation, it is not necessary to check this option to get the logons created.

Completing the Upgrade

After you have made all the necessary decisions, running the Upgrade program is simple. You will have several opportunities to review error messages, and you should do so. After the upgrade has been completed, you will find a subdirectory in MSSQL7\UPGRADE named *<MACHINENAME>_DATE_TIME*.

For example:

MYCOMPUTER_100699_120359

This folder contains files that refer to the upgrade in general. In this folder, there will be a folder for each database that was upgraded. This folder will be named *<NUMBER><DATABASENAME>*.

For example:

006MYDATABASE

The number has no meaning. These folders contain various scripts used in the upgrade.

When the upgrade completes, neither the 6.x or 7.0 server is running.

Compatibility Mode

After you have upgraded a database, it is in 60 or 65 compatibility mode. This preserves various behaviors that have changed in SQL Server 7.0. You can find descriptions of these changes in the "Backward Compatibility" section of Books OnLine.

You can determine the compatibility level of a database by issuing the following command:

```
sp_dbcmptlevel DATABASENAME
```

For example:

```
sp_dbcmptlevel MYDATABASE
```

You can also use this command to change the compatibility level (your choices are 60, 65, or 70) as shown in the following:

```
sp_dbcmptlevel MYDATABASE, 70
```

master, msdb, model, pubs, and Northwind, as well as any new databases you create, will be in 70 compatibility mode.

While you are in 6.x compatibility mode, you still get most of the new features of SQL Server 7.0 (such as the improved Query Optimizer and row-level locking). However, you will not have access to new Transact-SQL commands, such as BACKUP (the 6.x DUMP command is still be available) and TOP. You want to move to 7.0 compatibility mode as soon as possible so that you can take advantage of all the new and improved features.

> **❝❞ IMO**
>
> I suggest that you do a test upgrade of all your databases. Then you should put each of them into 70 compatibility mode. Review the documentation on backward compatibility so that you can identify where you might anticipate problems. Then, run all your existing applications, see what breaks, and fix it. After you have identified and fixed all the problem areas, you are ready to do another upgrade and put your production systems on SQL Server 7.0.

Advanced Topics

This section describes some things that you can do to tailor the installation and upgrade process, including an unattended installation, using SMS to install SQL Server, and customizing the upgrade by inserting your own scripts.

Unattended Installation

It is possible to do an unattended installation of SQL Server 7.0. This can be useful if you have many servers on which SQL Server 7.0 must be installed. You need a setup initialization file. You can create this file in a couple of ways. First of all, one will be created for you automatically as a result of a manual installation of SQL Server. It will contain all the choices you made when you did the installation. The file, SETUP.ISS, is located in the \MSSQL7\INSTALL directory. You can use this file to set up other SQL Servers that have the same configuration.

You can also have SQL Server generate a SETUP.ISS file without installing SQL Server. To do this, start a command-prompt session. Switch to either the X86\SETUP or ALPHA\SETUP directory on the Install CD. Issue the following command:

```
Setupsql k=Rc
```

The SETUP.ISS file will be written to the WINDOWS or WINNT folder. When the Setup program says that it is ready to copy files, just cancel the process.

You will need to modify the following two sections of the file that is generated because they will be incomplete:

```
[SdStartCopy-0]
Result=1
```

and

```
[SdFinish-0]
Result=1
bOpt1=0
bOpt2=0
```

You can also prepare the SETUP.ISS file from scratch using any text editor that can create an ASCII file. Refer to the Books OnLine for details if you want to do this.

Using SMS to Install SQL Server 7.0

It is possible to use Microsoft System Management Server 1.2 and later to install SQL Server. The install CD contains a *Package Definition Format* (PDF) file, SMSSQL70.PDF. This file automates creating a SQL Server package that can then be distributed and installed on SMS computers.

The package includes instructions for installing a full server, a full client, a desktop server, and a desktop client. You can follow the chain of .BAT and ISS files to find out the included options. If you want to do something different, you should copy the PDF file and modify it.

Customizing the Upgrade Process

You can customize the upgrade process by introducing your own scripts. When you run the upgrade, you have the option of pausing between steps. Between each upgrade step, you can run an EXE or a SQL script. This is most useful for *independent software vendors* (ISVs) who are distributing upgrade packages for their products. Most users do not need this capability.

3

Server and Client Configuration and Troubleshooting

With previous versions of SQL Server, as soon as it was installed, the DBA sat down to configure it. SQL Server 7.0's capability to configure itself removes much of that need. However, you may find some things useful in solving problems specific to your installation. This chapter covers the startup of SQL Server. Then, it looks at some of the configuration options that you may want to explore. Note that the most useful configuration options relate to how SQL Server performs. This chapter also covers SQL Server's interaction with Windows NT. The server-side discussion ends with a section on server troubleshooting. The discussion then turns to the client side, and covers client setup and configuration. Finally, because one of the most annoying tasks you will face as a SQL Server DBA involves dealing with connectivity problems, this chapter shows you a few tricks for dealing with this troublesome part of SQL Server.

Starting, Pausing, and Stopping SQL Server

When you installed SQL Server, you most likely checked the option to have SQL Server and the SQL Agent start when Windows NT starts. On some occasions, however, you may want to stop and start the server without taking down NT. You can do this with Enterprise Manager, or with the SQL Service Manager. I almost always use the Service Manager because it comes up quickly, and its traffic light icon is easily accessible from my Icon Tray. But there are other ways of stopping and starting the server, including the following:

- The Services applet in Control Panel
- From the command prompt

Starting SQL Server

You can start SQL Server from the command prompt in two different ways:

- NET START mssqlserver
- sqlservr

NET START starts SQL Server as a service just as Enterprise Manager, SQL Service Manager, or Control Panel do. When SQL Server is running as a service, you can log off NT and the server continues to run. If you start it by just typing sqlservr at the command prompt, however, it is not run as a service. This means that you must shut it down (by pressing Ctrl+C) before you log off of NT. Note that you shouldn't minimize the command window. When you start SQL Server this way, it runs as a foreground application. If you minimize the window, NT pages all the SQL Server memory out. You can specify some options on the command line; some of the most useful ones are discussed later in this chapter.

You can also start SQL Server from DMO with the Start method of a server object. The Start method has four parameters, as shown here.

Parameter	Description
StartMode	When set to true, an attempt is made to connect on successful start. When set to false, no attempt is made to connect after a successful start.
Server	This parameter is optional and is a string that specifies the SQL Server name. You can also provide the server name in the Name property of the SQL Server object.
Logon	This parameter is optional, and is a string specifying the SQL Server logon that will be used to connect after the server is started. (StartMode is true.)
Password	This parameter is optional and is a string specifying the SQL Server password that will be used to connect after the server is started. (StartMode is true.)

Pausing SQL Server

You can pause SQL Server with Enterprise Manager, SQL Service Manager, the Services applet in Control Panel, the command line, or DMO. You can pause the server only when it is running as a service. When you pause SQL Server, no new connections are allowed, but existing connections are allowed to complete their work. You should pause the SQL Server and broadcast a "Server going down in *x* minutes" message when you plan to take the server down. In Enterprise Manager, SQL Service Manager, and Control Panel, it is just a matter of clicking the Pause button. From the command line, just type the following:

```
NET PAUSE MSSQLSERVER
```

In DMO, use the Pause method of a SQL Server object. This method has no arguments.

You can restart a paused server with the Start/Continue button in SQL Service Manager, the Continue button in the Services applet, or the Continue choice in Enterprise Manager. To restart from the command line, use the following:

```
NET CONTINUE MSSQLSERVER
```

In DMO, use the Continue method of a SQL Server object. The method has no arguments.

General Tip

There doesn't seem to be any way to pause and resume SQL Server with Transact-SQL.

Stopping SQL Server

When you stop the SQL Server, SQL Server disallows new connections and allows existing connections to finish their work. Then, it takes a checkpoint in every database, and shuts down. It's possible to stop SQL Server with Enterprise Manager, Service Manager, the Services applet, the command line, DMO, and Transact-SQL. In the graphical tools, just click Stop. To stop SQL Server from the command line, use the following:

```
NET STOP MSSQLSERVER
```

 General Tip

Note that if you don't start SQL Server as a service, you must use Ctrl+C to stop it.

In DMO, just use the Stop method of the SQL Server object. This method has no arguments.

In Transact-SQL you can issue the following shutdown command:

```
SHUTDOWN [WITH NOWAIT]
```

If you don't specify WITH NOWAIT, SQL Server stops in the same fashion described previously. If you specify WITH NOWAIT, existing connections are stopped, their transactions are rolled back, and no checkpoints are taken. You should use the NOWAIT option only in an emergency and when you are certain that the server needs to stop immediately.

Startup Switches

Some startup switches are used when SQL Server starts. The default values are stored in the Registry. Any switches you provide on the command line override the Registry values. The following three switches are required.

Switch	Description
-dmaster_file_path	The fully qualified name of the master database file (for example, C:\MSSQL7\DATA\MASTER.MDF)
-lmaster_log_path	The fully qualified name of the transaction log for the master database (for example, C:\MSSQL7\DATA\MASTER.LDF)
-eerror_log_path	The fully qualified name of the SQL Server Error log file (for example, C:\MSSQL7\LOG\ERRORLOG)

You can change the default values for startup switches in several ways. In Enterprise Manager, highlight the server, right-click, and choose Properties. On the General tab, click the Startup Parameters button. Or you can edit the Registry, although I don't recommend doing that. The startup parameters are stored in the following: HKEY_LOCAL_MACHINE\SOFTWARE\Microsoft\ MSSQLServer\MSSQLServer\Parameters

The parameters are named SQLArg0, SQLArg1, SQLArg2, and so on. The order doesn't matter because the switch is part of the parameter.

You can also use the following useful switches at startup.

Switch	Description
-c	Starts SQL Server so that it does not run as a service. This shortens startup time, but there is no other advantage. When you start SQL Server this way, you cannot log off of NT without stopping SQL Server first.
-f	Starts SQL Server with a Minimal configuration. This is useful for recovering from a failed configuration.
-m	Starts SQL Server in single-user mode, and enables the Allow Updates to System Tables option (discussed later). This option is most often used when restoring master (see Chapter 6, "Backup and Recovery," for more information).
-pprecision_level	Specifies the maximum level of precision used for decimal and numeric datatypes. The actual precision allowed is 38; but by default, SQL Server only allows 28. If you need the additional 10 digits, use this start-up switch.
-sregistry_key	Starts SQL Server with a set of parameters stored under the key named in registry_key. You can only use this option from the command line, but it enables you to have many previously defined startup options.
/Ttrace_flag#	Specifies that the server should start with a trace flag.
-x	Turns off the recording of CPU and cache-hit ratio statistics. This can improve performance, but you will not be able to see these values in Performance Monitor. It may also interfere with Performance Condition alerts (see Chapter 8, "Jobs and Alerts," for more information on alerts).

When I'm going to use a switch once—for example, putting the server in single-user mode so that I can restore the master database—I set the switch with Control Panel. To do this, use the Services applet. Highlight the MSSQLServer service. You will see the display shown in Figure 3.1.

Figure 3.1   Specifying startup switches in Control Panel.

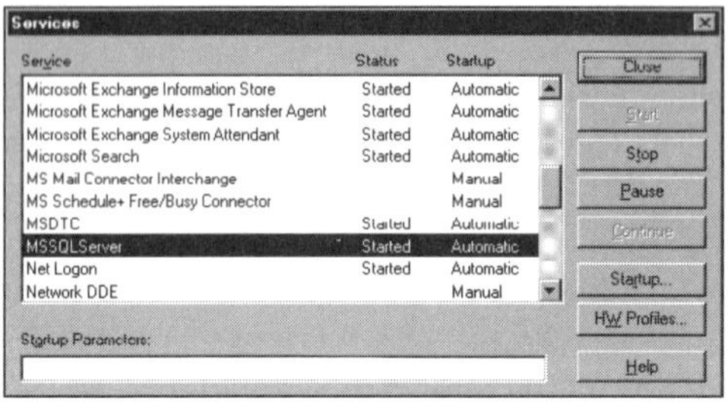

You can just type the **–m** switch (or another switch name) in the Startup Parameters box at the bottom of the screen. It applies for a single startup of SQL Server. I think this is much easier than going through Enterprise Manager to change the parameters, and then having to remember to change them back.

General Tip

There's no way to specify startup switches when you start the server with DMO. It uses the default settings from the Registry.

Setting the Polling Interval

Both Enterprise Manager and SQL Service Manager routinely poll the SQL Server to determine whether it (as well as SQL Server Agent, MSDTC, and Full-Text Search) is still running. If you look closely at the Service Manager icon at the bottom right of your screen, you will periodically see a little red "blip" when this polling happens. You can control the polling interval. In Enterprise Manager, highlight a server and choose Tools, Options. Choose the target service and specify the polling interval in seconds. If you uncheck the Poll Server box, Enterprise Manager will not poll. The only downside of this is that you won't see little red, green, and yellow indicators of server state in the console tree. The upside of not polling is that there's less demand on the server.

To specify SQL Service Manager's polling interval, open Service Manager and select the service. Then right-click the icon in the System Tray and choose Options. Enter the polling interval in seconds.

General Tip

There's no relationship between Service Manager's polling interval and Enterprise Manager's. They're both client programs operating independently.

Configuring SQL Server

SQL Server is largely self-configuring, and in many cases it works correctly "right out of the box." You should understand some options, however, in case your circumstances require changes from the default behavior. You can change all configuration options with Transact-SQL, many of them with Enterprise Manager, and all of them with SQL DMO.

This section discusses generic options, covering options that relate to specific tasks as the task is discussed. Configuration options are classified on two different dimensions:

- **Standard versus advanced.** Standard options are the most commonly changed, whereas advanced options are infrequently changed.
- **Static versus dynamic.** Static options do not take effect until the server is restarted, whereas the dynamic options take effect immediately.

In SQL Server 7.0, the advanced options are visible by default. If you turn off the Show Advanced Options, you can't modify any of the advanced options using Transact-SQL. In the following discussions on options, these categories are in parentheses at the end of the description of the option:

- **(S, S).** Standard option, requires restart
- **(S, D).** Standard option, takes effect immediately
- **(A, S).** Advanced option, requires restart
- **(A, D).** Advanced option, takes effect immediately

Use these category descriptions to understand when options take effect and when you are required to restart SQL for them to take effect.

Miscellaneous Options

Some options apply to the server as a whole and don't fit into a neat category such as "memory." I've grouped them here.

- **Allow Updates.** When this option is set to true, direct updates to the system tables are permitted. In most cases, you do not want this option to be turned on. In those rare cases in which you must modify system tables, I recommended that you do it with the server in single-user mode. Note that if this setting is true when you create a stored procedure, the stored procedure can modify system tables even after the option is turned off. (S, D)

 Danger

Updating system tables directly can cause your server to fail to start or to behave erratically.

- **Default Language.** This option specifies the ID (taken from syslanguages) for the default language, and controls default formats for displaying dates and gives meaning to the date parts.

  If you have a localized version of SQL Server (French, German, Spanish, Japanese), the default language specifies the language in which error messages display. If you have a Japanese SQL Server, and the default language is Japanese, for example, SQL Server error messages display in Japanese. If the default language on a localized SQL Server is not the local language, the messages displays in U.S. English. If you have a French SQL Server and specify Italian as the default language, for example, all error messages will be in U.S. English. (S, D)

- **Language in Cache.** This option specifies the number of languages that can be held in cache. The default is 3. (S, S)

- **Network Packet Size (B).** The network packet size specifies the network packet size in bytes. By default, SQL Server uses 4096 bytes as the packet size. If you routinely send large amounts of data across the network, you may benefit from a larger packet size. Conversely, if most of your transmissions are small, you might want to set this to 512 bytes, which is sufficient for many small data transmissions. If you have multiple protocols, set the network packet size to that which is appropriate for the most commonly used protocol. Note that a client application can specify a packet size that differs from the one specified here. (A, D)

- **Recovery Interval (Min).** This option specifies the number of minutes it will take SQL Server to recover all databases on the system at startup. It influences the frequency with which SQL Server takes checkpoints. By default, it is 0, which means that SQL Server configures it appropriately. In general, you should leave this option alone unless you find that checkpoints are being taken too frequently (see Chapter 6 for a discussion of checkpoints). In that case, you may want to experiment with increasing the value in small increments. (A, D)

- **Show Advanced Options.** This option determines whether you can see or change the advanced options when you run `sp_configure`. By default, it is set so that advanced options are visible.

  Note that if you run the Upgrade Wizard (see Chapter 2, "Installation and Upgrade," for more information on this) and ask to migrate SQL Server 6.5 configuration options, you will find that this option is set to off. (S, D)

Memory-Related Options

The options in this section all relate to how SQL Server uses memory. In SQL Server 7.0, memory is largely self-configuring. If you have a machine running only SQL Server, you probably won't have to modify these settings. If you are running other applications, however, you may want to adjust some of these settings.

By default, SQL Server monitors its environment. When the operating system has less than 5MB (± 200KB) of free memory, SQL Server gives memory it would have normally kept for its available pool back to the operating system. When there is more than 5MB free, SQL Server takes the memory back.

The memory options available are as follows:

- **Extended Memory Size (MB).** This option is primarily for forward compatibility. It will be available in future versions of SQL Server running on a future version of Windows NT that has support for 64-bit addressing. Some hardware vendors may support this capability under Windows NT 4.0. (A, S)

- **Locks.** In previous versions of SQL Server, the amount of space available for locks was fixed, and it was necessary to tinker with this option. In SQL Server 7.0, SQL Server allocates 2% of the available memory for locks. When additional memory is needed, SQL Server allocates it unless doing so would reduce the amount of free memory for the OS to less than 5MB. If this happens, SQL Server issues a message that you are out of locks. You should change the number of locks only if you receive this message. The default for this option is 0, which means that it is self-configuring. If you explicitly specify this value, the value must be between 5,000 and 2,147,483,647. (A, S)

- **Min Server Memory (MB), Max Server Memory (MB).** These two options work together. If you set Min Server Memory and Max Server Memory to the same value, SQL Server uses a fixed portion of memory. If SQL Server is the only application running on the machine, leave these settings alone. If other applications are running, setting a Max Server Memory influences how quickly they start up, because there is normally a delay between when the competing application begins and when SQL Server frees memory for it. If you want to guarantee that SQL Server has a set minimum amount of memory no matter what, specify a Min Server Memory. The smallest value you can specify for Max Server Memory is 4MB; the highest value is limited by the resources available on your system. If you specify Min Server Memory, and the server is involved with replication, the value must be greater than or equal to 16.

If your server is periodically idle for long periods of time, you may want to set Min Server Memory so that the memory is immediately available when a query does come. If you have other critical applications on the machine that might also have idle applications, you might want to set Max Server Memory so that memory is available to those applications when they become active. (A, S)

General Tip

If you have installed Full-Text Indexing and are running the MS Search Service, you must specify a Max Server Memory so that there is enough room for the Search Service to run. In this case, you must configure NT's virtual memory so that there is virtual memory (virtual memory for SQL Server and virtual memory for any other concurrently running applications equal to 1.5 times the machine's physical memory for the search service):

NT virtual memory ≥ 1.5 × physical memory

You also need to specify a Max Server Memory if you are running SQL Server on the same machine as Exchange Server.

- **Set Working Set Size.** This option reserves physical memory for SQL Server. If Windows NT must page, it must swap out other processes. By default, this option is off, and idle SQL Server memory can be swapped out. It is best to leave it off. (A, S)

- **Open Objects.** An open object is any table, stored procedure, view, and so on currently in use. Note that no matter how many users there are for an object, it is one open object. This option is self-configuring by default, and in most cases you should leave it that way. If you receive repeated instances of the following message in your Error log, you may want to consider setting it to some value:

 Warning

OPEN OBJECTS parameter may be too low; attempt was made to free up descriptors in localdes(). Run sp_configure to increase parameter value.

I would start with 10,000 and keep increasing it until the messages go away. Note that doing this reserves memory for open objects that cannot be reused for other purposes. (A, S)

Look, But Don't Touch Options

All the options listed in this section enable you to look at information. You should never modify the sort order ID or the Unicode information. The only successful way to change these is to reinstall SQL Server. Likewise, there is nothing to be gained from modifying the User Connections option. Following are the "look, but don't touch" options:

- **Default SortOrder ID, Unicode Comparison Style, Unicode Locale ID.** These options show you the sort order ID, Unicode comparison style, and Unicode locale that you chose when you installed SQL Server. These options are numbers; to find out what they mean, issue the following command:

```
sp_helpsort
```

- **User Connections.** In previous versions of SQL Server, it was necessary to specify the maximum number of concurrent connections to SQL Server. In this release, SQL Server manages the number of connections dynamically and there is no reason to specify a value for this option. If you set it too low, users may be denied access to SQL Server. (A, S)

General Tip

Don't confuse connection with user. Each user may have many simultaneous connections to the server. You can't use the User Connections option to limit concurrent users.

Options That Affect Applications

Some of the SQL Server options can change the behavior of applications. The following list identifies these options:

- **Two Digit Year Cutoff.** Since time immemorial, SQL Server has observed the rule that, if dates are entered without a century, values less than 50 are assumed to be in 20*xx* and values greater than 50 are assumed to be in 19*xx*. Therefore, 1/14/44 is interpreted as 1/14/2044, and 1/14/56 is interpreted as 1956. However, the OLE automation interface, including the capability to maintain data in Enterprise Manager (and ADO as well), has a cutoff of 30. With this rule, 1/14/44 becomes 1/14/1944. If at the time you are reading this you still have any applications that are not providing the century as part of the date, you probably have bigger things to worry about than this option. Your best option is to leave it alone and make sure the century is always supplied.

Danger

It is very easy to enter incorrect date data in Enterprise Manager's Open Table, Return All Rows dialog box because the dates display in mm/dd/yy format *without* century. Enterprise Manager, being a graphical tool going through OLE automation, uses 30 as the pivot point.

- **Nested Triggers.** When you are working with triggers, you can set up your applications so that a trigger on Table A performs some operation on Table B. With nested triggers, if there is a trigger on Table B, the trigger fires when Table A's trigger modifies Table B. This makes triggers much smaller and much more modular. It is unusual, although not impossible, for there to be situations in which this behavior is undesirable. In such a case, you turn nested triggers off. In most cases, you do not want to do so. Nested triggers has been SQL Server's default since 4.2; be very careful changing this if you have legacy applications that have been upgraded. This is a serverwide option. Don't confuse it with "recursive triggers," which are requested at a database level. (S, D)

- **User Options.** Many session-level (connection-level) settings control the behavior of applications. These options are specified with the SET statement. Some of these can be specified at the server level by using the appropriate bit masks for the User Options configuration option. The following options can be set at the server level.

SET Option	Bit Mask
DISABLE_DEF_CNST_CHK	1
IMPLICIT_TRANSACTIONS	2
CURSOR_CLOSE_ON_COMMIT	4
ANSI_WARNINGS	8
ANSI_PADDING	16
ANSI_NULLS	32
ARITHABORT	64
ARITHIGNORE	128
QUOTED_IDENTIFIER	256
NOCOUNT	512
ANSI_NULL_DFLT_ON	1024
ANSI_NULL_DFLT_OFF	2048

See the discussion of the SET statement in your SQL Server documentation for the meaning of these settings. If you are not comfortable working with bit masks, you can set these on or off through the Enterprise Manager graphical user interface. (S, D)

Changing Configuration Options with Transact-SQL

To change a configuration option in Transact-SQL, use the following command:

```
sp_configure [option [, value]
```

If you just issue the command sp_configure in Query Analyzer, a report appears showing all the configuration options available together with their minimum, maximum, current, and next values. This report looks like the one shown in here.

Name	Minimum	Maximum	config_value	run_value
Affinity Mask	0	2147483647	0	0
Allow Updates	0	1	0	0
Cost Threshold for Parallelism	0	32767	5	5
Cursor Threshold	−1	2147483647	−1	−1

Name	Minimum	Maximum	config_value	run_value
Default Language	0	9999	0	0
Default SortOrder ID	0	255	51	51
Extended Memory Size (MB)	0	2147483647	0	0

The Name column in this report is the name of the particular option, and what you use if you want to change that option. The column headed config_value is the value that will be used the next time SQL Server is started. The column headed run_value is the value SQL Server is currently using. A minimum and maximum of 0 and 1, respectively, indicates that it is a true-false option. If there is a minimum and maximum, but the run_value is 0, it's most likely one of the options that SQL Server manages dynamically.

If you issue the sp_configure command with just the name of an option, you will see the line of the preceding report for only that option. For example:

```
sp_configure 'allow updates'
```

This shows you the settings for just the Allow Updates option. You don't need to spell the option name out in full; any unique left substring works. Therefore, for Allow Updates, you can use 'al', 'allow', and so on.

To change the value of an option, add a value to the command such as this:

```
sp_configure 'allow', 1
```

After you have done this, you must use the reconfigure (or, in some cases, the reconfigure with override) command to make the option take effect. If the option is dynamic, the change is made immediately. If it's a static option, you must stop the server and restart it before the change takes effect.

Changing Configuration Options with Enterprise Manager

Not all configuration options can be changed in Enterprise Manager. To change options using Enterprise Manager, right-click the server in the console pane and choose Properties. The SQL Server Properties dialog box displays, which includes several various tabs and options. Two screens in this dialog box can be confusing if you've never worked in them before. The first is the Memory Configuration screen shown in Figure 3.2.

Figure 3.2   Memory Configuration screen.

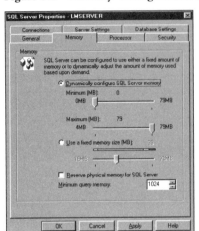

The check box labeled Reserve Physical Memory for SQL Server is the same as the Set Working Set Size option discussed previously.

Another confusing screen is the Connection Options screen shown in Figure 3.3.

Figure 3.3   Connection Options screen.

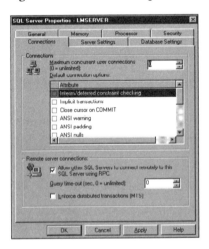

The check boxes for the Default Connection Options correspond to the bit masks for the User Options configuration option described previously.

In Enterprise Manager, the Apply and OK buttons cause the dynamic options to take effect. In addition, Enterprise Manager asks you whether you want to stop and restart the server when you modify a static option. If you are ready to stop the server, choose Yes. If you want to wait until a later time to stop the server (remembering that the option won't take effect until you do so), choose No.

Changing Configuration Options with DMO

The SQL Server object has a configuration object, which contains the ConfigValues collection. Each ConfigValue object has the following useful properties.

Property	Description
CurrentValue	Long
RunningValue	Long
MaximumValue	Long
MinimumValue	Long
Name	String
DynamicReconfigure	True if it's a dynamic option; false if it's a static option

To change a configuration option, you set the value for the appropriate option (using the names specified) as follows:

```
Set oConfigValue = oSQLServer.Configuration.ConfigValues("Show Advanced
➥Options")oConfigValue.CurrentValue = 1
```

When you are ready to apply the changes, you use the ReconfigureCurrentValues method of the configuration object. If the configuration option requires with override as does the Allow Updates option, use the ReconfigureWithOverride method instead. If any of the changes are to static options, you must use the Stop and Start methods of the SQL Server object to make the changes take effect.

Behind the Scenes

Information about configuration option settings is contained in two different tables, sysconfigures and syscurconfigs:

- **sysconfigures.** This table contains the options SQL Server started with as well as any changes made to dynamic options since the server was started.

- **syscurconfigs.** This table contains values used the next time SQL Server is started. Note that syscurconfigs is a dynamic table built only when it is referenced.

Setting Up and Configuring Remote and Linked Servers

One SQL Server can interact with other SQL Servers as well as many other heterogeneous data sources. This can be done in two ways: *remote* servers and *linked* servers. When you set up a remote server, another SQL Server can execute stored procedures that reside in the remote server. Remote servers must be SQL Servers. This architecture is far more limited than the linked server architecture, which permits users to issue select, insert, update, and delete queries against the linked server. The linked server need not be a SQL Server; in fact, using linked servers, it is completely possible to join data from tables residing in SQL Server, Oracle, and Excel. In most cases, you will want to use linked servers rather than remote servers, because the linked servers are more powerful. I am going to cover remote servers as well as linked servers, however, because you may have legacy systems using the older architecture and because replication is implemented with remote servers.

Remote and Linked Server Configuration Options

Four configuration options deal with remote and linked servers. In most cases, the defaults are what you want, but you must make sure that the settings have not been changed from the default when you set up remote servers.

Options That Apply to Both Remote and Linked Servers

The following options apply to both remote and linked servers:

- **Remote Login Timeout (S).** This configuration option affects both remote and linked servers. It specifies how long to wait when connecting to a remote server. If you try to connect to a remote server, and that server is down, for example, you might wait forever. The default is 0, which means that you want to wait indefinitely. You may want to set this to an interval, such as 5 or 10 seconds. (S, D).

General Tip

The Remote Login Timeout option cannot be set in Enterprise Manager; you must use Transact-SQL or DMO to set it.

- **Remote Query Timeout (S).** This option specifies the number of seconds that SQL Server should wait after issuing a request to a linked server or a remote server before timing out if no results have been returned. The default is 0, which means that you wait indefinitely. (S, D)

Options That Apply Only to Remote Servers

The following options apply only to remote servers:

- **Remote Access.** The default is 1, which allows other servers to access this server remotely. If you are planning to use remote servers, you should leave this option alone. If you set it to 0, other servers can't access the server remotely. (S, S)

- **Remote Proc Trans.** If this option is set to 1, all operations using remote servers will be distributed transactions managed by MSDTC. Because a lot of overhead is required to manage distributed transactions, you should leave this option set to 0 (the default) and explicitly request a distributed transaction only when you need one. (S, D)

 General Tip

You can read more about distributed transactions in the Books OnLine.

Remote Servers

Remote servers are set up in pairs. First, each server must be aware of the other's existence. Then, you must set up logins for the remote servers. These are effectively mappings between the login ID used on one of the servers to the login ID used on the other server.

Setting Up Remote Servers with Transact-SQL

This procedure must be done on both servers. First, use the following command:

```
sp_addlinkedserver 'server', 'SQL Server'
```

Suppose, for example, that you have two servers, one named ServerA and one named ServerB. On ServerA, issue the following command:

```
sp_addlinkedserver 'ServerB', 'SQL Server'
```

On ServerB, issue the following command:

```
sp_addlinkedserver 'ServerA', 'SQL Server'
```

Now, you must map the logins. The way you do this depends on whether the logins are SQL Server Authentication logins or NT Authentication logins. (See Chapter 9, "Security," for details on the different methods of authentication.)

Mapping SQL Server Authentication Logins

If the user has the same login name and password on both SQL Servers, it is not necessary to perform this step. If Tom has a login on ServerA and a login on ServerB, for example, the mapping is automatic. If the names differ, however, you must define the mappings. Assume for this example that ServerA has a login named Theresa, and you want that login to map to a login named RemoteUsers on ServerB. Use the command sp_addremotelogin, as follows:

```
sp_addremotelogin 'remoteserver', 'login', 'remote_name'
```

For example, on ServerB:

```
sp_addremotelogin 'ServerA', 'RemoteUsers', 'Theresa'
```

After this has been done, Theresa, running on ServerA, can execute any stored procedures that RemoteUsers have been given permission to on ServerB. If you want bidirectional logins (that is, from ServerB to ServerA), use a similar process on ServerA.

The final step is to specify whether a password is needed when Theresa wants to run a procedure on ServerB. In most cases, it is easiest if you do not request that the password be checked, because remote stored procedures are likely to be executed from local stored procedures and it is difficult to interact with a user for a password. You specify this with the command sp_remoteoption, as follows:

```
sp_remoteoption 'remoteserver', 'loginame',
'remotename', trusted, {true ¦ false}
```

To continue the preceding example, the command should look like this:

```
sp_remoteoption 'ServerA', 'RemoteUsers', 'Theresa',
  trusted, true
```

Mapping NT Authentication Logins

Mapping NT Authentication logins is done differently. Use the command sp_addlinkedsrvlogin, as follows:

```
sp_addlinkedsrvlogin 'remoteserver', {true ¦ false},
  'locallogin', 'remotename', 'rmtpassword'
```

The second argument must be false for an NT Authentication login. Assume that PINE\SHARON has an NT Authentication login on ServerA, and that you want to map this login to RemoteUsers on ServerB with no password. The command, issued on ServerB, should look like this:

```
sp_addlinkedsrvlogin 'ServerA', false, RemoteUsers,
  'PINE¦SHARON', NULL
```

Setting Up Remote Servers with Enterprise Manager

It's much easier to set up remote servers with Enterprise Manager than with Transact-SQL, but it's not possible to map NT Authentication logins in Enterprise Manager. In the Security folder in the console pane, right-click on Remote Servers and choose New Remote Server. The screen shown in Figure 3.4 displays.

Figure 3.4   Remote Server Setup screen.

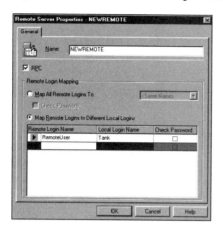

It is important to check the box labeled RPC near the top of the screen. You can map all users to a single login on the remote machine or you can map them individually as shown in Figure 3.3. To skip checking passwords on the remote server, don't check the box in the Check Password column.

Setting Up Remote Servers with DMO

You work with the RemoteServers collection, the RemoteServer object, the RemoteLogins collection, and the RemoteLogins object to set up remote servers with DMO.

To add a remote server, create a RemoteServer object. Specify its Name property and add it to the RemoteServers collection of a connected SQLServer object.

General Tip

You will see some other properties in the documentation and in the list that appears in Visual Basic for the object, but they all have to do with replication. You do not need to worry about setting these for a simple remote server.

To set up remote logins, create a RemoteLogin object. Set the RemoteName, LocalName, and Trusted properties. (Set these to true if password is not to be checked; otherwise set them to false.) Add the object to the RemoteLogins collection of a RemoteServer object.

General Tip

The RemoteLogin object seems to only handle SQL Server authentication logins.

Linked Servers

Linked servers are a new feature in SQL Server 7.0. They allow direct queries against many different data sources, including Oracle, Excel, Access, and ODBC data sources. After you have set up a linked server, you can query it by just including the linked server name as part of the table name, as follows:

```
SELECT * from MySpreadsheet...Sheet1$
SELECT * from ORACLEDB..Scott.Emp
```

Setting Up Linked Servers with Transact-SQL

Use the `sp_addlinkedserver` command to set up a linked server with Transact-SQL. This is the same command I described under remote servers, but there is a lot more information that you must provide when linking a heterogeneous server, as follows:

```
sp_addlinkedserver 'server', 'product_name',
provider_name','data_source','location',
'provider_string', 'catalog'
```

Server is a name you assign to the server, such as MyLinkedServer. The following table lists possibilities for the other parameters:

Remote Data	product_ name	provider_ name	Data_ Source	Location	provider_ string	Catalog
SQL Server	SQL Server (default)	SQLOLEDB (optional)	Network Name of SQL Server (optional)	N/A	N/A	Database name (option-al)
Oracle	Doesn't matter	MSDAORA	SQL*Net alias for Oracle database	N/A	N/A	N/A
Access/ Jet	Doesn't matter	Microsoft. Jet.OLEDB. 4.0	Full path name of Jet data-base file	N/A	N/A	N/A
ODBC data source	Doesn't matter	MSDASQL	System DSN of ODBC data source★	N/A	ODBC connection string★	N/A
File system	Doesn't matter	MSIDXS	Indexing Service catalog name	N/A	N/A	N/A

Microsoft Excel spread-sheet	Doesn't matter	Microsoft. Jet.OLEDB. 4.0	Full path name of Excel file	N/A	Excel 5.0	N/A
Text file***	Doesn't matter	Microsoft. Jet.OLEDB. 4.0	Full path name of text file	N/A	Text	N/A

*You establish this alias with Oracle client tools. Oracle connectivity must be installed on the machine to do this.

** Provide either the ODBC DSN or the full ODBC connection string, not both.

***You must have a SCHEMA.INI file in the same directory as the text file if you want to query text files. Preparation of this file is described in the Jet documentation that accompanies Microsoft Access.

If you want to set up an Excel spreadsheet as a linked server, the command should look like the following:

```
sp_addlinkedserver 'ExcelSpreadsheet', '',
'Microsoft.Jet.OLEDB.4.0',
'\\EXCEL:\MySpreadsheets\LastMonth.xls', '', 'Excel 5.0'
```

Remember that the path names are from the SQL Server's point of view; you must use share names accessible to SQL Server. Do not use your mapped drive letters. If the files do not reside on the SQL Server computer, SQL Server must be logging in with a domain account and that account must have permission to access the files.

When you set up linked servers, it's also necessary to configure logins for those servers. Use the command sp_addlinkedsrvlogin, as follows:

```
sp_addlinkedsrvlogin 'servername',{true ¦ false},
'SQL Server loginname',
'linked server login name',
'linked server password']
```

When you specify true for the second argument, the SQL Server login name is used to connect to the remote server. You can only use this if the SQL Server login is a SQL Server Authentication login. You may specify null for the SQL Server login name. In this case, all SQL Server logins will log in to the linked server with the linked server login name and password. If you provide a value, it must be a SQL Server login or a Windows NT login that has been granted access to the SQL Server. Assume, for example, that the Excel spreadsheet allows an Admin login with no password, and you want all SQL Server users to be able to log in to this linked server. The command to set this up is as follows:

```
sp_addlinkedsrvlogin 'ExcelSpreadsheet', FALSE,

     NULL, 'Admin', NULL
```

Setting Up Linked Servers with Enterprise Manager

It's very simple to set up linked servers with Enterprise Manager. In the Security folder, right-click Linked Servers and choose New. The screen shown in Figure 3.5 displays.

Figure 3.5   Setting up a linked server.

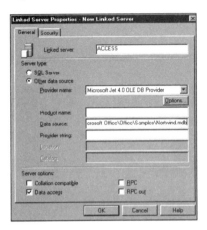

As annoying as it is, all linked server names must be in uppercase letters. Select the OLE DB Provider from the drop-down list, and provide the other elements using the parameters table in the preceding section. Leave Collation Compatible unchecked unless you are absolutely certain that the remote data source has the same character set as SQL Server. The RPC and RPC Out boxes only make sense for SQL Servers; they specify whether remote procedure calls from and to the server are allowed.

It's also possible to set up the logins with Enterprise Manager. You do so on the Security tab illustrated in Figure 3.6.

Figure 3.6   Specifying linked server logins in Enterprise Manager.

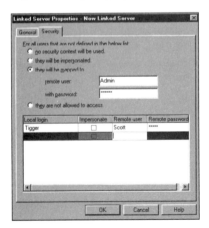

If you choose No Security Context Will Be Used, no logins at all are used. This makes sense for things such as Excel, if the spreadsheet isn't password protected, and text files, which have no security other than file-level permissions. If you choose They Will Be Impersonated, the SQL Server login is used to authenticate the user at the linked server. This only works for SQL Server Authentication logins. Checking this makes sense if the remote server is a SQL Server with the same logins as the server on which the linked server is defined. If you choose They Will Be Mapped To, all SQL Server users will connect to the linked server with the specified username and password. You should choose They Are Not Allowed to Access if you want to specify the logins individually in the grid at the bottom of the screen.

In the grid, provide the SQL Server login. In most cases, you won't choose Impersonate, because doing so requires that the logins be the same on both servers.

Refer back to Figure 3.6. With this setup, Tigger logs in to the linked server as a user named Scott with a password of Tiger. Any other users will log in as a user named Admin with a password of secret.

Setting Up Linked Servers with DMO

Each SQL Server object has a LinkedServers collection that contains LinkedServer objects. Each LinkedServer object has a LinkedServerLogins collection that contains LinkedServerLogin objects.

To add a new LinkedServer, instantiate a LinkedServer object and provide its Name property. Use the same properties you used for setting up linked servers with Transact-SQL to set up properties for DMO. When the properties of the LinkedServer object are complete, add it to the LinkedServers collection of a connected SQLServer object.

To define linked server logins, instantiate a LinkedServerLogin object. This object has four properties.

Property	Description
LocalLogin	SQL Server login
Impersonate	True if SQL Server login should be passed to the linked server; otherwise false
RemoteLogin	Username for linked server
RemotePassword	Password for linked server

Then, add the LinkedServerLogin object to the appropriate LinkedServerLogins collection.

Windows NT and SQL Server

When you install SQL Server, it modifies a couple of Windows NT settings. As long as the machine is dedicated to SQL Server, you should leave these settings alone. If the machine will run other applications, however, you may find it useful to change them.

SQL Server modifies the following Windows NT settings:

- **Application Performance.** SQL Server sets this so that foreground and background tasks are equally responsive. (The NT default gives priority to foreground tasks.)
- **Maximize Throughput.** SQL Server sets this to maximize throughput for network operations. (The NT default maximizes throughput for file-sharing operations.)

To change the setting for Application Performance, right-click My Computer and choose Properties. The System Properties dialog box shown in Figure 3.7 displays. The Application Performance option is on the Performance tab.

Figure 3.7   NT's Application Performance setting.

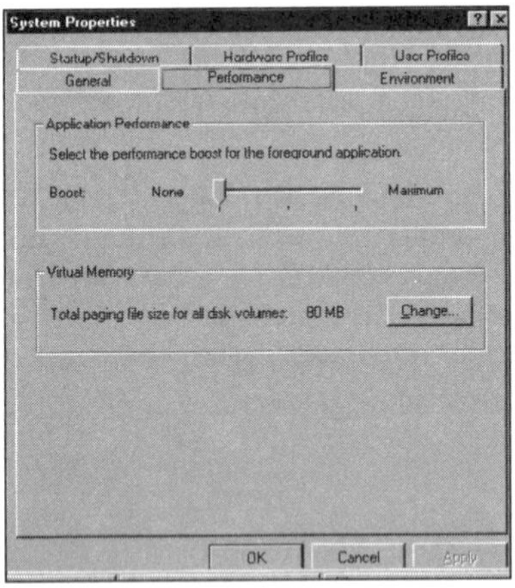

If you want to give more priority to foreground applications, move the slider to the right.

To modify the Maximize Throughput option, open the Network applet in Control Panel. On the Services tab, highlight Server and choose Properties. The screen shown in Figure 3.8 displays.

Figure 3.8   Server Properties dialog box in NT.

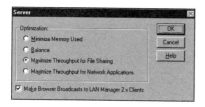

You can change the settings as necessary to benefit other applications on the machine. It's also a good idea to uncheck Make Browser Broadcasts to LAN Manager 2.x Clients if you don't have any of those (and you probably don't!). This broadcast could announce the name of your server to hackers.

Troubleshooting Server Problems

When SQL Server fails, it's often difficult to know where to start in terms of fixing it. This section examines how you can interpret SQL Server's Error log. Then, this section discusses something called trace flags, which you may be able to use to get information about what's happening. This section also shows you how to get the diagnostics you need when you call Microsoft Technical Support and how you can turn on SQL Server's "flight recorder." Most server troubleshooting is done "by guess and by golly," and there aren't many tools to help you. In the main, Enterprise Manager is useless; in fact, because it consumes so many resources, it may not even start when your server is having problems. You need to be comfortable with Query Analyzer, as well as operating system tools, such as the NT Event Viewer, and the always, reliable Notepad as well as the DOS prompt!

Error Log

SQL Server maintains a log of error and information messages. By default, this log is kept in the \MSSQL7\LOG folder, although you can change this by changing the location on the SQL Server startup (see the "Startup Switches" section earlier in this chapter). When you start SQL Server, SQL Server creates a new log and archives the old one. When you look in the folder where the Error logs are kept, you see the following files (assuming, for this example, that you have started SQL Server at least seven times):

File	Description
ERRORLOG	Current error log
ERRORLOG.1	Most recent error log
ERRORLOG.2	Second most recent log
ERRORLOG.3	Third most recent log

continues ▶

File	Description
ERRORLOG.4	Fourth most recent log
ERRORLOG.5	Fifth most recent log
ERRORLOG.6	Oldest log

If your server crashed, and you have restarted it, you may find the reason for the crash in ERRORLOG.1; if you haven't been able to restart it, look at ERRORLOG. You can view Error logs in Notepad. (It's also possible to view Error logs in Enterprise Manager; the logs are visible in the MANAGEMENT folder.) Many of the messages in the Error log are also visible in NT's Application Event log.

When you start SQL Server, it records the success and/or failure of its attempts to recover databases in the Error log. Normally, you see a series of messages and discover that all databases have been successfully recovered. Occasionally, you see a message that a database has been marked *suspect*. This usually means that one of the files that make up the database has been damaged or removed, and you will need to correct that problem. If you see errors that are Exception Access Violations, there is probably a bug in SQL Server and you will need to contact Microsoft Support. Other messages appear from time to time; for example, anytime that someone performs a non-logged operation, a message to that effect appears in the Error log. Following is one message that users often find troubling, but you shouldn't worry about it:

```
Failed to obtain TransactionDispenserInterface: XACT_E_TMNOT
AVAILABLE.
```

This message means that the MSDTC service isn't running. If you're not performing distributed transactions, you don't need MSDTC.

If your server crashes, you should start it in single-user mode and check the Error log to make sure that all the databases were successfully recovered and that there are no problems before you make the server available for general use.

Errors issued by applications in your organization may appear in the Event log as well. (Chapter 8 discusses this in more detail.)

Trace Flags

Trace flags are used to temporarily change the characteristics of SQL Server, or to turn off some particular behavior. Some trace flags are available for backward compatibility with previous versions of SQL Server. They can also provide additional information about locks, deadlocks, and query plans. Microsoft sometimes provides trace flags as a way of working around a bug. Trace flags normally write information to the Error log; there's a trace flag that you can use to override this and send the information back to a client. A few of the more useful trace flags are discussed here; you can get details about others from Books OnLine.

Trace Flags That Provide Detailed Information About Locks and Query Plans

Chapter 10, "Performance Tuning," discusses query plans in more detail, but the trace flags listed here can give you additional information when you are studying performance or contention problems:

Flag	Meaning
325	Prints information about the cost of using a non-clustered index or a sort to process an ORDER BY clause
326	Prints information about the estimated and actual cost of sorts
330	Enables full output when using the SET SHOWPLAN option, which gives detailed information about joins
1204	Returns the type of locks participating in the deadlock and the current command affected
1205	Returns more detailed information about the command being executed at the time of a deadlock

Managing Tape Compression

It's often desirable to compress data that is written to tape so that it takes up less space. By default, if a tape drive supports hardware compression, backups will be written in a compressed format. You can use the following trace flag to disable this compression if you want to exchange tapes with other sites or use other drives that don't support compression.

Flag	Meaning
3205	Disable hardware compression

Managing Trace Flags

As mentioned earlier, many trace flags send output to the Error log. You may want the output to come directly to you. Two trace flags control where the output is sent.

Flag	Meaning
3604	Sends trace output to the client. Used only when setting trace flags with DBCC TRACEON and DBCC TRACEOFF.
3605	Sends trace output to the Error log. (If you start SQL Server from the command prompt, the output also appears onscreen.)

Suppressing Unneeded Messages

The following trace flag that suppresses unneeded messages is an important flag, and you may want to include it on the SQL Server startup. Any time a statement that does not return results is executed in a stored procedure, SQL Server sends a Done in Proc message back to the client. For example, the following statement sends such a message:

```
IF @@error <> 0
```

Flag	Meaning
3640	Eliminates the sending of DONE_IN_PROC messages to the client for each statement in a stored procedure. This is similar to the session setting of SET NOCOUNT; but when set as a trace flag, every client session is handled this way.

The client has absolutely no interest in the Done in Proc message. It is a short message and can create bottlenecks across WANs. It also impairs the performance of stored procedures when they are run through the Job Scheduler.

Using Trace Flags

You can use trace flags in two ways:

- As a SQL Server startup parameter
- With DBCC TRACEON/OFF

To specify a trace flag as a SQL Server startup parameter, use **–T** or **/T** followed by the trace flag, as follows:

```
/T3640
```

Be sure to use a capital T; lowercase is for Microsoft internal trace flags.

To set a trace flag with DBCC, use the following command:

```
DBCC TRACEON (trace# [,...n])
```

If you are studying a problem and want the output to come back to the client (Query Analyzer, for example) instead of being written to the Error log, you should issue the following commands:

```
DBCC TRACEON (3604)
```

```
DBCC TRACEON (1205)
```

To turn off a trace flag, use the following command:

```
DBCC TRACEOFF (trace# [,...n)
```

To determine whether a trace flag is on or off, use the following command:

```
DBCC TRACESTATUS (trace# [,...n)
```

The resulting display shows the trace flag and a 0 if it is off, or a 1 if it is on.

Diagnostics

When you encounter problems with SQL Server, you need information that will help you solve the problem. If you have to contact Microsoft, they will ask you about your server configuration and want details as well. You have two ways of getting this information:

- The sqldiag utility
- SQL Server's "flight recorder"

You can also use these tools to collect information whether or not you are having problems. The flight recorder can help you isolate problem queries, and the output from sqldiag can provide a record of configuration settings, and other items as detailed in the following sections.

sqldiag

The sqldiag utility comes with SQL Server and gives you information whether or not SQL Server is running. When SQL Server is running, the report includes the following:

- Text of all Error logs
- Registry information
- DLL version information
- Output from the following:
  - `sp_configure`
  - `sp_who`
  - `sp_lock`
  - `sp_helpdb`
  - `xp_msver`
  - `sp_helpextendedproc`
  - `sysprocesses`
- Input buffer SPIDs/deadlock information
- Microsoft Diagnostics Report for the server, including the following:
  - Contents of <*SERVERNAME*>.TXT file
  - Operating system version report
  - System report
  - Processor list
  - Video display report
  - Hard drive report
  - Memory report
  - Services report
  - Drivers report
  - IRQ and port report

- DMA and memory report
- Environment report
- Network report

- The last 100 queries and exceptions (if you have turned on the recording of these)

  If SQL Server is not running, information about SPIDs, configuration information, and the output of the various stored procedures is not included. To run the diagnostics program, issue the following command at a DOS prompt:

  ```
  sqldiag [{-U login_ID] [-P password] ¦ [-E]}] [-O output_file]
  ```

  You must run sqldiag on the server; you cannot run it from a client workstation. You can specify a login ID and password, or use the **–E** switch to specify a trusted connection. By default, the output files are named SQLDIAG.TXT and SQLDIAG.TRC (if the query recorder is running) and are placed in the MSSQL7\LOG folder. You may specify a different name and location.

The Flight Recorder

It's possible to have SQL Server save the last 100 queries. If you do this, they are included in the output from sqldiag. The sqldiag utility produces a file that can be read by SQL Profiler. You can also have this file produced at any time (without running sqldiag) after the flight recorder has been enabled. The queries are stored in a wraparound list; when query 101 comes along, it overwrites query 1 in the list. To turn on the flight recorder, issue the following command:

```
xp_trace_setqueryhistory 1
```

After you have issued the command, `xp_trace_setqueryhistory` stored procedure is automatically executed each time SQL Server starts. To turn off the recorder, issue the following command:

```
xp_trace_setqueryhistory 0
```

You do not have to run sqldiag to find the most recent queries. Instead, you can issue the following command:

```
xp_trace_flushqueryhistory 'filename'
```

With this command, you can specify a full path as part of the filename. After the file has been created, you can view it using SQL Profiler. (See Chapter 10 for more information on SQL Profiler.)

 General Tip

I could not get the flight recorder to work until I stopped the server and restarted it. The commands appeared to work, but no query history file was created. The documentation did not mention the need to stop the server and restart it after issuing the `xp_trace_setqueryhistory` command.

After you have enabled the query history, SQL Server saves a trace automatically whenever there is a SQL Server–issued error with severity level 17 or higher. Note that if an application raises an error of level 17 or higher, the trace is not written. The trace is written to a file named BLACKBOX.TRC and saved to the \MSSQL7\LOG folder.

Client Configuration

Thus far, this chapter has discussed the server configuration. Now it's time to take a look at the client side.

Client/Server Architecture

SQL Server is a client/server database management system. That means that client processes, which are often running on remote machines, must communicate with SQL Server over the network, as shown in Figure 3.9.

Figure 3.9   Client/server architecture.

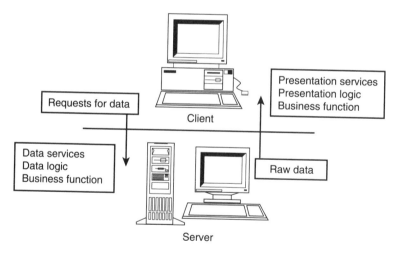

Client processes communicate with SQL Server in the following ways:

- **Open Database Connectivity (ODBC).** This is a native SQL Server driver used by many applications and developer tools including Visual Basic and Visual C++. The *Data Access Objects* (DAO), *Remote Data Objects* (RDO), and *Microsoft foundation classes* (MFC) all use ODBC.

- **OLE DB.** This is also a native SQL Server provider based on the *Component Object Model* (COM) and the *Distributed Component Object Model* (DCOM). It is less widely supported today, but support for it is expected to grow. It can be used from Visual Basic and Visual C++ as well as Visual Interdev. The *ActiveX Data Objects* (ADO) use OLE DB.

- **DB-Library (dblib).** This is the original *application programmer's interface* (API) to SQL Server. It is supported for backward compatibility, but has not been enhanced with SQL Server 7.0 features.

Regardless of which of these is being used, the communication process is identical, as Figure 3.10 shows.

Figure 3.10   Client/server communications.

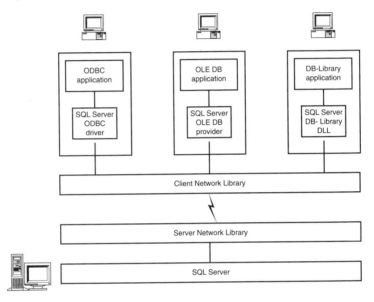

What's important is the network library. Chapter 2 discussed choosing network libraries for your server. It is important that the library each client is using match one on which the SQL Server is listening. Otherwise, there will be no communication.

The client and server network libraries are DLLs. The relationship between the netlib and the actual DLL is shown in the following table.

Netlib	32-bit DLL	16-bit DLL
multiprotocol	DBMSRPCN.DLL	DBMSRPC3.DLL
named pipes	DBNMPNTW.DLL	DBNMP3.DLL
TCP/IP Sockets	DBMSSOCN.DLL	DBMSSOC3.DLL
IPX/SPX	DBMSSPXN.DLL	DBMSSPX3.DLL
AppleTalk	DBMSADSN.DLL	n/a
Banyan VINES	DBMSVINN.DLL	DBMSVIN3.DLL
Shared Memory	DBMSSHRN.DLL	n/a
DECnet	DBMSDECN.DLL	n/a

Installing Client Connectivity

You install client connectivity with the same Setup program that you used to install SQL Server. You must choose a Custom install. The client workstation must have the Client Connectivity libraries installed. You can install the management tools (Enterprise Manager, Query Analyzer, and so on) and Books OnLine, but you do not need to. You might want to put these tools on developer workstations. Only C and C++ programmers need the development tools. Developers might also benefit from the code Samples. You specify what you want to install on the Components Selection screen shown in Figure 3.11.

Figure 3.11   Client Components Selection screen.

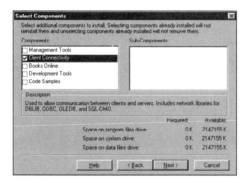

When you install Client Connectivity on Windows NT or Windows 9x, by default the client is using named pipes. If that client wants to connect to a server running on Windows 9x, you must change the default network library to TCP/IP. Do this with the Client Network utility.

> ⚠️ **Warning**
>
> A common misunderstanding has to do with how multiprotocol works. Although it can work over the NT network protocols—NetBIOS, TCP/IP, and NWLink IPX/SPX—it doesn't necessarily mean that the client can send requests using any of those network libraries. If you are using multiprotocol on the server, you must also use it on the client.

Troubleshooting Connectivity Problems

When a user reports that he or she can't connect, the first thing to do is to find out what message the user is getting. If the message says, Login Failed for User, the user most likely forgot his or her password. You can reset the password with sp_password. The command looks like this:

```
sp_password NULL, newpassword, loginid
```

Only the system administrator can issue this command.

`` IMO

The sp_password command should be available to members of the security admin role (Chapter 9 discusses that role in detail), but it is not.

If the user is getting messages, such as Specified SQL Server Not Found (named pipes) or General Network Error (Sockets), you most likely have a connectivity problem. These messages can also be issued if the server is down, so you want to make sure the server is running before doing anything else.

Unfortunately, most client connectivity problems have to be solved at the client workstation; so unless you have a utility such as PC Anywhere or Remotely Possible, you will have to visit the workstation of the user with the problem. You can try several things when you are at the user's workstation.

First, use the Client Network utility to check out the network library the client is using. This was installed along with Client Connectivity.

When you start the utility, the General tab shows you what the default network library is. A client can be set up to connect to more than one server, using different network libraries. You will see these aliases on the General tab as well. If the default network library or the one associated with a particular alias is not the one that SQL Server is listening on, just change the library. You can either select a different default, modify an existing alias entry, or add a new network library and alias. The Network Libraries tab shows you the network libraries available on the client workstation.

You might also need to check that the client and server are using the same underlying network protocol. If the server is using TCP/IP and the client is using NetBEUI, for example, there will be no communication even if the SQL Server netlibs are the same. You can find the installed network protocols by right-clicking on Network Neighborhood, and then choosing Properties. On a Windows 9x machine, highlight the network adapter and choose Properties. On an NT machine, look at the information shown on the Protocols tab.

If you can't resolve the problem with the Client Network utility, try the methods described in the following sections.

Troubleshooting Named Pipes Connectivity

At the operating system prompt, on the client workstation, type the following:

```
NET VIEW\\SERVERNAME
```

This tells you whether the workstation can see the server. If you get back information about the server, the workstation can see the server. If you get an Error 5 – Access Denied, there is a problem with the NT Authentication login. If the user can't see the server at all, you receive an Error 53. In this case, or if you get any other message, a network problem exists and you should contact the network administrator.

If this succeeds, but you still can't connect to the SQL Server, you should test the pipe with makepipe and readpipe. Unfortunately, you need to do part of this on the server and part of this on the client. makepipe runs on NT only; readpipe runs on NT, Windows 9x, and Windows 3.11. These tools install automatically when you install SQL Server. They are in the \MSSQL7\BINN directory. There is no icon for them, and they do not appear in the Start menu.

makepipe

You run makepipe on the server with the following command:

```
> makepipe
```

Upon running this command, you should see output that looks something like the following:

```
Making PIPE:\pipe\abc
read to write delay (seconds):0
Waiting for Client to Connect...
```

At this point, you can return to the client workstation and issue the readpipe command.

readpipe

You run readpipe on the client with the following command:

```
> readpipe /Sservername /Dstring
```

Assuming, for example, that you have run makepipe on a server named MyServer, run the following:

```
> readpipe /SmyServer /Dhello
```

If this command is successful, you should see output that looks like this:

```
SvrName:\\myserver
PIPE    :\\myserver\pipe\abc
DATA    :hello
Data Sent: 1 : hello
Data Read: 1 : hello
```

If you do not see the Data Read message, you have a network problem and should contact your network administrator. Press CTRL+C on the server to terminate the makepipe program.

Troubleshooting Sockets Connectivity

To test TCP/IP connections, use ping at the client workstation. It takes either a server name or an IP address, as shown here:

```
> ping MyServer
```

or

```
> ping 11.11.11.11
```

You should see results that look like this:

```
Pinging myserver [1.1.1.40] with 32 bytes of data:
Reply from 1.1.1.40: bytes=32 time<10ms TTL=128
Reply from 1.1.1.40: bytes=32 time<10ms TTL=128
Reply from 1.1.1.40: bytes=32 time<10ms TTL=128
Reply from 1.1.1.40: bytes=32 time<10ms TTL=128
Ping statistics for 1.1.1.40:
    Packets: Sent = 4, Received = 4, Lost = 0 (0% loss),
Approximate round trip times in milliseconds:
    Minimum = 0ms, Maximum =  0ms, Average =  0ms
```

If you get a message that the request timed out, you have a network problem and should contact your network administrator.

Troubleshooting ODBC Connectivity

If you have network connectivity but still can't connect to SQL Server, you may have a problem with ODBC connectivity. You can use ODBCPING to diagnose these problems. ODBCPING is in the \MSSQL7\BINN directory. There is no icon for it in your Start menu. You can use it to test a direct ODBC connection to a server and to test an ODBC *data source name* (DSN).

To test a direct ODBC connection, use the following command:

```
ODBCPING -Sservername -Uusername -Ppassword
```

If you don't get a response, you probably need to install a newer version of the ODBC driver.

If this works, you need to identify which ODBC DSN the client is using (you can probably determine this by looking at the ODBC applet in Control Panel), and then issue the following command:

```
ODBCPING -Ddatasourcename -Uusername -Ppassword
```

If the direct ODBC connection worked, but this one did not, you need to check the DSN for correctness. For example, is does the DSN specify a database the user does not have access to or provide an incorrect server name? Do this with the ODBC applet in Control Panel.

 General Tip

You can also test connectivity to an ODBC data source with the ODBC applet. Highlight the data source and choose Configure. Click Next, and then Finish. On the final screen, click the Test Data Source button.

If none of these tricks help, you can try using SQL Profiler (described in Chapter 10) to see what login message is actually getting to SQL Server. Tools such as the NT Network Monitor and the Network General Sniffer can also help you diagnose and correct connectivity problems. Ask your network administrator for help with these last two tools.

4

Storage Management

One of your tasks as a SQL Server administrator is the management of disk space. This chapter describes the underlying storage architecture of SQL Server. Then, it covers how to create and manage databases. The discussion then turns to troubleshooting techniques, even going "under the covers" to show you how SQL Server manages databases internally.

SQL Server Disk Storage Structures

Those of you who have worked with previous versions of SQL Server are going to find that the disk storage structures have completely changed. Instead of the hated devices and segments, now a much simpler architecture provides all the flexibility of the old architecture.

Files and File Groups

In SQL Server 7.0, databases are comprised of operating system files. SQL Server databases are stored in files. The files that comprise a database are operating system files and are visible in Windows Explorer.

Each SQL Server database is comprised of at least two files:

- **A primary data file.** Stores data and indexes, as well as other objects, such as stored procedures.

- **A Transaction log file.** Stores a record containing additions, changes, and deletions

A database may have secondary data files, and multiple files can be used for the Transaction log, as well. The files can be set up so that they grow automatically as space is needed. It is still possible to run out of space if you exceed the amount of space on the physical disk drive that contains the file.

This chapter discusses the architecture of the primary and secondary data files. Chapter 6, "Backup and Recovery," covers the architecture of the Transaction log in detail.

Files are not shared between databases. By convention, the primary data file has the file type MDF, secondary files have the file type NDF, and the Transaction log has the file type LDF. Although you can use something else, you should follow the conventions so that other people aren't confused. It is possible to have a variety of different file configurations for a database.

Figure 4.1 shows three different arrangements. The Payroll database has a single primary data file and a single log file. The inventory database is spread across two data files, a primary on the E: drive and a secondary on the F: drive. The Transaction log file is on the G: drive. The Sales database has only a primary data file but has two log files, each on a separate drive.

Figure 4.1   Sample database configurations.

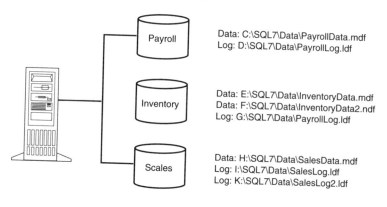

General Tip

It is always a good idea to put the Transaction log on a separate drive from the data because it is an important part of your ability to recover from disasters.

Figure 4.2 shows the simplest database configuration. This database has a single database file and a single Transaction log file.

Figure 4.2   A simple database.

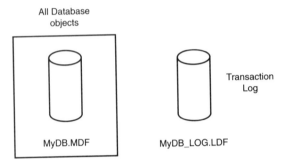

If you start with a single file, you can always add files later and end up with a configuration similar to the one shown in Figure 4.3.

Figure 4.3   A simple database containing multiple data and log files.

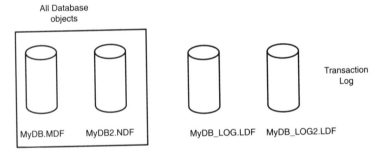

Database files can be organized into *file groups*. These are just named collections of files. A file group named *Primary* is defined when you create a database. You may define other file groups. File groups enable you to do the following:

- Control data placement to improve performance
- Back up certain sets of data at a more frequent interval than the rest of the database
- Mark a set of data as read-only

It's not possible to place data on a file or to mark a file as read-only; you must use file groups if you want to do either of these.

❝ IMO

It's possible to back up a file, but it doesn't make much sense to me to do that. If you don't use file groups, all data is distributed across all the files, and one file would just be a part of the database. Backing up each file separately would be equivalent to backing up the database, but a lot more work.

One file group, named Primary, is created for you when you create a database. The system objects are *always* placed in the primary file group. If you are going to use a design strategy that involves file groups, the primary file group should contain only system objects. All your user tables and indexes should go in the secondary file groups. This will help you work around a bug in recovery (see the discussion of this bug later in this chapter).

There is always a default file group. Initially, the default file group is the primary file group, but you can change this. If you do not specify a file group when you create a table or index, the table or index is placed on the default file group. Figure 4.4 shows a complex database configuration you can develop using file groups.

Figure 4.4   A complex database configuration.

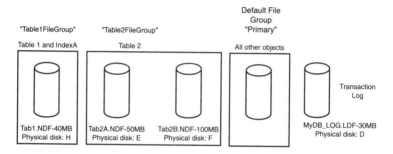

File groups are specific to a database, and databases cannot share file groups. A file can belong to only one file group. Files that comprise the Transaction log do not belong to any file group.

When a file group, database, or Transaction log has multiple files, data is placed in the files according to a proportional fill algorithm. Data is written to files based on the amount of free space in each file. Assume, for example, that the database has two files, File1 and File2. File1 has 200MB of free space, and File2 has 400MB. As data is added, SQL Server allocates one extent on File1 and two extents on File2. This prevents the situation in which one file gets full and grows automatically leaving the other files unused.

Data Storage Architecture

Inside each file, data is stored on *pages*. These pages make up the I/O unit that SQL Server uses. Each page is 8KB. There is a 96-byte page header, and Microsoft reserves some space for future use. Rows in SQL Server must fit on a page, so the maximum row length is documented at 8060 bytes. In practice, however, the actual limit is lower and varies depending on the datatypes used in the table. For example, I can create a table that looks like the following:

```
CREATE TABLE Test
(Col1 char(39), Col2 char(8000)
```

This gives me a row length of 8039. If I change Col1 to char(40), the CREATE TABLE fails. If I change the datatype of both columns to varchar as shown in the following, however, the command fails because varchar fields have more overhead than char fields:

```
CREATE TABLE Test2
(Col1 varchar(39), Col2 varchar(8000)
```

The command succeeds when I change Col1 to varchar(35). This does not include the *Binary Large Object* (BLOB) datatypes (text, image, and ntext). These columns can be as long as 2,147,483,647 bytes. A pointer to a separate structure is stored with the rest of the data in the row.

In each file, pages are numbered sequentially from 0 to the end of the file. If you expand the file, the numbering sequence continues. If you shrink the file, pages are removed starting at the high end and working backward. This ensures that the sequence is always contiguous. This makes it possible for SQL Server to identify any page in a database by specifying the database ID (assigned when the database is created), the file ID (assigned when the file is added to the database), and the page number.

Pages are allocated to tables or indexes in *extents*. These are blocks of eight contiguous pages. Normally, all pages in the extent contain data for a single table or index. So that space is not wasted for small tables, however, there is a provision for *mixed extents*. In these, any page contains data from only one table or index, but the extent may contain pages from different tables and indexes. When a table grows beyond eight pages, all subsequent extent allocations are uniform extents.

Pages can be organized in different ways depending on the table's structure. If the table has a clustered index (see the next section for an explanation of clustered indexes), it is said to be a *clustered* table. The data rows are sorted in order of the clustering key, and a doubly linked list is maintained between the pages.

If the table does not have a clustered index, it is said to be a *heap*. The data is in no particular order, and there are no pointers between pages.

Text, image, and ntext data are stored in a B-tree structure. All the columns of these datatypes from a given table are stored in the same place. Columns from multiple rows can be placed on a single page. It is possible to place the text and image columns of a table on a separate file group from the data.

❝❝   IMO

This architecture for text, ntext, and image columns is much more robust than the architecture used in previous versions of SQL Server. It wastes less space (in 6.5 and earlier versions, a minimum of one page was used for each row that contained a text or image value) and should have fewer problems than the linked-list structures of earlier versions.

There are six types of pages:

Page Type	Contents
Data	Data except text, image, and ntext columns
Index	Index entries
Text/Image	Text, ntext, and image data
Global Allocation MAP (GAM, SGAM)	Information about allocated extents
Page Free Space (PFS)	Pages with free space available
Index Allocation Map (IAM)	Extents used by a table or index

The function of the first three page types is obvious. However, the last three need a bit of explanation. They are used to manage the first three types of pages. The *Global Allocation Map* (GAM) keeps track of which extents have been allocated for any use. Each GAM covers 64,000 extents, or about 4GB of data. Each bit represents an extent. If the bit is 1, the extent is in use. If it is 0, the extent is free and can be allocated to a table or index. The *Secondary Global Allocation Map* (SGAM) records those extents which are mixed and which currently have at least one free page. The SGAM covers the same number of extents as the GAM.

The *Page Free Space* (PFS) pages keep track of whether a page has free space. Each PFS can keep track of free space in 8,000 pages, or 1,000 extents. For each page, there is a bitmap recording whether the page is empty, 1% to 50% full, 51% to 80% full, 81% to 95% full, or 96% to 100% full.

Finally, the *Index Allocation Map* (IAM) records the use of extents by a particular heap or clustered table. A pointer to the first IAM for each table or index is stored in the sysindexes table.

In any file, the first page is a file header. Then comes the first PFS page. Next is the GAM, and then the SGAM. After the SGAM are data pages. After 8,000 pages, there is another PFS page. After 512,000 pages, there is another GAM and SGAM. IAM pages are stored randomly in the file. Figure 4.5 illustrates this layout.

Figure 4.5   Layout of pages in a database file.

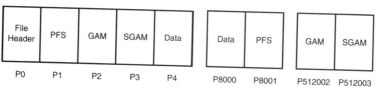

Index Architecture

SQL Server has two different types of indexes:

- **Clustered.** The data is stored in order of the clustering key.
- **Non-clustered.** The data is in no particular order, but the leaf nodes contain the keys in sorted order.

A table can only have one clustered index. SQL Server indexes are built with B-trees. This is a common technique and is used in most database management systems and even some file systems such as VSAM. One of the major features of this architecture is that the path from the root node of the index to any row is always the same regardless of the actual content of the key. There is no skewing of the tree because some keys appear more frequently than others appear. B-trees consist of nodes, which contain key value-pointer pairs. The root node is the entry point into the index structure. Leaf nodes are the bottom level of the tree and are the only nodes that point to data. Other nodes in the B-tree are referred to as intermediate nodes. In a clustered index, the actual data is the leaf node. Each node in a SQL Server index is one page.

 General Tip

The number of branches (pointers) in any given node determines, to some extent, the depth of the tree. The depth of the tree defines how many disk accesses are required to retrieve data using the index. If you can place more keys in a node, there will be fewer levels and hence fewer accesses. For this reason, it is best to have short keys so that there will be more branches.

SQL Server manages non-clustered indexes in one of two ways. If the table has a clustered index, each node-pointer pair consists of the key for the non-clustered index and the key of the clustered index. If the table is a heap (does not have a clustered index), each node-pointer pair consists of the key for the non-clustered index and the record ID, which is built from the file number, page number, and row number on the page.

Example

Assume that you have an employee table, and the data in this table looks like the data listed here.

EmpID	LastName	FirstName	Record ID (Hypothetical)
1	Jones	John	020501
2	Smith	Mary	020502
3	Sanchez	Pedro	020503

You build a non-clustered index on LastName, FirstName. If there were a *clustered* index on EmpID, the nodes in that non-clustered index would look like the following:

Non-Clustered Index Node for a Clustered Table

Jones	John	1
Smith	Mary	2
Sanchez	Pedro	3

Performance Tip

This use of the clustering key in non-clustered indexes is another reason to keep clustering keys short. Doing so reduces the amount of space each non-clustered index node requires, and permits more nodes per page.

If you do not have a clustered index on the employee table, and you build a non-clustered index on LastName, FirstName, the nodes would look like the data listed here:

Non-Clustered Index Node for a Non-Clustered Table

Jones	John	020501
Smith	Mary	020502
Sanchez	Pedro	020503

General Tip

The record ID is strictly internal to SQL Server; you do not have access to it.

Planning the Physical Structure of Databases

A great deal of work is done in designing a database that is only briefly described here. (Database design is a book in itself.) Someone must define the tables needed to serve the business function that the database must support. Usually this is done through a process that has a *logical design* phase in which the entities and attributes of interest to the organization are identified, together with the relationships among entities. In this process, an activity called *normalization* is used to remove redundant data. Referential integrity and other business rules are identified at this time. Quite often, physical design is performed at this time as well so that high performance can be ensured. During this process, the normalized design can be denormalized to improve performance. Appendix A, "Bibliography," lists many excellent books on these topics.

This discussion about the database creation process starts at the point where all the tables and indexes in the database have been identified and the estimated number of rows in each table is known. You can create a database without this information, of course; but with this information, you can estimate what the size of the database should be. In addition, you can use this information to determine what file groups you need. The following sections explain why this is important.

Sizing a Database

It is possible to set up a database so that it can grow automatically when space is needed. Some overhead accrues in the growth process, however, and the files are likely to be fragmented rather than contiguous on the disk drive. So you should figure out the approximate size you need the database to be before you create it. To do this, you need to figure out how much space is required for each table and index in the database. You can find formulas for doing this in the Books OnLine. These calculations are tedious, however, to say the least, and the process is easier when using a couple of automated tools. The BackOffice Resource Kit 4.5 contains an Excel spreadsheet that helps with these calculations. (This software is available as part of both TechNET and MSDN, or you can purchase the entire Resource Kit, including hard-copy documentation.)

You can also create a test database, define all the tables and indexes, and use a stored procedure to compute the amount of space needed for each table. The Web site for this book (www.newriders.com/ 0735708649) lists the source code for this stored procedure.

These techniques just give you estimates; you should add a "fudge factor" depending on your confidence in the estimates of number of rows. Computing the size of the Transaction log is not a science. In most cases, your Transaction log should be from 10% to 25% of the size of your database. If you are planning on using replication, it may go as high as 50%.

Determining What Files and File Groups You Need

First of all, if you are starting with a new machine, you will have had to select your NT file system. Your choices for a SQL Server machine are NTFS and FAT. In general, you want NTFS because it is more fault tolerant, allows for file-level security, and supports larger files than FAT does. If you must dual boot Windows 9x or DOS with NT, however, you need to use FAT. The two have no significant performance differences.

An aside about RAID: In the past, the standard recommendation for RAID architectures has been to put the database on a RAID 0 device and the Transaction log on a RAID 1 (mirrored device). This gave the best combination of performance and fault tolerance. Now, however, the new RAID architecture called 0+1 is your best choice for both data and log files.

> **! Important!**
>
> It is important that you place the Transaction log on a separate physical device from the data. You want the most fault-tolerant device possible for the Transaction log.

When you know what total space you need, you should lay out your files and file groups. Your decisions regarding files and file groups should be based on four factors:

- Maintenance requirements
- Performance requirements
- Hardware layout
- Ability to recover databases up to the point of failure

Grouping by Maintenance Requirements

You might want to put tables with similar maintenance requirements into the same file group. Back up and restore can be performed at the file group level. If a table is updated frequently, for example, you might want to assign it to its own file group so that it can be backed up more often than the rest of the database.

Grouping for Performance Reasons

Files or file groups can be used to distribute data across different physical devices. This means that multiple read/write heads can be used, producing a performance gain. Also, a file is the unit of parallelism for sequential reads of data (a common activity). SQL Server can manage one thread per file. You should consider having as many files as you have physical drives. When you have more than one file, SQL Server uses a proportional fill strategy to make sure that the data is spread across all the files, and simple striping can be achieved. If you have hardware striping, you should consider maintenance decisions as a way of defining files and file groups before considering performance. You can let the RAID architecture handle the striping.

Grouping by Hardware Layout

If you have multiple disk controllers, you can potentially improve performance. With this approach, you configure each of the drives as a stripe set. To get a configuration that uses the best features of both hardware striping and SQL Server striping, point each controller to a hardware stripe set. Then, define a file group that includes multiple files (as many as there are striped devices) spread across all the devices.

Recovering Databases up to the Point of Failure

Chapter 6 covers database recovery more thoroughly, but it's mentioned here. SQL Server 7.0 has a flaw that makes it impossible to back up the Transaction log if the primary file is damaged. If your operation requires this type of recovery (this is most often needed in 24 × 7 shops and those shops with a very high transaction rate), you will want to do the following. Create the database so that it has a primary file group (the default) and another file group. Place the primary file group on an extremely fault-tolerant drive, preferably a mirrored drive. After you create the database, but before you create any object, make the other file group the default.

Creating a Database

After you have figured out how big the database should be and what files and file groups you need, you are ready to actually create the database. Like most operations in SQL Server 7.0, you can do this with Enterprise Manager, Transact-SQL, or SQL-DMO.

General Considerations

Keep in mind the following considerations when creating your databases:

- The database name is a *sysname* and can be up to 128 characters.
- Database and log files can grow automatically when they need additional space. There is a slight performance degradation each time a file needs to grow. You want to minimize the number of times the files must grow. Suppose you have decided that your database is going to take 100MB. If you use the default of 10% growth, it grows by 10MB the first time, 11MB the second time, and so on. You can reduce the number of auto-grows by setting this percentage of growth to a larger number (perhaps 25%) or using an absolute number of MB. If you choose unrestricted file growth, the file expands until it has filled up every byte of available space on the drive. You can restrict this to a specific amount. Keep in mind that when the file has reached the specified maximum size, any attempts to add data are likely to produce an error message. You need to monitor both the number of autogrows and the absolute size of the database. If you do not want the file to grow beyond its original size, set the percentage or amount by which the file should grow to 0.

" IMO

I recommend that you create the database at the maximum size you expect it to be. In doing this, you need to consider how long it will take the database to reach its maximum size. For example, if it will be 100GB two years from now but currently is 10MB, you probably won't allocate all the space now. You might allocate enough for 6 months. Turn on autogrow, and specify an increment that is reasonable relative to the original size; for example, if your initial size was 100MB, you would probably want to grow in 10-20MB (10%-20%) increments rather than 1MB increments..

- Choose your logical filenames carefully; they cannot be changed after the database has been created.

Creating Databases with Transact-SQL

The syntax for creating a database in Transact-SQL looks very complicated, but in fact can be quite simple, as shown here:

```
CREATE DATABASE database_name
[ ON [PRIMARY]
        [ <filespec> [,...n] ]
```

```
            [, <filegroup> [,...n] ]
    ]
    [ LOG ON { <filespec> [,...n]} ]
    [ FOR LOAD ¦ FOR ATTACH ]
    <filespec> ::=
      ( [ NAME = logical_file_name, ]
      FILENAME = 'os_file_name'
      [, SIZE = size]
      [, MAXSIZE = { max_size ¦ UNLIMITED } ]
      [, FILEGROWTH = growth_increment] ) [,...n]
    <filegroup> ::=
    FILEGROUP filegroup_name <filespec> [,...n]
```

Example:

```
CREATE DATABASE MyDB2 ON PRIMARY
        (NAME='MyDB2_Data',
        FILENAME='c:\mssql7\data\MyDB2_Data.mdf',
        SIZE=10,
        MAXSIZE=30,
        FILEGROWTH=10),   — MEGS
FILEGROUP MyDataFiles
        (NAME='MyDB2_SecondData',
        FILENAME='c:\mssql7\data\MyDB2_SecondData.ndf',
        SIZE=10,
        MAXSIZE=30,
        FILEGROWTH=10)   — MEGS
LOG ON
        (NAME='MyDB2_Log',
        FILENAME='d:\Logs\MyDB2_Log.ldf',
        SIZE=3,
        MAXSIZE=10,
        FILEGROWTH=5%)   —percent
```

> ✔ **General Tip**
>
> The Transact-SQL example shows the data files being placed in the default directory, \MSSQL7\DATA. In most cases, you don't want to put them in this directory. By default, it's on the C: drive, which is probably where your swap file is as well, along with all the NT and SQL Server code. I find it easiest to manage with separate folders for each database.

Two options in Transact-SQL are not available to you in Enterprise Manager:

- **FOR LOAD** is used when you are creating a database just to restore from a backup. It is a carryover from earlier versions of SQL Server and has no meaning for SQL Server 7.0.

- **FOR ATTACH** is used when you need to create a database to which you are going to attach files (as discussed later in this chapter). You need to do this only when you are attaching a database that has more than 16 files.

Be careful when you specify the growth_increment for the FILEGROWTH option. You can specify a number followed by MB (megabytes), KB (kilobytes), or %. If you specify nothing, megabytes is assumed. If you specify 0, the file does not autogrow. If you do not use this clause, the default is 10% growth.

Creating Databases with Enterprise Manager

In Enterprise Manager, you get to the new database dialog box by right-clicking the DATABASES folder and choosing New Database. Figure 4.6 shows the Database Properties dialog box that you use to create and modify databases.

Figure 4.6   Database Properties dialog box.

Something interesting appears in the screen shown in Figure 4.6. Although it would not appear so, it is possible to define a file group when you add files to the database. Just position the cursor in the File Group box, and type the name of the file group you want to create. It is then available in the drop-down list for additional files.

Creating a Database with SQL-DMO

To create a database in SQL-DMO, you need to create both a Database object and a DBFile object. You also need a LogFile object. If you are planning to use file groups other than the primary file group, you need a FileGroups collection object. You need to follow these steps:

1 Create a Database object and set its Name property.

2 If you want file groups other than the primary file group, create a FileGroup object for each file group and add it to the FileGroups collection of the Database object.

3 Create a DBFile object for each file. Set its Name, PhysicalName, Size, Growth, and Maximum properties. Add the file objects to the DBFiles collection of the appropriate file group.

4 Create LogFile objects for each file that will comprise your Transaction log. Set the Name, PhysicalName, Size, Growth, and Maximum properties. Add these LogFile objects to the LogFiles collection of the Database object's TransactionLog object.

5 Add the Database object to the Databases collection of a SQL Server.

Setting File Group Properties

You can set three file group properties:

- **Default**   All objects created without specifying a file group are placed on this file group.
- **ReadOnly.**   This file group is read-only.
- **ReadWrite.**   This group reverses the read-only property; file groups are read/write when created.

I haven't found a way to set file group properties in Enterprise Manager. However, it is easy to do in both Transact-SQL and DMO.

 General Tip
The file group must contain at least one file before you can modify its properties.

Setting File Group Properties with Transact-SQL

Syntax

To set the file group properties with Transact-SQL, use the following syntax:

```
ALTER DATABASE databasename
MODIFY FILEGROUP filegroupname
{DEFAULT ¦ READONLY ¦ READWRITE}
```

Examples

```
ALTER DATABASE Test MODIFY FILEGROUP GROUP1 DEFAULT

ALTER DATABASE Test2 MODIFY FILEGROUP WAREHOUSE READONLY
```

Setting File Group Properties with DMO

You need to connect a SQLServer object, and then refer to the target file group of the database's FileGroups collection. There are two FileGroup properties: Default and ReadOnly. These properties can be set to true or false.

Examples

```
oDatabase.FileGroups("GROUP1").Default = TRUE
oDatabase.FileGroups("WAREHOUSE").ReadOnly = TRUE
```

Managing Database Space Usage

Although you can set databases to grow automatically and to shrink automatically, most of the time you want to monitor database size and manage it yourself. In addition, even when files are allowed to grow automatically, there is the potential of running out of disk space. Overhead is associated with automatically growing databases, and even more associated with automatically shrinking them. You want to leave the autogrow options set for each file, however, so that databases do not shut down because they are out of space. In general, if the data files are nearing 90% full, and you anticipate further additions of data, you want to consider increasing the amount of space available to the database. It is harder to give a figure for the Transaction log, because it tends to be somewhat "self-cleaning" (as discussed in Chapter 6). You can monitor how much space is used in a database or any given file with Enterprise Manager, Transact-SQL, and DMO. The following sections tell you how to monitor database space.

Monitoring Space with Transact-SQL

To find out how much space is allocated for a file, as well as other attributes of the file, make sure that the database you are concerned about is selected in the drop-down list in Query Analyzer, and then use the following command:

```
sp_helpfile filename
```

If you leave off the filename, you get a listing for all the files in the database.

To find out how much space is used in a file, use the following statement:

```
SELECT FILEPROPERTY('MyFile', 'SpaceUsed')
```

The following Transact-SQL command shows you the total space available in all files in the database and the amount used:

```
sp_spaceused
```

This command isn't as useful because all the space, including the Transaction log, is lumped together and it is hard to determine whether you need data space in a specific file group space or Transaction log space.

Monitoring Space Usage with Enterprise Manager

To view how space is used in Enterprise Manager, you highlight the
database in the console tree. The task pad in the Details pane shows
you how space is used in each file when you click the Space Allocated
button at the top of the screen.

Monitoring Space with DMO

The Database and TransactionLog objects have a float property,
SpaceAvailableInMB, which tells you how much space is *left*. They also
have a long property, SpaceAvailable, which gives you available space in
KB. The DBFile object has a long property, SpaceAvailableInMB, which
also tells you how much space is left.

The Database, TransactionLog, DBFile, FileGroup, and LogFile objects
all have a Size property that returns a long property containing the total
size of the referenced object in MB. The DBFile object also has a Float
property, SizeInKB, which returns the size of the file in KB.

Expanding Databases

Despite your careful planning, you may find that new applications or unantic-
ipated data require that the database be expanded. You can expand existing
files, as long as they will still fit on the physical disk drive. You can add new
files and you can add file groups.

Expanding Databases with Transact–SQL

To change the size of a file with Transact-SQL, use the ALTER DATABASE
statement:

```
ALTER DATABASE
        MODIFY FILE (NAME= filename
            [,SIZE = megabytes]
    [,MAXSIZE = {megabytes | UNLIMITED} ]
                [,FILEGROWTH = increment}]
```

The documentation implies that you can only change one of these in a
single statement, but that is incorrect, as the example in BOL clearly
shows.

It's not possible to move a file to a different physical location with this command; you learn how to do that later in this chapter. The one exception is tempdb. You are allowed to issue the following command:

```
ALTER DATABASE tempdb
    MODIFY FILE (NAME = 'tempdev',
                FILENAME = 'f:\SQL Tempdb\tempdb.mdf')
```

This command relocates tempdb. It does not take effect until the SQL Server is stopped and restarted. If you want to move a file from any other database, you need sp_detach_db and sp_attach_db (as discussed later in this chapter).

To add a new file or set of files to a database, you also use the ALTER DATABASE statement:

```
ALTER DATABASE database
{    ADD FILE (NAME = logical_file_name
        [, FILENAME = 'os_file_name' ]
        [, SIZE = size]
        [, MAXSIZE = { max_size ¦ UNLIMITED } ]
        [, FILEGROWTH = growth_increment] ) [, … n]
        [TO FILEGROUP filegroup_name]
```

You also add new log files with the ALTER DATABASE statement:

```
ALTER DATABASE database
    ADD LOG FILE (NAME = logical_file_name
        [, FILENAME = 'os_file_name' ]
        [, SIZE = size]
        [, MAXSIZE = { max_size ¦ UNLIMITED } ]
        [, FILEGROWTH = growth_increment] ) [, … n]
```

If you want the new data file or file to be in a new file group as well, you must add the file group *before* you add the file(s):

```
ALTER DATABASE database
ADD FILEGROUP filegroup_name
```

Expanding Databases with Enterprise Manager

In Enterprise Manager, just use the Database Properties screen on which you originally created the database, and either increase the size of existing files or add a new file. You can expand the database files or the Transaction log files with the same techniques.

Expanding Databases with DMO

To increase the size of a file, modify the Size, Growth, and/or Maximum properties of a DBFile or LogFile object.

To add data files to a database, create a DBFile object for each file. Set its Name, PhysicalName, Size, Growth, and Maximum properties. Add the file objects to the DBFiles collection of the appropriate file group.

If you want to add a new file group, you must create a FileGroup object and add it to the FileGroups collection of the Database object. You must create the new file group before you can add files to it.

To add new log files, create LogFile objects for each file. Set the Name, PhysicalName, Size, Growth, and Maximum properties. Add these LogFile objects to the LogFiles collection of the Database object's TransactionLog object.

Shrinking Databases and Files

You may find, as records are deleted and not replaced, that your databases have a lot of wasted space. You might want to make this disk space available to other applications by shrinking files or databases. It is possible to set a database option that allows the database to shrink automatically, but there is quite a heavy overhead penalty associated with this, and I recommend that you not set this option. (There's more about database options later in this chapter.)

 General Tip

Autoshrink is false by default in the Standard and Enterprise editions. However, it is true by default in the Desktop Edition. It is okay to leave it set to true in a Desktop Edition because systems using that edition should have a very small number of users and not have significant performance requirements.

When you shrink a database, you have three options for how unused space should be handled. The default is to move all used pages to the front of a file and return the unused space to the operating system. You can specify that you want all the used pages moved to the front, but that space should not be given back to the operating system (NOTRUNCATE). It's also possible to give just the empty space back to the operating system (TRUNCATEONLY). When you shrink a file, you can move all of its pages to other files in the file group, and then remove the file from the file group (EMPTYFILE).

You can also shrink the Transaction log, but the truncation options don't apply.

Shrinking a Database or Files with Transact-SQL

To shrink either a database or files with Transact-SQL, you use a command named DBCC. You are going to see this command appearing in a variety of places. The command stands for Data Base Consistency Checker, and it still performs that function. That function is discussed later in this chapter. Over the years, however, many different capabilities have been hung onto this command. (My theory is that it was just an easy place for developers to plug in new functions without having to develop a whole harness for executing them.) As you will see throughout this book, and as you delve further into SQL Server capabilities, the DBCC commands are very inconsistent. But it's the only way to do a lot of important tasks.

Using DBCC *to Shrink a Database*

Syntax

Use the following syntax to shrink a database using the DBCC command:

```
DBCC SHRINKDATABASE
    (    database_name [, target_percent]
        [, {NOTRUNCATE ¦ TRUNCATEONLY}]
    )
```

target_percent specifies the amount of free space that should be left in the database after the shrinking operation. Unless the database will never have any more data added to it, you should leave a reasonable amount of free space. Otherwise, the database automatically grows immediately. A good starting point for the amount of free space to leave is the amount by which you have set it to grow. SQL Server calculates a size for each file based on the amount of data the file contains and the amount of free space you have specified in the target percent. Assume, for example, that you have a database that contains one data file that is 20MB in size. The file contains 10MB of data, and you want 10% free space (1MB). SQL Server moves any pages from the last 9MB of the file to the front and shrinks the file to 11MB (10MB of data plus 1MB of free space). If you use the NOTRUNCATE option, the database files do not shrink. If you use the TRUNCATEONLY option, the target percent is ignored, and only free space after the last allocated extent is returned to the operating system.

The minimum size a file will shrink can be any of the following:

- The size it was originally created
- The last explicit size it was increased to by ALTER DATABASE MODIFY FILE commands, or
- The last explicit size it was shrunk to by a DBCC SHRINKFILE command.

If you don't specify a target percent, the database shrinks as much as possible.

Shrinking the Transaction log is different. First of all, instead of being examined file by file as data files are, the log files are examined as a group. This must be done because the architecture of log files differs significantly from the architecture of the data files. The target percent is used to calculate the amount of free space in the log as a whole. In addition, the Transaction log files don't shrink immediately like the data files do. The shrinking takes place when you back up the Transaction log or set the Truncate Log on Checkpoint option to true. The shrinking operation does not necessarily shrink the file to the amount you request because it can only shrink the log to the size of a virtual log file.

Shrinking Files with DBCC

You can shrink databases without regard to the database in which you are currently positioned. However, you must be in the database that contains the files to shrink the files. If you are using Query Analyzer, just select the database from the drop-down list. If you are writing a script to shrink files, issue the USE statement before you issue the DBCC SHRINKFILE statement.

Syntax

The following syntax is used to shrink files with the DBCC command:

```
DBCC SHRINKFILE
    ({file_name ¦ file_id }
      { [, target_size]  [, {EMPTYFILE ¦ NOTRUNCATE ¦ TRUNCATEONLY}] }
    )
```

 General Tip

The syntax in BOL implies that you choose between target_size and the three options; in fact, however, you do not need to. You may specify a target size and either the TRUNCATEONLY or the NOTRUNCATE option, although the target size ignored with the TRUNCATEONLY option. You cannot specify a target size when you use the EMPTYFILE option.

Here's your first example of DBCC inconsistency! The SHRINKFILE command takes either a filename or the file's internal identifier! And it takes a target *size*, not a target percent!

 General Tip

You can find a file's internal identifier by doing a select from the *sysfiles* table or by using the FILE_ID function, as shown here:

```
SELECT FILE_ID('MyDataFile')
```

I recommend using the function because system tables are subject to change by Microsoft, and the function insulates you from those changes.

The target size is the number of MB you want the file to be. (It must be an integer.) DBCC SHRINKFILE does not make a file smaller than needed to contain all the data. If the file is currently 10MB, and contains 7MB of data, and you specify a target size of 6MB, for example, the file shrinks only to 7MB. The target size can be smaller than the original allocation or the latest explicit MODIFY FILE size, however. If you specify a target size with the NOTRUNCATE option, DBCC SHRINKFILE moves pages above the target size to available space earlier in the file. However, the free space is not given back to the operating system.

You want to specify a target size that allows a reasonable amount of free space in the file if you expect that more data will be placed in that file. A reasonable amount of space is an autogrow increment. If you don't specify a target size, the file is shrunk as much as possible.

The EMPTYFILE option moves used pages to another file in the file group. After you have used this option, SQL Server will not place any more data on the file that was emptied. You can remove the file from the database with the ALTER DATABASE command, as follows:

```
ALTER DATABASE databasename
        REMOVE FILE filename
```

Just as you saw with DBCC SHRINKDATABASE, the shrinking behavior of DBCC SHRINKFILE differs for the files that comprise the Transaction log. The target size specifies the number of MB for the log in total. Based on that, SQL Server calculates the amount of free space to be left in each log file so that the log uses the desired amount of space. Shrinking requested with DBCC SHRINKFILE does not happen until the Transaction log is backed up or truncated. The log may not shrink to the amount you request because it can only shrink to the size of a virtual log file.

Shrinking Databases with Enterprise Manager

It is not possible to shrink files with Enterprise Manager. You must shrink the entire database. Enterprise Manager also does not enable you to specify how much the database should shrink by, although you can do that with Transact-SQL and DMO. You get to the dialog box for shrinking a database by right-clicking the database, choosing All Tasks, and then choosing Shrink Database. You then see the Shrink Database dialog box, as shown in Figure 4.7.

Figure 4.7   Shrink Database dialog box.

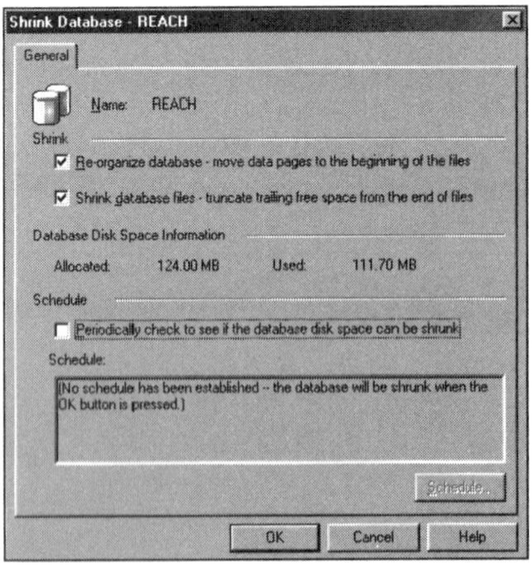

If you uncheck the box that says Reorganize and leave Shrink checked, you get the TRUNCATEONLY behavior. If you leave the box that says Reorganize checked and uncheck the box that says Shrink, you get the NOTRUNCATE behavior. With them both checked, used pages are moved to the front and empty space is given back to the operating system.

The options are applied to all files in the database. It is possible to schedule the database shrink to run on a regular basis or at a specific time. You can then use the scheduling features of SQL Server to set up a job to run at a time when users are not active.

IMO

In most cases, you probably won't want to do schedule database shrinks so that they run on a regular basis; you should determine by your monitoring routines when it is appropriate to shrink a database or files.

Performance Tip

It's possible to shrink a database while users are active in it. However, this could have a severe impact on the performance of applications those users are running.

Shrinking Databases with DMO

You can use DMO to shrink a database, a file, or a Transaction log. The Database object, the DBFile object, and the LogFile object have a Shrink method:

```
Object.Shrink(NewSize, Truncate)
```

NewSize is a long integer specifying the target size. If it is negative, the database or file will be shrunk to the smallest possible size. If it is positive, and you are using the Shrink method of the Database object, the number specifies the percentage of free space to remain in the database after it is shrunk. If it is positive, and you are using the Shrink method of either a DBFile or LogFile object, it is the number of megabytes you want the file to be after the shrink. You can find more details about how this works by reading the preceding sections on using Transact-SQL to shrink a database or a file.

Truncate is a long integer that can be specified with the constants shown here.

Constant	Meaning
SQLDMOShrink_Default	Data in pages located at the end of the file(s) is moved to pages earlier in the file(s). File(s) are truncated to reflect allocated space.
SQLDMOShrink_EmptyFile	Migrate all data from the referenced file to other files in the same file group. (DBFile and LogFile object only).
SQLDMOShrink_NoTruncate	Data in pages located at the end of the file(s) is moved to pages earlier in the file(s).
SQLDMOShrink_TruncateOnly	Data distribution is not affected. File(s) are truncated to reflect allocated space, recovering free space at the end of any file.

Setting Database Options

You can set many different options for each database. These options control various behaviors, such as enforcement of certain ANSI standards, database access, behavior of SQL statements, behavior of triggers, Transaction log management, and replication activities. This section covers some of these options; others are covered in the appropriate chapters.

Many of these options can be set at three different levels: connection, database, and server. Options are specified at a connection level with the Transact-SQL SET statement. Options at the database level can be specified with Transact-SQL, Enterprise Manager (most, not all), and DMO. Some (not all) connection options can be specified at the server level with Transact-SQL, Enterprise Manager, or DMO. Some of the tools, such as Query Analyzer and EM, may set options that override your database settings. Also, ODBC data sources set default options for the connection that may differ from the ones you set for the database. Applications using ADO or OLE DB may also override some of your settings when they connect to the database.

The options are all true/false; that is, they are either on or off. The only options that are on by default for NT SQL Servers are Auto Create Statistics and Auto Update Statistics. (Chapter 10, "Performance Tuning," discusses both of these.)

The following tables list access options, ANSI options, performance options, Transact-SQL options, and two miscellaneous options that control torn page detection and Transaction log behavior.

Access Options

The following options limit database access:

- **DBO Use Only.**   When set to true, only the database owner can use the database. Active users can continue to access the database after this setting has been changed, but new users other than the DBO cannot access the database. You may want to use this option when performing administrative functions such as schema changes.

- **Read Only.**   When set to true, users can only read data in the database, but not modify it. The master database is the exception, and only the system administrator can use the master while the Read Only option is being set.

Performance Tip

When this option is set, SQL Server won't lock resources, which can be a performance benefit.

- **Single User.** When set to true, only one user at a time can access the database. You can set this option to true while there are active users. Those users continue to access the database, but no new users will be allowed to access it. After all the active users disconnect, only a single connection is allowed. Be careful that you don't compete with yourself; you can't have two windows open in Query Analyzer, nor can you be using the database in Enterprise Manager while also using it in Query Analyzer. Restoring a database puts it in single-user mode automatically.

- **Offline.** When this option is set to true, the database is offline.

❝❝ IMO

It's not clear to me why we need this option. I think it's a carryover from the old ways of dealing with removable media databases. Today, with `sp_detach_db` (see Chapter 6) the option does not seem to apply, but it is still there.

ANSI Options

Some default behavior of SQL Server does not conform to the ANSI standard for SQL; you can use these settings to enforce ANSI-compliant behavior:

- ANSI null default   When true, CREATE TABLE follows the SQL-92 rules to determine if a column allows null values. By default, SQL Server assumes a column does not allow nulls when the nullability property (NULL, NOT NULL) is not specified. The ANSI standard states that a column allows nulls when the nullability is not specified. Setting this option will make SQL Server behave like ANSI.

 General Tip

However, I recommend that you explicitly specify nullability for each column when you create a table. Then you will get exactly what you ask for. In addition, your table definitions will produce the same results in all relational database systems.

- ANSI nulls   When set to true, all comparisons to a null value evaluate to UNKNOWN. When set to false, comparisons of non-UNICODE values to a null value evaluate to TRUE if both values are NULL.

 General Tip

This option is meaningful for legacy SQL Server systems (that are not in 6.x compatibility mode) where the non-standard practice of writing X = NULL has been used. Better practice dictates writing X IS NULL or X IS NOT NULL and leaving this option alone.

- ANSI Warnings   When set to true, errors or warnings are issued when conditions such as "divide by zero" occur.

- concat null yields null   When set to true, if either operand in a concatenation operation is NULL, the result is NULL. This is the ANSI behavior of nulls, although it has not been observed in all versions of SQL Server, particularly with respect to character string data.

 General Tip

It's not clear to me that the concat null yields null option accomplishes anything. For example, in the Northwind database the TitleOfCourtesy column in the Employees table allows nulls. If I set this option to true, and issue a statement that looks like the following:

```
SELECT TitleOfCourtesy + ' ' FirstName,
```

I get NULL when TitleOfCourtesy is null. When I set this option to false, I get exactly the same result.

- Cursor Close on Commit   When set to true, any cursors that are open when a transaction is committed or rolled back are closed. When set to false, such cursors remain open when a transaction is committed. When false, rolling back a transaction closes any cursors except those defined as INSENSITIVE or STATIC.

- Quoted Identifier   When set to true, double quotation marks can be used to enclose delimited identifiers that contain spaces or characters that are not permitted in SQL Server identifiers. For example, you could have a column named My Column, which you would refer to by enclosing it in double quotation marks: "My Column".

❝ IMO

In general I don't recommend using quoted identifiers, particularly on legacy SQL Server systems where people may have used double quotation marks to delimit literal strings. In addition, many of the front-end tools don't understand quoted identifiers. If you must have non-conforming names, use the SQL Server 7.0 delimited identifier, and enclose the name in square brackets as shown here: [My Column].

❝ IMO

I recommend that you explicitly specify nullability for each column when you create a table. Then you will get exactly what you ask for. In addition, your table definitions will produce the same results in all relational database systems.

ANSI database options that can be controlled for a connection with the SET command include the following:

- SET ANSI_NULLS
- SET ANSI_WARNINGS
- SET ANSI_NULL_DFLT_ON
- SET CURSOR_CLOSE_ON_COMMIT
- SET ANSI_PADDING
- SET QUOTED_IDENTIFIER

Performance Options

Chapter 10 contains more information about the performance options. They are included here just for completeness:

- Auto Create Statistics   When set to true, any missing statistics needed by a query for optimization are automatically built during optimization.

- Auto Update Statistics   When set to true, any out of date statistics needed by a query for optimization are automatically built during optimization.

- Autoclose   When set to true, the database is shut down cleanly and its resources are freed after the last user exits.

- Autoshrink   When set to true, the database files are candidates for automatic periodic shrinking.

Options That Control Transact-SQL Behavior

The following options control Transact-SQL behavior:

- Default to Local Cursor   When this option is set to true, the cursor declarations default to LOCAL. This option is of interest to programmers who are making use of global cursors. In general, you should leave this option off. If a programmer needs a global cursor, the cursor can be explicitly declared to be global when it is defined.

- Recursive Triggers   When set to true, this option enables recursive firing of triggers.

 General Tip

You should leave this option off. Triggers that fire recursively are difficult to code, and will quickly run into the limit of 32 levels of recursion.

- Select Into/Bulkcopy   When true, the SELECT INTO statement and fast bulk copies are allowed.

 General Tip

This is an important and extremely useful option. The effects of SELECT … INTO and fast bulk copy are not recorded in the Transaction log, so using them has an impact on your backup strategy. Chapter 6 discusses this in more detail.

Miscellaneous Options

Following are a couple of useful options that are difficult to categorize:

- `Torn Page Detection`   When set to true, incomplete pages can be detected. A SQL Server page is 8KB, but NT does I/O in 512KB segments. A power failure or other system problem could cause the page to be only partially written. If the first part of the page were written, however, it would appear to SQL Server to be complete when in fact it is not. If you have battery-backed disk caches or other devices that guarantee all-or-nothing I/O, you can leave this option false. With less-sophisticated disk hardware, you may want to turn it on.

 Performance Tip

This option uses very little CPU time. However, it can increase contention, because when this option is set to true, a page cannot be read while it is being written to disk.

- `Trunc. Log on Chkpt.`   When set to true, a checkpoint truncates the inactive part of the log when the database is in log truncate mode. This is the only option you can set for the master database.

 General Tip

Chapter 10 describes this option in detail. In most cases, you want to leave it set to off.

Specifying Database Options with Enterprise Manager

After you have created a database, the Options tab becomes visible when you right-click on a database and choose Properties. Just check or uncheck the desired options. Not all database options can be specified with Enterprise Manager.

Specifying Database Options with Transact-SQL

You use the command `sp_dboptions` to set or reset database options in Transact-SQL.

Syntax

Following is the syntax for `sp_dboptions`:

```
sp_dboption [databasename [, option [, value]]]
```

If you issue the command with no parameters, as follows, you see the complete list of settable options:

```
sp_dboption
```

If you specify a database name, as follows, you see a list of the options set to true for the database:

```
sp_dboption Northwind
```

If you specify both the database name and an option, as follows, you see the setting of that particular option:

```
sp_dboption Northwind, 'SELECT'
```

Note that you need to specify only enough of the option to make it unique, and that the name of the option must be enclosed in single quotation marks.

If you specify the database name, the option name, and a value, the setting of the option changes, as shown here:

```
sp_dboption Northwind, 'SELECT', TRUE
```

As just noted, valid values are either TRUE or FALSE, and are not enclosed in single quotation marks.

You can also interrogate the state of any particular option with the DATABASEPROPERTY function, as shown here:

```
DATABASEPROPERTY(databasename, property)
```

The property for the preceding must be one of the following values:

- `IsAnsiNullDefault`
- `IsAnsiNullsEnabled`
- `IsAnsiWarningsEnabled`
- `IsAutoClose`
- `IsAutoShrink`
- `IsAutoUpdateStatistics`
- `IsBulkCopy`
- `IsCloseCursorsOnCommitEnabled`
- `IsDboOnly`
- `IsDetached`
- `IsEmergencyMode`
- `IsFulltextEnabled`
- `IsInLoad`
- `IsInRecovery`
- `IsInStandBy`
- `IsLocalCursorsDefault`
- `IsNotRecovered`
- `IsNullConcat`
- `IsOffline`
- `IsQuotedIdentifiersEnabled`
- `IsReadOnly`
- `IsRecursiveTriggersEnabled`

- IsShutDown

- IsSingleUser

- IsSuspect

- IsTruncLog

- Version

To find out what the setting of the Read Only option is in the Northwind database, issue the following command:

```
SELECT DatabaseProperty(Northwind, IsReadOnly)
```

In addition to the database options that can be set, the database properties you can interrogate include status information such as IsEmergencyMode and IsSuspect.

Specifying Database Options with DMO

A database object has a dbOptions property, and each of the settable options is a property of it. You set a database option in DMO with statements that look like the following:

```
Dim oDB as Database
oDB.dbOption.SelectIntoBulkCopy = True
```

The dbOption properties are as follows:

- AssignmentDiag

- AutoClose

- AutoCreateStat

- AutoShrink

- AutoUpdateStat

- ColumnsNullByDefault

- CompareNull

- ContactNull

- CursorCloseOnCommit

- DBOUseOnly

- DefaultCursor

- Offline

- QuoteDelimiter

- ReadOnly

- RecursiveTriggers

- SelectIntoBulkCopy

- SingleUser

- TornPageDetection

- TruncateLogOnCheckpoint

The names of most of these properties are similar to the names used for the Transact-SQL options, so I won't expand upon them. However, a couple of property names differ and can therefore be confusing. The first of these is `AssignmentDiag`. This property corresponds to the ANSI `Warnings` option. (Personally, I can't imagine where they came up with this name!)

The `ColumnsNull` property corresponds to the ANSI `Null Default` option, and the `CompareNull` property corresponds to the ANSI `Nulls` option. `ContactNull` is clearly a typo, it is definitely the name of the property: When I get VB to give me its automatic Help, the property appears this way. It corresponds to the `Concat Null` option; somebody clearly made a typo here.

Routine Maintenance and Troubleshooting

SQL Server 7.0 is quite robust and manages its storage system well. It is possible, however, for corruption in the database to occur. Routine inserts can cause the database to have internal fragmentation, affecting the performance of the system. Indexes also may need periodic reorganization. You will probably want to perform routine maintenance tasks, such as the following, on a regular basis:

- Check for, and possibly repair, database corruption
- Check for, and repair, fragmentation
- Reorganize indexes

All these tasks can be performed with Transact-SQL. You can also use DMO to check for database corruption or to reorganize indexes. Enterprise Manager enables you to reorganize indexes only.

❝❝   IMO

SQL Server 7.0, like its predecessor, includes a Database Maintenance Plan Wizard and a command-line executable named SQLMAINT. You can use either of these to carry out some troubleshooting tasks (as well as some tasks that are not listed here) on a scheduled basis. However, I do not recommend doing so because the wizard and the underlying utility operate on an all-or-nothing basis. That is, every index on every table gets reorganized whether it needs it or not. These operations can be time-consuming and impact the performance of the system. You will want to manage them at a much lower level—for example, reorganizing the indexes on a particular table or even just reorganizing a specific index.

Checking for Database Corruption

SQL Server 7.0 databases are much more robust than the databases of previous versions. Most of us still feel more comfortable running periodic checks, however, to make sure that there is no corruption in our databases. I'm not talking about bad data here, or data that violates referential integrity constraints. Instead, I'm talking about corruption in SQL Server's internal storage structures—bad pointers, duplicate keys in indexes, and so forth. These consistency checks are much faster with SQL Server 7.0 than they were in previous versions.

You can check several different aspects of the storage structures, including the following:

- Allocation and structural integrity of database objects
- Allocation and use of all pages in the database or in a particular file group
- Consistency of system tables
- Correctness of identity values
- Physical integrity of data and indexes for a table

When a column is defined with the IDENTITY property, SQL Server assigns a new value when rows are inserted into the table. This is sometimes referred to as an autoincrement column. It's the equivalent of Access's Counter datatype.

You determine how frequently you should check for corruption. You need to balance the time it takes to do the checks against the volatility of your data. Tables that have a lot of insert, update, and/or delete activity should be checked more frequently than more static tables.

Checking for Database Corruption with Transact-SQL

Use the Transact-SQL DBCC command to check for database corruption. This command has several different forms, as described in the following sections.

DBCC CHECKDB

The DBCC CHECKDB command performs the most comprehensive checks of all the DBCC commands. It checks the structural integrity and allocation of every object in the database, ensuring the following:

- Index and data pages are correctly linked.
- Indexes are in their proper sorted order.
- Pointers are consistent.
- Data on each page is reasonable.
- Page offsets are reasonable.

Note that data checking is not about validating your business data; it is just about making sure that the row sizes and structures are correct.

DBCC CHECKDB requires shared table locks on all tables and indexes. (See Chapter 5, "Transaction Management," for more information on locks.) You cannot make changes to table definitions while DBCC is running.

Syntax

Following is the syntax for DBCC CHECKDB.

```
DBCC CHECKDB ('database_name' [, NOINDEX            ¦
{REPAIR_ALLOW_DATA_LOSS                    ¦
➡REPAIR_FAST                  ¦ REPAIR_REBUILD}])
[WITH {ALL_ERRORMSGS ¦ NO_INFOMSGS}]
```

If you use the NOINDEX keyword, DBCC does not check non-clustered indexes, except on the system tables. This saves time. It's okay to skip these checks because non-clustered indexes, unlike clustered indexes, can be rebuilt very quickly.

If you use the WITH ALL_ERRORMSGS option, DBCC displays all messages. If you use the WITH NO_INFOMSGS, DBCC doesn't show you any informational messages or the report of space used. If you don't use either option, you see information and error messages. The report lists a maximum of 2,000 messages; the messages you see are the first ones encountered.

DBCC can repair some database corruption. Not all database corruption can be repaired by DBCC, however, and if you have a seriously damaged database, you may have to recover from your backups. (See Chapter 6 for more information on database recovery.)

The three DBCC repair options are as follows:

- REPAIR_FAST fixes minor errors, such as the same key occurring twice in an index. All the repairs done by this option can be done quickly and are completely safe; there is no risk of data loss.

- REPAIR_REBUILD does everything that REPAIR_FAST does, as well as performing other repairs that may be more time-consuming, such as rebuilding an index. There is no risk of data loss with this option either.

- REPAIR_ALLOW_DATA_LOSS does everything that REPAIR_REBUILD does, but it also corrects allocation errors, structural row or page errors, and it deletes corrupted text objects. There is a possibility of losing data with this option, and you should use it with extreme caution.

The database must be in single-user mode if you want to use any of the repair options.

DBCC CHECKFILEGROUP

The DBCC CHECKFILEGROUP command performs the same checks as DBCC CHECKDB, but for a specific file group.

Syntax

Following is the syntax for the DBCC CHECKFILEGROUP command.

```
DBCC CHECKFILEGROUP ( [{'filegroup' ¦ filegroup_id}]
[, NOINDEX])
[WITH {ALL_ERRORMSGS ¦ NO_INFOMSGS}]
```

You can specify either the file group name or its ID. To find a file group ID, use the FILEGROUP_ID function or use sp_helpfilegroup.

It is possible that some tables that are not in the specified file group can also be checked as a result of this command. If the file group contains a non-clustered index for a table in a different file group, for example, that table is also checked.

> ❝ **IMO**
>
> The Microsoft documentation does not list any repair options for DBCC CHECKFILEGROUP. However, they are accepted on the command. Because there is no documentation of the effects of the options, I don't recommend using them.

DBCC CHECKTABLE

The DBCC CHECKTABLE command performs the same checks as DBCC CHECKDB, but does those checks for a specific table.

Syntax

Following is the syntax for the DBCC CHECKTABLE command.

```
DBCC CHECKTABLE ('table_name' [, NOINDEX ¦ index_id
                ¦{ REPAIR_ALLOW_DATA_LOSS
                        ¦ REPAIR_FAST
                        ¦ REPAIR_REBUILD}])
                [WITH {ALL_ERRORMSGS ¦ NO_INFOMSGS}]
```

If you specify an index_id, DBCC will only check that index. If you specify a table_name, and don't use the NOINDEX keyword, DBCC will check the table and all its indexes.

The other options of DBCC CHECKTABLE are identical to those for DBCC CHECKDB.

DBCC CHECKALLOC

The DBCC CHECKALLOC command performs a subset of the checks performed by DBCC CHECKDB. It just checks the allocation and use of all pages in the database. It is not necessary to run this command if you have already run DBCC CHECKDB.

Syntax

Following is the syntax for the DBCC CHECKALLOC command:

```
DBCC CHECKALLOC ('database_name' [,NOINDEX
                ¦
                {REPAIR_ALLOW_DATA_LOSS
                    ¦ REPAIR_FAST
```

```
                        | REPAIR_REBUILD}])
   [WITH {ALL_ERRORMSGS | NO_INFOMSGS}]
```

All the options for CHECKALLOC have the same meaning that they do for DBCC CHECKDB.

DBCC CHECKIDENT

The DBCC CHECKIDENT command checks and repairs, if necessary, the current identity value for a table. This value is the last one assigned when a row was inserted.

Syntax

```
DBCC CHECKIDENT ('table_name' [, { NORESEED | {RESEED [,
new_reseed_value]} }])
```

If you just specify DBCC CHECKIDENT (MyTable) or DBCC CHECKIDENT (MyTable, RESEED), the identity is checked and corrected if necessary. By default, the identity value is set to the maximum value in the table. If the current identity is larger than the maximum value in the table, however, the change is not made. If you use the NORESEED option, the value isn't changed. If you use the RESEED option with a new_reseed_value, the current value of the identity is set to that value. Use caution when you do this. If the value you specify is lower than the value currently in use, people receive duplicate violation messages when they attempt to insert new data into the table.

DBCC CHECKCATALOG

This command checks for consistency between some of the system tables. Specifically, it checks to ensure that every datatype in the syscolumns table has a matching entry in the systypes table and that each table and view in the sysobjects table has at least one column in the syscolumns table.

Syntax

```
DBCC CHECKCATALOG ('database_name') [WITH NO_INFOMSGS]
```

Checking for Database Corruption with DMO

Methods exist at the database, file group, and table level for checking for database corruption with DMO. The object methods for each of these levels are listed and described in the following sections.

Database Object Methods

The Database object has several methods that correspond to the DBCC commands described previously. The CheckTables method is the same as DBCC CHECKDB; the CheckTablesDataOnly method is the same as DBCC CHECKDB with the NOINDEX option.

Method	DBCC **Command**
CheckTables	DBCC CHECKDB
CheckTablesDataOnly	DBCC CHECKDB NOINDEX
CheckAllocations	DBCC CHECKALLOC
CheckAllocationsDataOnly	DBCC CHECKALLOC NOINDEX
CheckIdent	DBCC CHECKIDENT on all tables in the database. The Reseed and No Reseed options are not available in DMO.
CheckCatalog	DBCC CHECKCATALOG

The CheckTable, CheckTableDataOnly, CheckAllocations, and CheckAllocationsDataOnly methods require a parameter that specifies the type of repair you want to perform, as shown in the following table.

Constant	Meaning
SQLDMORepair_Allow_DataLoss	Attempt all database repair regardless of the possibility of data loss. For example, delete corrupted text objects.
SQLDMORepair_Fast	Attempt database repair tasks that do not incur data loss.
SQLDMORepair_None	Default. Do not attempt database repair on database inconsistencies encountered.
SQLDMORepair_Rebuild	Attempt database repair tasks that do not incur data loss. Rebuild indexes on successful database repair.

FileGroup Object Methods

The FileGroup object has a CheckFileGroup method that is the same as running DBCC CHECKFILEGROUP and a CheckFileGroupDataOnly method that is the same as running DBCC CHECKFILEGROUP with the NOINDEX option. No repair options are permitted.

Table Object Methods

The Table object has a CheckTable method that is the same as running DBCC CHECKTABLE, and a CheckTableDataOnly method that is the same as running DBCC CHECKTABLE with the NOINDEX option. As nearly as I can determine, there are no repair options; they are not documented and when I use the method in VB, no arguments are presented as they normally would be. There is also a CheckIdentityValue method, which takes no arguments. It's the same as DBCC CHECKIDENT with no optional arguments.

Discovering and Repairing Fragmentation

As data is inserted into and deleted from tables and indexes, fragmentation can occur. SQL Server automatically takes care of fragmentation within each page. However, fragmentation can occur at the data level when a table has a clustered index, and in both clustered and non-clustered indexes. As index splits occur, it can become necessary for SQL Server to use additional extents that are not contiguous. These extents can cause more disk read/write head movement during sequential read operations and can impair performance.

You can use Transact-SQL to detect and repair fragmentation. You can also use DMO to repair fragmentation but not to discover it. Fragmentation can be repaired in the data pages of tables that have a clustered index and in the index structures of both clustered and non-clustered indexes. Fragmentation in data pages of a table that does not have a clustered index can only be repaired by copying all the data out of the table, deleting all the data, and reloading the data from a copy.

Warning

Note that I am not talking about the fragmentation of files on the disk. I am talking about internal-to-SQL Server fragmentation. I don't recommend using disk defrag utilities such as DiskKeeper on SQL Server files. There's no evidence that it does any good, and Microsoft's position on whether they will support databases that have been defragged is fuzzy. With sophisticated disk subsystems, such as RAID arrays, the need for defragging is becoming obsolete. If you create correctly sized databases on a freshly formatted drive, there will not be any disk fragmentation anyway.

Discovering Fragmentation with Transact-SQL

You can use a DBCC command to determine whether a table or index is fragmented.

Syntax

Following is the syntax for the DBCC command.

```
DBCC SHOWCONTIG (table_id [, index_id])
```

You must provide the table_id. If you do not provide the index_id, only the table is checked. If you provide the index_id, only the index is checked. To find the ID of a table, use the OBJECT_ID function (you cannot substitute this function for the ID in the DBCC command), as shown here:

```
SELECT OBJECT_ID('tablename')
```

To find an index ID, use the following SQL statement:

```
SELECT indid FROM sysindexes
WHERE name = 'indexname'
AND id = OBJECT_ID('tablename')
```

When you issue the DBCC SHOWCONTING command, you get output that looks like the following:

```
DBCC SHOWCONTIG scanning 'Categories' table...
Table: 'Categories' (181575685); index ID: 1, database ID: 6
TABLE level scan performed.
- Pages Scanned................................: 1
- Extents Scanned.............................: 1
```

```
- Extent Switches.............................: 0
- Avg. Pages per Extent.......................: 1.0
- Scan Density [Best Count:Actual Count].......: 100.00% [1:1]
- Logical Scan Fragmentation .................: 0.00%
- Extent Scan Fragmentation ..................: 0.00%
- Avg. Bytes Free per Page....................: 7502.0
- Avg. Page Density (full)....................: 7.31%
```

Three parts of this output are particularly meaningful:

- Scan Density
- Extent Switches
- Avg. Page Density

Scan Density is the most important. If it shows 100%, as the preceding output sample does, that there is no fragmentation. The further below 100% the Scan Density is, the more fragmented the table or index is. Extent Switches are just another measure of fragmentation; the more of them there are, the more fragmented the table is. Avg. Page Density is a measure of how much of each page is used. Ideally, 100% of each page is used but this is difficult to achieve in practice, because it is unusual to have a row size that exactly divides the bytes available for data storage. However, it is desirable to have as high an Avg. Page Density as possible.

Repairing Fragmentation with Transact-SQL

Use DBCC DBREINDEX to repair fragmentation in a clustered index (and in the table as well) or a non-clustered index.

Syntax

Following is the syntax for DBCC DBREINDEX command.

```
DBCC DBREINDEX('tablename' [, 'indexname'])
```

If you do not specify an index name, all the indexes on the table are rebuilt. If you specify an index name, only that index is rebuilt.

Repairing Fragmentation with DMO

To repair fragmentation with DMO, use the RebuildIndexes method of the Table object. This method rebuilds all the indexes on the table. To repair fragmentation in a single index, use the Rebuild method of the Index object.

Reorganizing Indexes

Often, you'll want to reorganize indexes so that there is free space for insertions and deletions. You need to do this if you find that operations are slowed by frequent page splits. You can monitor page splits with Performance Monitor. (See Chapter 10 for more information on Performance Monitor.)

Not all indexes require reorganization. If a table is static or has a very low update frequency, there is no point in leaving "holes" in the indexes; you will only waste disk space. You are always trading off the cost of leaving empty space against the time it takes to do inserts, updates of index keys, and deletions. In addition, leaving these "holes" results in SQL Server having to read more pages for the same amount of data, because the pages are not tightly packed. Reads tend to outnumber writes in database systems, so you want to be careful that you don't leave too much space. You can measure SQL Server reads and SQL Server writes with Performance Monitor. Explore leaving free space if the number of writes is at least 30% of the number of reads.

You specify the amount of free space to be left in an index when you create the index. However, over time this free space is used up. You can reorganize the index and use the original amount of free space or you can change it.

When you create an index, there are two different ways to influence the amount of space that is left empty:

- **Fill Factor.** This factor specifies how full each leaf node of an index should be. The default value of Fill Factor is 0, which means that leaf nodes are completely full and other nodes have space for at least one additional entry. If you specify a value of 100, all the nodes are completely full. This is appropriate for tables that will never be updated, because there is no wasted space. If you specify any other value, the leaf nodes will be filled to that percentage, and all other nodes will have space for one additional entry. Remember that the actual data is the leaf node of a clustered index.

- **Pad Index.** Pad Index works with Fill Factor and specifies that the intermediate nodes should also only be filled to the percentage. There is no point to specify Pad Index if you are using the default fill factor or a fill factor of 100.

 General Tip

Reorganizing indexes has the nice side effect of getting rid of fragmentation even if you didn't know it was there.

You can reorganize indexes with Enterprise Manager, Transact-SQL, and DMO.

Reorganizing Indexes with Enterprise Manager

You can reorganize an index in Enterprise Manager by highlighting a table, right-clicking it, and choosing All Tasks, Manage Indexes. An Index dialog box displays. Select the index you want from the drop-down list and choose Edit. You can modify the Fill Factor if you choose. If you don't check the Fill Factor box, the original fill factor is used. You can also choose Pad Index by checking the option for it. When you click OK, the index is rebuilt.

Reorganizing Indexes with Transact-SQL

You can reorganize an index in Transact-SQL with the CREATE INDEX statement or with DBCC DBREINDEX.

Reorganizing Indexes with the CREATE INDEX Statement

Syntax

Following is the syntax for the CREATE INDEX statement.

```
CREATE [UNIQUE] [CLUSTERED ¦ NONCLUSTERED]
        INDEX index_name ON table (column [,...n])[WITH [PAD_INDEX]
            [[,] FILLFACTOR = fillfactor]
            [[,] DROP_EXISTING]
```

You use the CREATE INDEX statement just as you would when creating a new index, but you add the DROP_EXISTING clause. This makes SQL Server destroy the existing index before it builds the new one. Use the PAD_INDEX option to get the padding behavior described previously, and the FILLFACTOR option to specify a fill factor. If you do not specify PAD_INDEX, there will be no free space left in the intermediate nodes, even if you used PAD_INDEX when you originally created the index. If you do not specify a fill factor, the original fill factor is used.

Note that if you are reorganizing an index that implements a primary key or unique constraint, you must use the DROP_EXISTING keyword. For other indexes, you can use a DROP INDEX statement followed by a CREATE INDEX statement if you want, although there are some performance benefits to using DROP EXISTING, particularly on clustered indexes, because it stops SQL Server from sorting data that is already sorted.

Reorganizing Indexes with DBCC

Syntax

```
DBCC DBREINDEX (table_name' [, index_name
        [, fillfactor ] ])
        [WITH NO_INFOMSGS]
```

If you specify a table name, but no index name, all the indexes on the table are rebuilt. To specify a fill factor to apply to all indexes, write your statement like this:

```
DBCC DBREINDEX ('MyTable', '', 70)
```

Note that you use an empty string (one apostrophe followed immediately by another) in place of the index name.

Reorganizing Indexes with DMO

You can reorganize indexes with DMO by re-creating them or by rebuilding them.

Re-Creating the Indexes with DMO

It is not as straightforward to reorganize indexes by re-creating them in DMO as it is in Transact-SQL. You must start with a connected Table object that represents the table you want to work on, and then proceed as follows:

1 Use the Table object's BeginAlter method to signal the start of the operation.

2 Use the Indexes collection's Remove method to remove the index from the collection.

3 Use the Table object's DoAlter method to cause the change to be made in SQL Server.

4 Instantiate an Index object, and set its properties. There is a FillFactor property but not a PadIndex property. You also need to set the Name, IndexedColumns, and the Type properties.

5 After the Index object has been completed, use the BeginAlter method of the Table object, add the Index object to the Indexes collection, and use the DoAlter method to cause the change to be made in the database.

General Tip

There is no equivalent to the DROP_EXISTING keyword, and I suspect that this approach won't work on indexes that implement primary key and unique constraints.

Using the Objects' Rebuild Methods

You can use the RebuildIndexes method of the Table object to reorganize all the indexes on the table. This method takes two arguments:

- IndexType   This is an optional argument used to maintain compatibility with earlier versions of DMO.

- FillFactor   This is a long argument specifying the fill factor.

To reorganize a single index, use the Rebuild method of the Index object. If you want to change the fill factor, set the FillFactor property of the Index object before using the Rebuild method.

Under the Covers

This section briefly discusses some of the system databases and system tables that relate to storage management.

The Model Database

Each new database starts out with the contents of model. When you create a database, the contents of model are copied to the new database. This includes the system tables present in every database as well as any objects you may have added to model. If you have some common objects (tables, user datatypes, stored procedures, and so on) that you want to appear in every database you create, add them to model and they will appear in any new databases created after that. Even tempdb is re-created from model each time the server starts. If model is corrupt or damaged in some way, it won't be possible to create tempdb and SQL Server won't start.

sysdatabases

When you create a database, an entry for that database is added to sysdatabases, which is in the master database. This entry includes the database name, two status columns, and the full operating system path to the database's primary data file, as well as the creation date and some internal identification data. The columns *status* and *status2* hold bit maps that represent the database options you have set. See the Books OnLine if you want to know how to decode these fields.

sysfilegroups

Each file group you define gets an entry in sysfilegroups. This table is in the database itself, not in master. Information stored in this table includes the file group name, its status (read-only, default, and so on), and a mysterious column named *allocpolicy*, which is described as "reserved for future use." One can only speculate as to what its purpose will be. The documentation implies that the status field is a bit mask, but in fact the data is actually stored in it as integers; so a status of 10 means default and a status of 8 means read-only.

sysfiles

Information about each of the files that comprises your database is stored in sysfiles. This table is also in the database itself. Information in this table includes the file's logical name, physical path, the Id of the group to which it belongs, its size, its maximum size, and how much growth is allowed. There is a Status field that contains information such as whether growth is in percentage and how the file was created. It also has a mysterious column named *perf*, which is simply described as "reserved." There's also a mysterious, undocumented table called *sysfiles1*. This table contains different status values, the file's logical and physical names, and the file's ID. Who knows what it is for! Perhaps it's a predecessor to sysfiles, or something for future use.

sysaltfiles

This table, in the master database, is a copy of the all the information in each database's sysfiles table. It has an additional column that is the database ID. It is clearly what Microsoft should be using to find the location of transaction log files (see previous discussion and Chapter 6), but apparently isn't. At the time of this writing, I have not yet been able to determine its use.

sysindexes

The fill factor used in the most recent CREATE INDEX statement for each index is stored in sysindexes, along with a lot of other information about indexes. However, no information about Pad Index is saved. It's often confusing to people when they discover that each table has an entry in sysindexes. The index ID in the rows that represent tables is 0. The index ID of the clustered index, if any, is always 1. Non-clustered indexes are number from 2 to 250.

5

Transaction Management

This chapter is not about "transactions per second" or any other measurement of performance. It is about what many people would call "logical units of work." First, this chapter talks about transactions and what they are capable of. Then, the discussion focuses on how SQL Server locks resources, and how these locks interact with transactions. Finally, this chapter covers problems that may occur because of transactions and locks, and shows you some of the things you can do to troubleshoot these problems. Please have patience while reading the first two sections of this chapter that cover transactions and locks; these topics present a "chicken-and-egg" type of problem. I promise to tie it all together in the end.

Transactions

A *logical unit of work* is a set of database update activities that must be complete in its entirety or does not happen at all. In the SQL Server world, we usually call these sets of database activity transactions because of the command we use to define where the logical unit of work begins and ends. Transactions must adhere to the *ACID* properties shown in the following table:

Property	Description
*A*tomicity	The update is indivisible. All parts of it must be complete or the database must be left in the state it was in before the transaction started.
*C*onsistency	At the conclusion of the transaction, the database must be in a physically and logically consistent state.
*I*solation	Two concurrently executing transactions must result in the same database state that would have existed if they had executed one after the other.
*D*urability	After a transaction has completed, its effects cannot be lost even if there is a system software or hardware failure.

Applications have the responsibility of ensuring that the first two properties, Atomicity and Consistency, are observed. SQL Server has responsibility for ensuring that the last two properties, Isolation and Durability, are observed. SQL Server ensures isolation by using locks on resources, and it ensures durability by recording changes in the Transaction log.

Any Transact-SQL updating DML (INSERT, UPDATE, DELETE) is a transaction in its own right. If a DELETE statement updates more than one row, either all the rows will be deleted or none of them will be. If the logical unit of work involves multiple UPDATE statements, however, it's the application's responsibility to define the transaction boundaries. Consider, for example, the following statements that transfer money from a savings account to a checking account:

```
UPDATE Savings SET Balance = Balance - 500
WHERE AccountNumber = '12S'
UPDATE Checking SET Balance = Balance + 500
WHERE AccountNumber = '12C'
```

If the system were to crash after the first update, both the principles of atomicity and consistency would be violated. If the money never actually makes it to the checking account and it is no longer in savings, the total amount of money in all accounts no longer adds up. To prevent this from happening, you must use the following code:

```
BEGIN TRANSACTION
UPDATE Savings SET Balance = Balance - 500
WHERE AccountNumber = '12S'
        UPDATE Checking SET Balance = Balance + 500
WHERE AccountNumber = '12C'
COMMIT TRANSACTION
```

Note that the requirement to explicitly begin a transaction differs from the ANSI standard and from the behavior of most other relational database management systems. In the standard, a logical unit of work begins with the first SQL statement and continues until the application issues a COMMIT WORK or ROLLBACK WORK statement. Then another logical unit of work begins. You can make SQL Server behave like the ANSI model by issuing either of the following statements:

```
SET IMPLICIT_TRANSACTIONS ON
```

or

```
SET ANSI_DEFAULTS ON
```

These are connection-level options and must be set for each connection. It is possible to set up the SQL Server so that all transactions conform to the ANSI standard by setting the User Options configuration option with sp_configure, as follows:

```
sp_configure 'user options', 2
```

You can also check the appropriate box on the Connections tab in Enterprise Manager's Server Properties dialog box. Note that either of these approaches affects only transactions. It does not change any of the other configuration or database options that deal with other deviations from the ANSI standard. (See Chapter 2, "Installation and Upgrade," and Chapter 4, "Storage Management," for more information on this.)

After a transaction has started, it runs until it is either rolled back or committed. The SQL Server can roll the transaction back, or the application can. Transactions can be nested, but a rollback is always to the *state* before the *first* begin transaction.

If you are developing stored procedures or other applications you must learn a great deal more about transactions. The mission here is administration, and that is enough theory to carry us through the chapter.

Concurrent Update Problems

When many people are concurrently updating data, four problems can arise:

- **Lost updates.** One user's update overlays another user's update, causing it to be lost.
- **Dirty data.** One user sees another user's uncommitted changes.
- **Non-repeatable reads.** When a record is read for the second time during a transaction, its values have changed.
- **Phantoms.** Records appear or disappear during a transaction.

Lost Updates

A lost update occurs when one user's changes overlay changes made by another user, as shown in the following table.

User 1	User 2

`SELECT @lname=LastName,`
`@fname=FirstName,`
`@phone = Phone FROM Employee`
`WHERE LastName = 'Smith'`
`and FirstName = 'John'`
@phone is 610-555-1212.
	Inactive.

Interacting with user.
User changes phone number
to 212-999-9999.
	`UPDATE Employee set`
	`Phone = '215-123-4567'`
	`WHERE LastName =`
	`'Smith' and FirstName =`
	`'John'`
	Phone is now 215-555-1212 in the database.

`UPDATE Employee SET Phone = Inactive`
`@phone WHERE LastName =`
`'Smith' and FirstName = 'John'`
Phone is now 212-999-9999 in database. User 2's change is lost.
	Inactive.

Dirty Data

The following table illustrates what could happen when users can see dirty data.

User1	User 2
Current balance in account 1 is $10000. `BEGIN TRANSACTION`	Inactive.

```
UPDATE Accounts
    SET Balance = Balance - 9000
    WHERE AccountNumber = 1
```
Balance is now 1000.

```
                                        SELECT Balance from
                                        Accounts
                                        WHERE AccountNumber = 1
                                        IF Balance < 5000
                                                Credit denied
```

```
UPDATE Accounts
    SET Balance = Balance + 15000
    WHERE AccountNumber = 1
```
Balance is now 16000.

```
COMMIT TRANSACTION
```

The customer was denied credit because the balance update was incomplete at the time User2 issued a dirty read.

Non-Repeatable Reads

Some applications must make multiple passes over the same data and find it unchanged. These applications include various statistical calculations and many kinds of period-end reporting. The following table illustrates this problem.

User 1	User 2

`SELECT SUM(Salary)`
`FROM Employees`
`Where DepartmentNumber = 300`
	Inactive.

Share locks are released after the query.	

Working with the data received.	`UPDATE Employees`
	`SET Salary = Salary * 1.1`
	`WHERE DepartmentNumber =`
	`300`

`SELECT SUM(Salary)`
`FROM Employees`
`Where DepartmentNumber = 300`	

Total of department 300 salaries is now different from the first value retrieved.	

Phantoms

Phantoms are records that appear or disappear during a transaction. Suppose, for example, that the transaction is performing an operation on all the employee records for a particular department. Simultaneously, another transaction inserts an employee into that department. The first transaction does not know about this newly added employee, and therefore, the operation does not get performed for that employee. Deletion can also cause phantoms. If the first transaction is processing records sequentially, for example, a concurrent transaction might delete an employee that the first transaction hasn't gotten to yet.

Locks

The problems described in the previous sections are not unique to SQL Server; they can happen in any system that allows concurrent updates. Operating systems, other DBMS, and SQL Server all use locks to prevent these problems from occurring. SQL Server's lock manager manages all the locking internally, although the application developer can in some ways influence the types of locks used.

SQL Server uses several *lock types*. These can be applied at many different levels (see the discussion of lock granularity that follows). Regardless of the level at which they are applied, locks have the effects shown in the following table.

When a Resource Is Locked with a Lock Type Of	Result
Shared (S)	Others can read, but no one can change.
Exclusive (X)	No one else can read or change.
Update (U)	An update is planned; no one else can get an exclusive lock.
Intent shared (IS)	A lower-level resource has a shared lock.
Intent exclusive (IX)	A lower-level resource has an exclusive lock.
Shared with intent exclusive (SIX)	This resource has a shared lock, but a lower level resource has an exclusive lock.
Schema stability (Sch-S)	Used while a query plan is being developed for a table to prevent changes to the definition of the table.
Schema modification (Sch-M)	Used while a table is being altered or created.
Bulk update (BU)	Used when a bulk copy operation is placing data into a table (requires explicit table lock request).

Some of these lock types are compatible, which means that more than one person can have a lock of that type. Some lock types are incompatible. In the following table, *Y* means that User 2's request will be granted; *N* means that it will not be granted. The column and row labels are the same abbreviations that are in parentheses in the table of lock types.

User 2 wants	User 1 holds S	X	U	IS	IX	SIX	Sch-S	Sch-M	BU
S	Y	N	Y	Y	N	N	Y	N	N
X	N	N	N	N	N	N	Y	N	N
U	Y	N	N	Y	N	N	Y	N	N
IS	Y	N	Y	Y	Y	Y	Y	N	N
IX	N	N	N	Y	Y	N	Y	N	N
SIX	N	N	N	Y	N	N	Y	N	N
Sch-S	Y	Y	Y	Y	Y	Y	Y	N	Y
Sch-M	N	N	N	N	N	N	N	N	N
BU	N	N	N	N	N	N	Y	N	N

When a process requests an incompatible lock, it must wait until the lock is freed before it can proceed. This can create contention problems. Monitoring and resolving these problems is discussed later in this chapter in the section "Monitoring Locks and Troubleshooting Conention Problems."

The SQL Server lock manager applies locks at many different levels. The size of the resource that is locked is called *granularity*. When locks are applied to small units, such as a row, there is more concurrency. However, there is also more overhead in managing the locks. When locks are applied to large units, such as a table, there is much less opportunity for concurrent use of that table. However, the overhead is much lower.

In fact, sometimes it's better to lock at the largest granularity. Because of the reduction in management overhead, the process may actually take less time and other users may be able to get to data more quickly. SQL Server 7.0 will apply locks at the following levels:

- Rows
- Pages
- Keys
- Key ranges
- Tables
- Indexes
- Databases

You will also see extent locks, which are used when tables or indexes grow. These aren't something you have to worry about; they just ensure that the physical structure of the database is maintained correctly.

SQL Server uses a dynamic strategy to determine which type of lock will be best for each query. The Query Optimizer determines part of the locking strategy when it develops the execution plan for the query. A query that is going to update every row of a table, for example, will probably get an exclusive table lock. It is possible that the locking strategy may change while the query is executing. The lock manager uses dynamic lock escalation to raise lower granularity locks to a higher granularity. Suppose, for example, that a process has acquired a number of row locks for records that are all on the same page. SQL Server may decide that the operation would be faster if it just granted a page lock. After it has done this, it frees the memory that was being used to keep track of the row locks.

Interaction of Locks and Transactions

As stated in the preceding section, four problems can arise when people are concurrently using a database. The ANSI standard defines four isolation levels that specify which of these problems will be prevented. The following table lists these isolation levels and the problems that can occur at each level.

Isolation Level	Lost Update	Dirty Reads	Non-Repeatable Reads	Phantoms
Read Uncommitted	Not possible	Possible	Possible	Possible
Read Committed	Not possible	Not possible	Possible	Possible
Repeatable Read	Not possible	Not possible	Not possible	Possible
Serializable	Not possible	Not possible	Not possible	Not possible

By default, SQL Server operates at the *read committed* level. This is reasonable, because you don't ever want lost updates. Applications that require dirty reads, repeatable reads, and serializable transactions are less common. Occasionally, however, one of the other isolation levels is necessary or desirable.

Operating at the *read uncommitted* level may improve the performance for readers, because it enables a reader to access a resource even though that resource is exclusively locked. You need to exercise caution when you work in this level, however, because the reader may see changes that are incomplete or might subsequently be rolled back.

Serializable guarantees that the end result of the concurrently executing transactions is identical to running them sequentially. It is the only level that prevents phantoms.

In general, locks are held until the transaction commits or rolls back. The isolation level determines which locks are required and how long they must be held. The following table shows the shared and exclusive locks and their isolation-level status. These are the important locks.

	Isolation	Level		
Lock Type	Read Uncommitted	Read Committed	Repeatable Read	Serializable
S	None	Freed when no longer needed	Held until end of transaction	Held, on *key ranges*, until end of transaction
X	Ignored by readers	Held until end of transaction	Held until end of transaction	Held, on *key ranges*, until end of transaction

As you can see, when the isolation levels become stronger, more data is locked. This can result in contention problems (as discussed later in this chapter).

Note that SQL Server must lock key ranges when it operates at the Serializable level. If you issue the following query (inside a transaction), for example:

```
SELECT LastName, FirstName
FROM Employee
WHERE LastName BETWEEN 'Smith' AND 'Stevens'
```

SQL Server must make sure that no one with last names between Smith and Stevens can be inserted and deleted. This means that no other user can add a record, for example, for an employee named 'Snow', and no one can delete any of the employees in the range.

 General Tip

It's possible that records close to the key range will also be locked. If SQL Server is applying page locks, and other records on the page contain Smith, they may also be locked.

Modifying Default Locking Behavior

By default, SQL Server operates at the Read Committed isolation level. You can modify the isolation level at the connection level with the following SET statement:

```
SET TRANSACTION ISOLATION LEVEL
{READ COMMITTED
¦ READ UNCOMMITTED
¦ REPEATABLE READ
¦ SERIALIZABLE}
```

You should use some caution when you set the isolation level at the connection level because it applies to *all* queries and updates on *all* tables until it is reset. It is possible to specify the isolation level for a specific table or tables in a query by using *locking hints*. This localizes the isolation level to a single table.

Several hints specify different isolation levels, including the following:

- **SERIALIZABLE, HOLDLOCK.** When you use either of these hints, SQL Server operates at the Serializable level, holding shared locks on resources and key ranges until the end of the transaction
- **READUNCOMMITTED, NOLOCK.** When you use either of these hints, SQL Server does not apply share locks and ignores exclusive locks on the table.
- **READCOMMITTED.** Perform a scan with the same locking semantics as a transaction running at the Read Committed isolation level. By default, SQL Server operates at this isolation level.
- **REPEATABLEREAD.** When you use this hint, SQL Server will operate at the Repeatable Read level, holding shared locks on the resources (but not on key ranges) read until the end of the transaction.

 General Tip

Other locking hints specify what type of lock SQL Server should apply; Chapter 10, "Performance Tuning," covers those.

Locking hints can be specified in the SELECT statement and, in some cases, in the INSERT, UPDATE, and DELETE statements. The READUNCOMMITTED hint can only be used in the SELECT statement. In the following example, assume that SQL Server is operating at its default isolation level (Read Committed).

```
SELECT au_lastname, au_firstname, title
FROM authors
INNER JOIN titleauthor (READUNCOMMITTED)
      ON authors.au_id = titleauthor.au_id
      INNER JOIN titles (READUNCOMMITTED)
ON titleauthor.title_id = titles.title_id
```

This query enables the user to see data that has been modified in the titles or titleauthor table even if the transaction that is doing the modifications has not committed its changes. However, "dirty reads" against the authors table are not allowed.

To use a locking hint in an INSERT statement, you must use the keyword WITH, as follows:

```
INSERT INTO tablename WITH (lockinghint)
```

You can specify READCOMMITTED, REPEATABLEREAD, or SERIALIZABLE as the lockinghint value.

In UPDATE or DELETE statements, you can use locking hints in two places.

```
UPDATE tablename WITH (lockinghint)
SET …
FROM tablename (lockinghint)
INNER JOIN tablename (lockinghint) …
DELETE tablename WITH (lockinghint)
FROM tablename (lockinghint)
        INNER JOIN tablename (lockinghint) …
```

❝ IMO

In general, my practice is to use SQL Server's default isolation level as much as possible. When a specific application has a requirement for dirty reads, repeatable reads, or serializable transactions, however, I prefer to use the locking hints. I would much rather permit dirty reads against a single table than allow them against all tables, for example. And I would rather have repeatable reads and serializable activities limited to specific tables, because they limit the availability of resources for concurrent users.

Monitoring Locks and Troubleshooting Contention Problems

We need locks and transactions to ensure that our databases contain consistent data. But they do introduce some problems. You need to be prepared for two different problems:

- Contention
- Deadlock

Contention comes about when one process is using a resource and another process must wait. Process two is *blocked* by process one. This is a normal situation and cannot be avoided. Normally, after a short interval, process one will finish its work and process two can then access the resource. It can become a problem, however, if process one never finishes. This may happen if process one has "gone out to lunch," or because of poor application design.

Deadlock comes about when two processes have competing demands for resources. Assume, for example, that the following transactions are running concurrently.

Time	Transaction 1	Transaction 2	State
1	Begin	Begin	
2	Update savings	Update checking	
3	... thinking	... thinking	
4	Update checking	... thinking	Transaction 1 is blocked
5	... waiting	Update savings	Deadlock

Until Transaction 2's request for an exclusive lock on Savings at time 5, everything is normal. Transaction 1 is waiting for transaction 2 to release the lock on Checking. But at time 5, Transaction 2 creates a deadlock. Neither transaction's requests can ever be satisfied. SQL Server detects the deadlock, selects one of the transactions as a victim, and rolls the transaction back. Typically, the transaction that is rolled back is the one whose request created the deadlock, or Transaction 2 in this example. You have some say in this matter, as you'll discover in the following section.

Monitoring Locking and Contention

You can monitor locks and contention with Transact-SQL, Enterprise Manager, or DMO. There is also some general information on the total number of locks, the total number of blocking locks, and so on available from Performance Monitor.

> **IMO**
>
> I've never found this information particularly helpful, because I rarely care how many blocking locks there are. I'm far more interested in *where* they are.

When you encounter contention problems, often your only recourse is to terminate the process blocking other processes. Contention problems can be caused by poorly formed queries that lock resources for longer than they should or a connection that is actually orphaned. Processes can be orphaned by applications that have terminated abnormally. It's my experience that crashing the Visual Basic Interactive Debugging Environment is a sure way to create orphaned connections!

> **! Important!**
>
> Remember, it is normal for processes to be blocked for a short time when multiple users are on the system. It is not a red flag if you suddenly notice a blocked process, because the process might block other users for only a short time.

It is possible that you will attempt to terminate a process and it will not terminate. A DBA colleague of mine refers to these processes as *zombies*. When this happens, you need to shut down SQL Server and restart it.

Monitoring Locking and Contention with Transact-SQL

You can use two commands to look at contention and locks. sp_who and sp_who2 both show information about processes. I find the output of sp_who2 a little more useful, because it shows CPU utilization and disk activity. I can quickly decide that if a blocking process is using CPU and disk, it's probably still alive. It may be behaving badly, but it is running.

General Tip

It's important to remember that sp_who2 creates some tables in tempdb. If you are experiencing blocking problems in tempdb, this command will exacerbate them. Use sp_who instead.

Syntax

```
sp_who [loginame | spid]

sp_who2 [loginame | spid]
```

❝❝ IMO

sp_who2 does not seem to really use the loginname parameter. If I give it an NT Authentication login, it says the login doesn't exist. If I give it a SQL Server Authentication login, it displays everything anyway. sp_who does not exhibit this behavior.

Figure 5.1 shows some of the output of sp_who2.

Figure 5.1   Output of sp_who2.

SPID	Status	Login	HostName	BlkBy	DBName	Command	CPU...	Di...	LastBatch	Pr
3	BACKGROUND	sa	.	.	pubs	LAZY WRITER	0	0	01/18 16:...	
4	sleeping	sa	.	.	pubs	LOG WRITER	0	0	01/18 16:...	
5	sleeping	sa	.	.	pubs	CHECKPOINT ...	0	99	01/18 16:...	
6	BACKGROUND	sa	.	.	pubs	AWAITING CO...	0	1371	01/18 16:...	
7	RUNNABLE	sa	SHARONP350	.	pubs	SELECT INTO	0	67	02/11 10:...	MS
8	sleeping	PINE\Administrator	LMSERVER	.	msdb	AWAITING CO...	0	11	02/09 11:...	SQ
9	sleeping	PINE\Administrator	LMSERVER	.	msdb	AWAITING CO...	0	7...	02/11 10:...	SQ
10	sleeping	sa	SHARONP350	.	pubs	AWAITING CO...	0	11	02/11 10:...	MS
11	sleeping	sa	SHARONP350	.	pubs	AWAITING CO...	0	14	02/11 10:...	MS
12	sleeping	sa	SHARONP350	.	pubs	AWAITING CO...	0	0	02/11 10:...	MS
13	sleeping	sa	SHARONP350	.	pubs	AWAITING CO...	0	0	02/11 10:...	MS
14	sleeping	sa	SHARONP350	11	pubs	SELECT	0	0	02/11 10:...	MS

The interesting column in this part of the output is the one labeled *BlkBy*. If there's no value in this column, the process is not blocked. If there is a number in this column, it is the *server process ID* (spid) blocking the process. This figure shows that spid 14 is blocked by spid 11.

To see the Transact-SQL that was issued by the blocking process (or any other process, for that matter), use the following command:

```
DBCC INPUTBUFFER (spid)
```

This shows only the first 255 characters of the command.

To see why process 14 is blocked, use sp_lock, as shown in the following:

```
sp_lock [spid1, [spid2]]
```

This produces a report similar to that shown in Figure 5.2.

Figure 5.2   `sp_lock` **output.**

spid	dbid	ObjId	IndId	Type	Resource	Mode	Status
11	5	0	0	DB		S	GRANT
11	5	261575970	2	PAG	1:192	IX	GRANT
11	5	261575970	1	PAG	1:189	IX	GRANT
11	5	261575970	2	KEY	(4709c79bf149)	X	GRANT
11	5	261575970	2	KEY	(f60751aaa47f)	X	GRANT
11	5	261575970	1	KEY	(5d0164fb1eac)	X	GRANT
11	5	261575970	2	KEY	(de178f5ceb58)	X	GRANT
11	5	261575970	1	KEY	(5801526lc2ba)	X	GRANT
11	5	261575970	2	KEY	(bf0a36c9bbb7)	X	GRANT
11	5	261575970	2	KEY	(ef0d89919da1)	X	GRANT
11	5	261575970	1	KEY	(6001c93f41fe)	X	GRANT
11	5	261575970	1	KEY	(7701b418f8aa)	X	GRANT
11	5	261575970	1	KEY	(6501b9ef5fed)	X	GRANT

It is clear that process 11 is holding an IX (intent exclusive) lock on the
entire table. This is preventing process 14 from seeing it. To determine
which table is involved, you need to use the OBJECT_ID function, as
shown here:

```
SELECT OBJECT_ID(18575685)
```

 General Tip

SQL Server 6.5 has an sp_lock2 that actually does the ID-to-name translation for
you. I missed this feature, so I wrote my own procedure. The Web site for this book
contains the code for sp_lock3, which gives more meaningful information about
locks. It shows names rather than internal identifiers. It's pretty easy to do this sort
of thing. I started with sp_lock and modified it. You can't script system procedures
in Enterprise Manager, but you can use sp_helptext to get the complete text. You
can save the text to a file and modify it. Make sure you change the name of the
procedure if you do this!

If you have determined that the blocking process should be terminated,
you use the kill command as shown here:

```
KILL spid
```

You cannot kill your own process or the internal SQL Server processes
(Log Writer, Lazy Writer, Checkpoint, as well as some of the replication
agents) that will also be listed by sp_who2.

Monitoring Locking and Contention with Enterprise Manager

You will find Enterprise Managers' activity monitor in the MANAGE-
MENT folder. There are three different views. The Process Info view is
not very interesting. The Locks, Process view is the one you want when
you want to see whether there are any contention problems. You will
see a display that looks like the one in Figure 5.3.

Figure 5.3   Locks/Process Info display.

The diagram clearly shows that spid 8 is blocking spid 9. (spid stands for server process ID; each connection to SQL Server gets its own spid.)

If, in fact, spid 8 is truly idle—perhaps the application terminated abnormally—spid 9 will never get a chance to run. At this point, you should decide that process 8 should be killed. Unfortunately, you cannot do this on this display. Instead, you must remember the spid and switch to the Process Info view. When you double-click the process, the process details display, as shown in Figure 5.4.

Figure 5.4   Inspecting and killing a process.

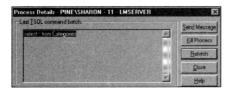

You can send a message (this goes via NET SEND; it's not necessary to set up mail) to see whether the user is still alive, or you can kill the process. You may want to make a note of the SQL statement, because it's possible that some badly behaved application keeps acting as a blocking process.

You can use the Locks/Object display if you need further information about the locks being held by the blocking process, as shown in Figure 5.5.

Figure 5.5   Locks/Object display.

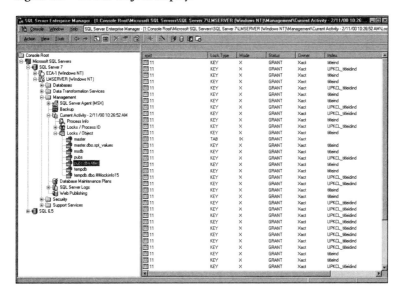

Monitoring Locking and Contention Problems with DMO

Use the EnumProcesses method of a connected server object to get a result set containing process information. The method takes an optional string parameter that can be either a login name or a process ID. The EnumProcesses method returns a QueryResult object that contains the values shown in the following table.

Column	Description
spid	SQL Server process ID.
status	Execution state, such as running or sleeping.
loginname	Name of the SQL Server login.
hostname	This is usually the network name of the client work-station, but an application might set this to some other value.
program_name	If applicable, name of the client application.
cmd	Abbreviated indicator of current command. AWAITING COMMAND when no command is current.
dbname	Database currently in use by process.
cpu	Cumulative CPU time for process. Note: This isn't necessarily CPU time at all. It's taken from the CPU column of sysprocesses, and that column will only be updated when the SETSTATISTICSTIMEON command has been issued (see Chapter 10).
memusage	Number of pages in the procedure cache currently allocated to this process. A negative number indicates that the process is freeing memory allocated by another process.
blocked	When non-zero, process ID blocking a request of the process ID listed by the row.

Use the EnumLocks method of a connected server object or a database object to get a QueryResults object that describes the locks. This method has an optional parameter, a long integer containing a server process ID. The contents of the result set are shown in the following table.

Column	Description
req_spid	Process ID of the process requesting the lock.
locktype	A text description of a locking mode. For more information about interpreting values, see the description of the system table *syslockinfo* column req_mode.
tablename	If applicable, the name of the table against which the lock is applied.
indexname	If applicable, the name of the index against which the lock is applied.

Column	Description
dbname	Name of the database in which the locked resource is defined.
status	An integer indicating lock application status. For more information about interpreting values, see the description of the system table *syslockinfo* column req_status.

To terminate a blocking process, use the KillProcess method of a connected server object. This method takes one parameter, a long integer specifying the process ID that is to be killed.

Avoiding Contention Problems

Many contention problems can be avoided with proper application design and use. Following are recommendations for application design and use:

- Applications should keep transactions as short as possible. Transactions should begin after the user has pressed the Save button, not while the application is soliciting data from the user.

- Where possible, applications should use optimistic concurrency methods (see Chapter 10 for more information on this) to keep lock duration short.

- Applications should always clean up after themselves when shutting down and make sure that they disconnect from SQL Server.

- Some contention problems can be avoided by proper scheduling. Resource-intensive jobs should be run at a time when interactive use is low.

Setting a Lock Timeout

A *lock timeout* causes a process to return, rather than wait forever, when its resource request is not granted after a certain interval. This favors the blocking process, because the processes that would like the resource held by the blocking process go away. (The users of the applications who are blocked may not like this solution.)

The lock timeout is a connection-specific setting; it cannot be set globally for the server as a whole. To set a lock timeout, use the following command:

```
SET LOCK_TIMEOUT timeout_period
```

> **IMO**
>
> I wish it were possible to set a lock timeout for the server as a whole, but Microsoft did not include this option in the set that can be specified at the server level.

The timeout_period is in milliseconds. If you specify −1, the connection waits forever. If you specify 0, the connection won't wait at all. If you specify any other value, it waits the specified number of milliseconds before giving up.

Monitoring Deadlocks

Usually, deadlocks are detected and broken before you even hear about them. Applications receive an Error 1205 (or 1204), and then you will hear about it, when it is too late to do anything about it. Applications should anticipate deadlocks and prepare an error handler that deals with Error 1205. The normal practice is to wait for a short time, and then retry a small number of times (3–5). Usually, the resources will be freed by then and the application will succeed.

If you are experiencing frequent deadlocks, you may want to use SQL Profiler to capture information about the deadlocks so that you and the application designers can figure out why they are occurring. An easy way to do this is to use the Create Trace Wizard in Enterprise Manager. Select Identify the Cause of a Deadlock from the Problems drop-down list and all the right events and counters are automatically selected for you.

Avoiding Deadlocks

It is impossible to prevent deadlock completely. But it can be substantially minimized by the way applications are coded. Applications should always request resources in the same order: savings, then checking, *or*, checking then savings, for example. When applications are coded like this, the scenario discussed earlier changes to resemble the one shown in the following table.

Time	Transaction 1	Transaction 2	State
1	Begin	Begin	
2	Update savings	Update savings	Transaction 2 is blocked.
3	… thinking		
4	Update checking		
5	Commit		Transaction 2 gets savings.
6		Update checking	
7		Commit	

The database design may cause deadlocks. For example, a database might contain two tables that must be kept in synchronization. When Table A is updated, fields in Table B must be set to match the corresponding fields in Table A. When Table B is updated, fields in Table A must also be updated so that they match the corresponding fields in

Table B. Business requirements dictate the need for retaining both tables, and updating both tables. This design causes the two transactions to request resources in the opposite order.

Another frequent cause of deadlock is transactions that run at a higher isolation level (either because the isolation level has been set for the connection or because they use the HOLDLOCK locking hint) are likely to increase the number of deadlocks.

As mentioned previously, long-running transactions can cause contention problems. They can also increase the deadlock frequency. It's always best to keep transactions as short as possible.

Setting Deadlock Priority

As stated previously, SQL Server normally selects the process that causes the deadlock as a victim. You can request that a process be chosen as the victim, however, regardless of who caused the deadlock. You do this with the following command:

```
SET DEADLOCK_PRIORITY {LOW ¦ NORMAL }
```

If you set the priority to LOW, you are requesting that the process be chosen as a victim. Setting it to NORMAL causes SQL Server to use its normal method of choosing a victim. Note that when you set deadlock priority to LOW, SQL Server returns Error 1204, not 1205.

Under the Covers

The information behind all the displays of process and lock information is kept in two virtual tables that reside in the master database: sysprocesses and syslocks. Neither of these tables actually exists; the data that they contain is gathered when the virtual tables are queried. The data comes from SQL Server's internal memory structures.

sysprocesses

The sysprocesses table contains one record for each connection. In addition to the information displayed by sp_who2, it has other process information that can be useful, such as the name of the application running on the connection and the network address from which the connection originated.

syslockinfo

syslockinfo is just information from the lock manager's internal structures presented as a table.

6

Backup and Recovery

Probably the most important task you will ever perform as a SQL Server administrator is the design and implementation of your backup strategy. You must prepare for all kinds of disasters that might never happen. Furthermore, if a disaster does happen, you must be able to recover from it. Your job is definitely in the balance here.

This chapter first discusses the kinds of backups that are available to you, and shows you how to develop your backup strategy. After that, you learn how to carry out the backups and how to recover from various types of crashes. Finally, the chapter finishes by focusing on maintaining a warm backup server.

Developing a Backup Strategy

No matter how many fault-tolerant devices you have, you still need backups. Those of us who lived through the heavy flooding on the East Coast this year know how much damage can be done, despite uninterruptible power supplies and mirrored drives. You must have a backup strategy that protects you from the following:

- Media failure
- System software failure
- Inadvertent or malicious use of DELETE or UPDATE statements, such as the following:

  DELETE prod_table

  DROP DATABASE ProdDB

  FORMAT C:

  UPDATE Employee SET Salary = 50000
- Destructive viruses
- Natural disasters
- Man-made disasters

You must continually expect that the worst possible thing can happen, and you must prepare for it. Hopefully, you will never need your preparation, but if you do, you will be glad that you have done it.

SQL Server backups can be done while users are logged on; it is not necessary to throw users off the system or to shut down the server. However, you cannot do backups while users are running DBCC CHECKALLOC, DBCC SHRINKDATABASE, bcp, SELECT INTO, or while users are restructuring the files and file groups that make up the database.

SQL Server 7.0 enables you to perform several different kinds of backups. You can back up the following:

- The entire database
- A file or a file group
- The transaction log

General Tip

Note that if you have set the database option Truncate Log on Checkpoint to true, you cannot make backups of the transaction log.

When SQL Server does a *full database backup*, it copies all the pages of the database, together with any part of the transaction log needed to make the backup consistent, to a disk or tape file. It's possible to do a *differential database backup*. A differential backup is much faster than a full backup because fewer pages have to be written. SQL Server copies all the pages that have changed since the last full backup to a file. When SQL Server does a *transaction log backup*, the transactions recorded in the transaction log are copied to a file. With a *file or file group* backup, all the pages that comprise the file or file group are copied to a file.

Important!

If you are using SQL Server's Full-Text Indexing facilities, you need to be aware of the fact that the indexes are not stored in the database. A full database backup will not include any full-text indexes you have defined. These files are stored in the operating system and need to be backed up with operating system backup commands.

You can develop a simple backup strategy that uses just one of these methods or you can combine all of them in a complex strategy. The strategy you choose depends on the volatility of your data. You can have different backup strategies for different databases on the same server. In developing your backup strategy, the main question you must ask yourself is, "How much work can I afford to lose" (also called *exposure*)? You need to look at two possible situations:

- The transaction log that was in use at the time of the crash can be backed up.

- It is not possible to back up the transaction log that was in use at the time of the crash.

Either situation can occur. If you can make a backup of the current transaction log, you can recover more data. The following chart shows you the recovery point for four major backup strategies in both situations.

Backup Strategy	Recovery Point If Log Is Not Available	Recovery Point If Log Is Available
Only full database backups at regular intervals	Most recent database backup	Point of failure
Full database backups and differential backups at regular intervals	Most recent differential backup	Point of failure

continues ▶

continued ▶

Backup Strategy	Recovery Point If Log Is Not Available	Recovery Point If Log Is Available
Database at regular intervals and log at regular intervals	Most recent log backup	Point of failure
Full, differential, and log backups at regular intervals	Most recent log backup, more quickly	Point of failure, more quickly

 General Tip

When you use a combination of database, differential, and log backups, your recovery goes much faster, because the differential backup contains the latest image of the data. The transaction log may contain multiple images if the data changed many times.

! **Important!**

Your backup strategy must always include full database backups or a full set of file group backups. If you are not using file group backups, the full database backup is the starting point for any restore. If you use file group backups, you can restore a single file group by starting with its first backup.

Full Database Backups at Regular Intervals

A strategy that involves only full database backups at regular intervals is appropriate in the following situations:

- The amount of data to be lost is small (for example, test databases).
- The cost of managing transaction log backups is greater than the cost of re-creating the data manually.
- Database changes are infrequent. (Database is primarily read-only.)
- Data is easily re-created from batch loads that take place nightly and replace all or most of the contents of the database.
- You require the simplest strategy because you do not have a full-time database administrator.

Figure 6.1 shows an example of a backup strategy that uses only full database backups.

With this strategy, if you lost both the database and the log at 2 p.m. on Wednesday, when you restored the database, you would only have its contents as of 11 p.m. on the preceding Monday. There is nothing necessarily wrong with this; if there were little or no changes during the intervals between backups, there is little to lose with this strategy. It is also very simple to implement.

Figure 6.1   Full database–only backup strategy.

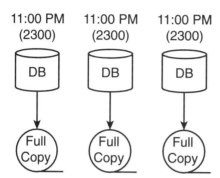

Full Database and Differential Backups

A strategy that combines full and differential backups is appropriate in the following situations:

- The amount of data to be lost is small.
- The resources needed for backup are limited (time or space).

In the preceding example, full backups were done every 48 hours. This means that up to two days of work can be lost. Scheduling a differential backup on Tuesday and Thursday reduces the exposure to 24 hours.

 General Tip

It would be possible to lose even more work if the backup was corrupted or the tape or other medium damaged.

Full Database and Transaction Log Backups

Many organizations find the combination of log and database backups to be the best strategy. This strategy is appropriate in the following situations:

- Any loss of data is unacceptable.
- You need to recover to the point of failure.
- Database changes are frequent.

You can include differential backups in this strategy, saving you some time if you need to recover from a disaster.

Figure 6.2 shows a complex backup strategy that uses a combination of full database backups, differential backups, and transaction log backups.

Figure 6.2   A complex backup strategy.

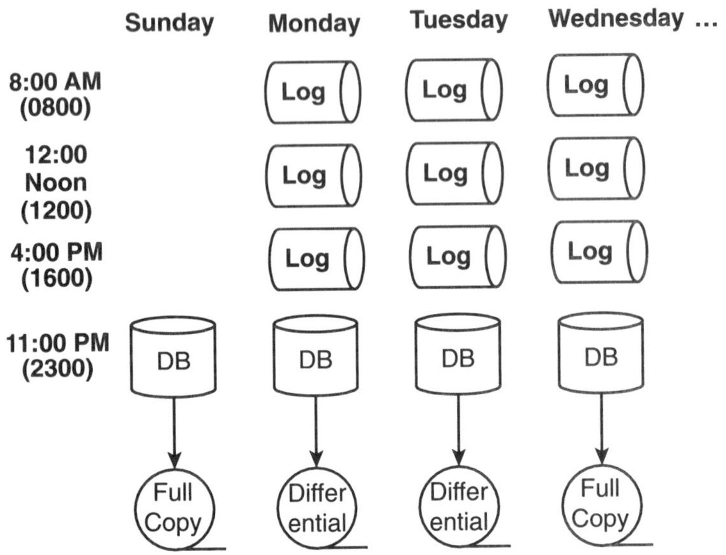

With this strategy, if you lose both the database and the transaction log at 2 p.m. on Wednesday, you can recover everything that happened up to the latest transaction log backup, or up to noon on that same Wednesday. This schedule is appropriate if most or all of the work in the organization takes place between the hours of 8 a.m. and 4 p.m. If the transaction log in use at the time of the crash were available, you would be able to recover up to the time of the crash. You have a maximum exposure of 4 hours between 8 a.m. and 4 p.m., 7 hours between 4 p.m. and 11 p.m., and 9 hours between 11 p.m. and 8 a.m.

To recover from a crash, you would need to restore the full database backup from Sunday, Tuesday's differential (differentials are cumulative), and the log backups made at 8 a.m. and noon on Wednesday.

In looking at your backup strategy, you also want to consider how long you want to keep the backups and where you are going to store them. It is customary to keep at least three generations, commonly called "grandfather, father, son," of backups. Usually the most recent is close at hand and the oldest is stored off-site. I also find it a good practice to back up the log right before I do a full database backup. This reduces the size of the log and gives me extra security. If something goes wrong with the full backup (like the tape breaking), I have the backed up log that together with my "father" backup, has approximately the same (exactly the same if there were no users on the system) information as the "son" backup.

General Tip

You might want to consider using either a hardware or software solution that will create two copies of your most recent backup. Then one can be stored close at hand and the other copy can be stored off-site.

File and File Group Backups

Your backup strategy may include some file or file group backups or consist entirely of files and file group backups. If you have placed highly volatile data on a file group, you may want to back up that file group more frequently than you back up other file groups. If you have a *very large database* (VLDB) where, for example, each file group maps to a big RAID 5 array, you need file group backups because the database backup might just be too big.

Backing Up Databases

You can store backup files on disk or on tape. If you write the backups to disk, you can use a local drive or a remote drive. If you are backing up to a remote drive, you must refer to it by its UNC name; you can't use a redirected drive letter.

General Tip

Remember, SQL Server is performing the backup, and it doesn't know about your mapped drives.

There is one exception to this rule: If you use T-SQL, and use xp-cmdshell to issue the NETUSE command, you can then refer to the mapped drive in your backup command.

It's also possible to back up to a named pipe; this option is primarily for independent software vendors who build backup and recovery tools.

By default, backups are appended to the backup file. They grow indefinitely if you do this. You will probably want to append for a certain time period, and then overwrite. Suppose, for example, that you do a full backup on Sunday, a differential on Monday, and another differential on Tuesday, and then start over with another full backup on Wednesday, and differentials on Thursday and Friday. You might put the Sunday, Monday, and Tuesday backups in one location, and the Wednesday, Thursday, and Friday backups on another. When Sunday comes around again, you can overwrite the backups on your first location.

If you choose to keep your backups on disk, you should locate them on a different physical drive from either your database files or your transaction log files. A tape drive must be local to the SQL Server computer. If you use multiple disk drives or tape arrays, SQL Server can use parallel I/O and make backup and restore operations faster. You can have up to 32 different locations for a single backup. They must all be of the same type; you can't mix tape and disk. If you are backing up to a remote drive or drives, the SQL Server Login account (see Chapter 2, "Installation and Upgrade," for more information) must have explicit write permissions to those drives. If SQL Server is logging in as LocalSystem, you must add the UNC name of the remote drive to the NullSessionShares Registry key as shown here:

```
\\HKEY_LOCAL_MACHINE
     \System
          \CurrentControlSet
               \Services
                    \LanmanServer
                         \Parameters
     Name: NullSessionShares
     Type: REG_MULTI_SZ
     Data: COMCFG
```

 General Tip

SQL Server 7.0 backups are written in Microsoft Tape Format, so you can store them on the same tape as NT backups. This was not possible in earlier versions.

 Important!

Any database options set at the time of the backup are copied and are restored when you restore the database. If you make significant option changes, you probably want to make a full database backup.

 Danger

Many people think that they just need to allow their NT backup software to make backups of the files that comprise the database. This is not a good idea. First of all, if SQL Server is running, the files are in use and most backup programs cannot copy them. Second, even if the backup software can copy open files, you aren't guaranteed consistency if there are active users. It is only safe to back up the files as files when SQL Server is stopped. Even then, I don't recommend using this method. Use SQL Server's native backup tools to back up SQL Server databases.

Several third-party backup products that have hooks to SQL Server are available. Many people find they encounter various problems when using these. I recommend that you use SQL Server's native backup facilities. You can then use your third-party backup tool to copy the backups to other media and to catalog them. The following lists summarize the advantages and disadvantages of third-party backups.

Advantages of third-party backup software include the following:

- It's potentially faster than native backups, depending on the performance of the drivers supplied.
- Integrates database backups with Windows NT backups with one schedule for both. With SQL Server 7.0 native backups, you can use the same tapes as NT backups but you still need to schedule the jobs separately.

- Potentially enables you to back up to a remote tape drive.

- May take advantage of software *redundant array of independent tapes* (RAIT). Third-party vendors typically support RAID 0, 1, 3, 5, and 10. SQL Server's backup facilities support only RAID 0 (striping). To get a higher level, you need to have hardware RAIT.

- May support jukeboxes and stackers.

- May provide better notification and management of tape-swaps.

- May integrate with barcode readers/writers.

- May support software compression. (SQL Server backups don't provide this feature.) Most backup devices offer hardware compression; if yours does not, however, a third-party tool with this capability can enhance backup performance.

- May provide multiplatform support and enable you to have a single backup interface for different operating systems such as UNIX and Windows NT.

Disadvantages of third-party backup software include the following:

- It is something that can go wrong, and it's in an area where you don't want anything to go wrong. Microsoft doesn't test third-party products, so it is up to each vendor to support new or changed SQL Server features for each release or service pack. Most vendors have had problems with full SQL 7.0 support. Make sure you get the latest release/patches for your product.

- In many cases they are slower than SQL Server's native backups.

- A product that performs a function other than backup might need to be able to access the backup files and would expect them to be in SQL Server backup format. The backup software vendor would write the backups in its proprietary format. An example of this is the Platinum Log Analyzer product (not available for SQL Server 7.0), which needs to read native SQL Server backups of the transaction log.

- Some third-party products require exclusive use of the tape drives they control, meaning you can't use it for SQL Server backups even if you need to.

- Often, there is a lag between the time Microsoft implements functionality, and the time the third-party vendors can support it.

General Tip

Note that it is possible to back up a corrupt database. If you do so, you might not be able to restore from the backup. It's a good idea to run DBCC checks (see Chapter 4, "Storage Management," for more information on this) before you do a backup.

Predefining Backup Locations

You can predefine backup locations or you can specify them when you set up the backup. The only difference that I can see between the two methods is that, in Enterprise Manager, you can see the contents of the predefined backup device without going to the restore dialog box, so you save one mouse click.

You can predefine a backup location in Enterprise Manager, Transact-SQL, and DMO.

Predefining a Backup Location with Enterprise Manager

To predefine a backup location with Enterprise Manager, first locate a Backup icon in the MANAGEMENT folder. Right-click it and choose New Backup Device. Give it a logical name, such as MyDB Full Backups, and fill in the full filename, remembering to use a UNC name if the drive is remote. That's all there is to it.

General Tip

In Enterprise Manager, you can't specify either a named pipe or a Zip/JAZ drive as a backup location. You can do this in Transact-SQL.

Predefining a Backup Location with Transact-SQL

To define a backup location with Transact-SQL, use the `sp_addumpdevice` command, as shown here:

```
sp_addumpdevice 'device_type', 'logical_name',
  'physical_name' [, {controller_type | 'device_status'}]
```

`device_type` is *disk* or *tape* or *pipe*. The logical name is what it is referred to in SQL Server; the physical name is the full filename where the backup will be stored. Neither `controller_type` nor `device_status` is required. If you specify `controller_type`, it will be ignored. Valid values are 2 when `device_type` is disk, 5 when `device_type` is tape, and 6 when `device_type` is pipe. `device_status` specifies whether ANSI tape labels are read or ignored. Valid values are SKIP to ignore labels, NOSKIP to read them. If you do not specify this parameter, NOSKIP is assumed. You cannot specify both `controller_type` and `device_status`.

General Tip

The odd name of the `sp_addumpdevice` command comes from the fact that in previous versions of SQL Server, the command used to make a backup called DUMP, and a dump device was the location to which the backup was written.

Predefining a Backup Location with DMO

To predefine a backup location with DMO, you must follow these steps:

1 Create a BackupDevice object.

2 Set its Name and PhysicalLocation properties.

3 Set the SkipTapeLabel property to true if you want to ignore ANSI tape labels; set it to false to read them.

4 Set the Type property to one of the following constants:

Constant	Description
SQLDMODevice_CDROM	Reserved for future use.
SQLDMODevice_DiskDump	Device is a disk file.
SQLDMODevice_PipeDump	Device identifies a named pipe.
SQLDMODevice_TapeDump	Device is a tape.

5 Add the BackupDevice object to the BackupDevices collection of a connected SQL Server.

Performing a Full or Differential Database Backup

You can perform a full or differential backup with Enterprise Manager, Transact-SQL, or DMO.

Performing a Full or Differential Database Backup with Enterprise Manager

There are many ways to get to the Backup dialog box; I find it simplest to highlight the database, right-click, and choose All Tasks, Backup Database. This brings you to the Backup dialog box shown in Figure 6.3.

Figure 6.3   SQL Server Backup dialog box, General tab.

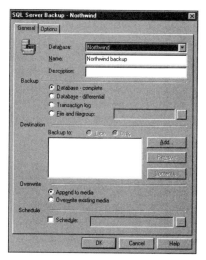

The Description field is optional; it serves as documentation. Choose whether to do a complete (full) backup or a differential backup. (Remember that your cycle must always start with a full backup.) Choose tape or disk. To specify where the backup should go, click the Add button. This brings you to a screen where you can either specify the physical location or select from your predefined backup locations. You can specify multiple locations.

 General Tip

You can use "append to media" even if the file does not exist. (This was not true in previous versions of SQL Server.) If you want to control expiration date and media labeling, however, you should choose Overwrite the first time you back up to the location.

If you check the Schedule box, you will have an opportunity to schedule a backup. The Browse button next to the default schedule takes you to the SQL Agent Scheduling screen (discussed in more detail in Chapter 8, "Jobs and Alerts"). Figure 6.4 shows the Options tab of the Backup dialog box.

Figure 6.4   SQL Server Backup dialog box, Options tab.

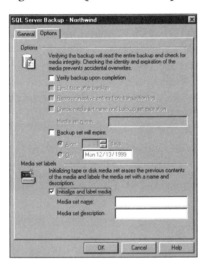

If you check the box next to Verify Backup on Completion, SQL Server checks that the backup is readable. Note that this does not check for corruption in the database; see Chapter 4 for the methods of checking for corruption.

If you choose Overwrite on the General tab, the options look like those shown in Figure 6.4. You can specify an expiration date or the number of days that must elapse before the backup file can be overwritten. You can also specify the Media set name and a description for it. This is used to label the media. Subsequently, when you append backups to this location, you can check to see that the media set name is correct. Both of these options protect you from having a backup file inadvertently overwritten. Note that a tape can still be erased and a file can be deleted.

After you have set up everything, just click the OK button and the backup runs immediately.

Performing Full and Differential Database Backups with Transact-SQL

The command to perform backups in Transact-SQL is a bit daunting, as shown in the following:

```
BACKUP DATABASE database_name
TO <backup_device> [,...n]
[WITH [BLOCKSIZE = blocksize]
[[,] DESCRIPTION = text]
[[,] DIFFERENTIAL]
[[,] EXPIREDATE = date ¦
 RETAINDAYS = days]
[[,] FORMAT ¦ NOFORMAT]
[[,] {INIT ¦ NOINIT}]
[[,] MEDIADESCRIPTION = text]
[[,] MEDIANAME = media_name]
[[,] [NAME = backup_set_name]
[[,] {NOSKIP ¦ SKIP}]
[[,] {NOUNLOAD ¦ UNLOAD}]
[[,] [RESTART]
[[,] STATS [= percentage]]]
```

database_name is self-explanatory; that is, it's the database's name. backup_device can be either a predefined backup location (use the logical name you used when you created it) or a full specification in the following form:

```
{DISK ¦ TAPE ¦ PIPE} = 'physical file name'
```

Here's an example of a simple command that does a full backup of the Northwind database:

```
BACKUP DATABASE Northwind to
DISK = 'F:\My Backups\Nwind.bak'
```

All the other options are part of the WITH clause. Separate them with commas if you specify more than one of them. You have the following options:

- BLOCKSIZE is irrelevant for backups written to disk. If you plan to copy the disk backup file to a CD-ROM and restore from the CD-ROM, you must specify 2048 as the block size. Any block size you specify for tape applies only if you also use the FORMAT option.

- DESCRIPTION is just documentation for the backup.

- DIFFERENTIAL says that a differential backup should be done rather than a full backup. To do a differential backup of Northwind, your command would look like this:

```
BACKUP DATABASE Northwind to
DISK = 'F:\My Backups\Nwind.bak'
WITH DIFFERENTIAL
```

- EXPIREDATE and RETAINDAYS are mutually exclusive; you can only use one of them. Use EXPIREDATE to specify the first date on which the backup file can be overwritten. Use RETAINDAYS to specify the number of days that must elapse before the file can be overwritten. These options protect you from inadvertent overwrites of the file.

- FORMAT and NOFORMAT specify whether the tape should be formatted. Formatting destroys any data on the device (either the disk file or the tape) and should be used with caution. If you are using a new tape, you should use FORMAT to make sure that the tape is in Microsoft Tape Format. When you specify FORMAT, both SKIP and INIT are implied.

- INIT and NOINIT specify whether the backup should overwrite the existing backups or should be appended. Use INIT when you want to start a new set of backups, NOINIT when you want to append a backup to the backups already on the file. NOINIT is the default. INIT will check the expiration dates and will not overwrite files that have not expired.

- MEDIADESCRIPTION is documentation about the media set.

- MEDIANAME is the name of the media set. It is required when NT backups and SQL Server backups will be placed on the same tape. It is also necessary if you want to check that the media name is correct before writing on the file.

- NAME is the name of the backup set.

- NOSKIP and SKIP specify whether the expiration dates and names should be checked. If you specify NOSKIP, the checks will be performed.

- NOUNLOAD and UNLOAD specify whether the tape should be ejected. Use NOUNLOAD to keep the tape in the drive, UNLOAD to eject it.

- RESTART tells SQL Server to restart a backup operation that was interrupted. This option applies only to tape backups and only if there are multiple tape volumes.

- Use STATS if you want a comforting display of the progress of the backup. It causes SQL Server to put out messages every *n* percent of the way through:

```
12 percent backed up.
22 percent backed up.
32 percent backed up.
42 percent backed up.
```

If you don't specify a percentage, it defaults to 10.

 General Tip

If your database is in 6.x compatibility mode (see Chapter 2), you cannot use the keyword BACKUP. You must use the old keyword, DUMP.

- The BACKUP command does not include an option to verify the readability of the backup like Enterprise Manager does. If you want to verify the backup, use the following:

```
RESTORE VERIFYONLY
FROM <backup_device> [,...n]
[WITH [FILE = file_number]
[[,] {NOUNLOAD ¦ UNLOAD}]
[[,] LOADHISTORY]
```

- File_number is a number assigned to each backup on the file. I show you how to find file numbers in the "Restoring Databases with Transact-SQL" section later in this chapter. If you don't specify a file number, it verifies the first file. LOADHISTORY causes historical information about this backup to be placed in the media and history tables in MSDB (see the "Under the Covers" section later in this chapter).

Performing Full and Differential Backups with DMO

 General Tip

There's an excellent example of all the code you need to manage backups with DMO in Books Online.

You must create a Backup object to do backups with DMO. Then, assign the name of the database to the Database property of the object. If you are using predefined backup locations, use the Devices property (it's a multistring property). If you are not using predefined locations, specify the filenames in either the Files or the Tapes property. Set the action property to one of the following values:

Constant	Description
SQLDMOBackup_Database	Back up the database
SQLDMOBackup_Incremental	Back up rows changed after the most recent full database or differential backup

The Backup object has lots of other properties that correspond to the options available in the Transact-SQL BACKUP command. The following table lists each property and the corresponding Transact-SQL option.

Property	Transact-SQL Option
BackupSetDescription	DESCRIPTION
BackupSetName	NAME
BlockSize	BLOCKSIZE
ExpirationDate	EXPIRATIONDATE
FormatMedia	FORMAT | NOFORMAT
Initialize	INIT | NOINIT
MediaDescription	MEDIADESCRIPTION
MediaName	MEDIANAME

continues ▶

continued ▶

Property	Transact-SQL Option
PercentCompleteNotification	STATS
Restart	RESTART
RetainDays	RETAINDAYS
SkipTapeHeader	SKIP | NOSKIP
UnloadTapeAfter	NOUNLOAD | UNLOAD

When the object is complete, use its SQLBackup method to perform the backup. You can also generate the SQL statement with its GenerateSQL method.

The object has three events that enable you to monitor the progress of the backup:

- The PercentComplete event fires for every 10% of the backup that is complete. If you specify a different interval in the PercentCompleteNotification property, this event fires at that interval rather than at 10%.

- The Complete event happens when the backup is complete.

- The NextMedia event fires if the disk space or tape being used for the backup is full.

Performing Transaction Log Backups

Before I cover the mechanics of backing up a transaction log, I want to discuss some important concepts. Remember that every database has its own transaction log in which all additions, deletions, and changes are recorded. The log is used when applications issue a rollback command, and when the server is restarted. You can also use transaction log backups as part of your backup strategy.

The transaction log is comprised of a series of virtual log files. You do not need to worry about these log files; they are created for you. They may vary in size at different times. One thing you do want to be careful about is how you define the size and growth of the transaction log. (See Chapter 4 for more information on how to do this.) If you have a small log, and a small growth increment, and the file has grown many times, there will be a lot of virtual log files, which will make recovery slower than if you have fewer, larger files.

Each record in the transaction log is identified with a number called the *Log Sequence Number* (LSN).

The transaction log is a "wraparound" file. Records are first written at the beginning of the file. When the end of the file is reached, it wraps back and writes over entries at the beginning that are no longer needed.

SQL Server's transaction log is a *write-ahead* log. As data is read, it is kept in memory. When data is modified, information about the modifications is written to the log but not necessarily to the database itself. This guarantees the highest level of recovery and is the technique used by most relational database management systems.

SQL Server handles all the management of the transaction logs, including writing appropriate records to it, automatically. An important part of this process is the *checkpoint*. The checkpoint thread is responsible for the following:

- Writing changed data pages to the database
- Recording a list of active transactions in the log
- Recording a list of dirty (changed) pages in the log
- Marks where recovery should begin when the server is restarted

The marker is called the Minimum Recovery Log Sequence Number (LSN) and is the lowest of the following values:

- The LSN of the checkpoint itself
- The LSN of the oldest dirty data page
- The LSN of the oldest uncommitted transaction
- The LSN of the oldest unreplicated transaction

Figure 6.5 illustrates a theoretical transaction log after the SQL Server has been running for a while. In this example, there is still unused space at the end of the log. Eventually, this space will be used and log records will spill over into Virtual Log 1.

Figure 6.5   Transaction log architecture.

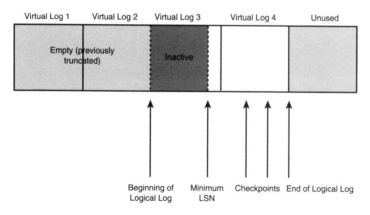

Notice that a portion of the log shown in Figure 6.5 is marked "Inactive," and a portion is marked "Empty (previously truncated)." The inactive portion contains transactions that have already been recorded in the database or that have been rolled back. This inactive portion is not needed for recovery (but may be needed for a restore), so the default behavior of SQL Server is to remove, or *truncate*, this inactive portion when the log is backed up. There is a database option that you can set, Trunc Log on Checkpoint, which modifies this behavior. If you set this option, the inactive portion will be truncated, for committed transactions, each time a checkpoint is taken. When you set this option, you cannot make backups of the transaction log. If you have determined that a backup strategy using only full database backups or a combination of full and differential backups is appropriate, you may want to set this option to true so that the log won't grow forever. Otherwise (and this is true for most high-volume update situations), you should set this option to false. (See Chapter 4 for details on how to set database options.)

General Tip

Note that if you set the Trunc Log on Checkpoint option to true, you cannot do file or file group backups.

Certain activities can prevent you from backing up the transaction log. You cannot back up the log if you have performed any non-logged operations, such as: fast bulk copy, SELECT INTO (outside of tempdb), WRITETEXT, or UPDATETEXT. These operations are not recorded in the log, so there is information in the database that is not in the log, and therefore, the sequence is interrupted. If you need to perform non-logged operations, back up the database, do the operation, and then back up the database again. You can then resume your schedule of log backups. You must also do a full backup after adding a file or a file group to the database. You cannot do a log backup until you have done so.

Although the normal behavior is to remove the inactive portion of the log after the log has been backed up, there are two other possibilities. These are typically used in emergency situations. The first option is to back up the log without removing the inactive portion. You normally do this after a database crash so that you have all the information (which should be in the crashed database, but might not be there) just in case you need it. The second option is to just remove the inactive portion without making a backup. Use this option when the transaction log is full and you need to free space. When you truncate the log in this fashion, your transaction log backups are no longer usable; you should make a full database backup as soon as possible.

Performing a Transaction Log Backup with Enterprise Manager

Backing up the transaction log with Enterprise Manager is done with the same dialog box as the one you use for backing up a database. Just click the radio button next to transaction log rather than the one for database or differential.

When you are doing a transaction log backup, the Options tab shows the Remove Inactive Entries from the Transaction Log option. It is checked by default; you can uncheck it if you do not want the inactive entries removed.

You cannot use this dialog box to remove inactive entries without backing up the log. Instead, you must right-click the database, and choose All Tasks, Truncate Log.

Performing a Transaction Log Backup with Transact-SQL

To back up the transaction log with Transact-SQL, use the same command that you use to do a full or differential backup. All the options available for a database backup are also available for a log backup. You do have some additional options, however, as follows:

```
BACKUP LOG database_name
{ [WITH {NO_LOG ¦ TRUNCATE_ONLY} ¦
TO <backup_device, [, … n]
WITH NO_TRUNCATE
```

Notice that there are two *different* WITH clauses. Use the first one when you want to remove the inactive portion of the log without making any backup of it. You can use either the NO_LOG, or TRUNCATE_ONLY options (they are synonyms) when you just need to remove the inactive portion. The following sample illustrates truncating the log for Northwind without making a backup:

```
BACKUP LOG Northwind WITH NO_LOG
```

To back up a log with the default behavior of removing the inactive portion, don't use any of these options. (You can use others, such as name, media set, expiration, and so on.) The command would look like this:

```
BACKUP LOG Northwind TO DISK =
'f:\My Backups\NWINDLOG.bak'
```

If you want to back up the log without removing the inactive portion, use the NO_TRUNCATE option. The command looks like this:

```
BACKUP LOG Northwind to DISK =
'f:\My Backups\NWINDLOG.BAK'
WITH NO_TRUNCATE
```

Performing a Transaction Log Backup with DMO

The process of performing a transaction log backup with DMO is essentially the same as that for a full or differential backup. The Action property of the Backup object should be set to the following:

Constant	Meaning
SQLDMOBackup_Log	Back up only the database transaction log

You also need to set the `TruncateLog` property to one of the following values:

Constant	Description
SQLDMOBackup_Log_Truncate	Default. Transaction log is backed up. Records referencing committed transactions are removed.
SQLDMOBackup_Log_NoTruncate	Transaction log is backed up. Records referencing committed transactions are not removed, providing a point-in-time image of the log.
SQLDMOBackup_Log_NoLog	Records referencing committed transactions are removed. Transaction log is not backed up.
SQLDMOBackup_Log_TruncateOnly	Same as SQLDMOBackup_Log_NoLog.
SQLDMOBackup_Log_NoOption	Same as SQLDMOBackup_Log_Truncate.

Performing File and File Group Backups

It is possible to back up a specific file or file group. You need to be somewhat careful with your design if you plan to do this. You need to make sure all related data is in the backup. If you have a parent-child relationship between two tables, and the parent is on File Group 1 and the child is on File Group 2, for example, you could end up with things out of sync if you only back up File Group 2. If you restore only File Group 2, you might have children whose parents had been deleted from File Group 1.

 General Tip

All the indexes of a table must be backed up with the table, whether or not they are on the same file group of a table. You need to keep this in mind when you design the placement of objects.

The process for performing file and file group backups is the same as that for full and differential database backups.

Backing Up System Databases

The basic tools for backing up system databases, such as master and msdb, are identical to those used for backing up user databases. However, you need to know some things about these databases.

First, you can only do full backups of the master database. Transaction log and differential backups are not permitted. You should back up master on a regular schedule even if there have been no changes to it. SQL Server cannot function without the master database. You may want to do extra backups of master for the following scenarios:

- When you create or delete databases
- When you add logins or make other login-related security changes
- When you change server or database configuration options

Because master isn't usually very big, backing it up can be done very quickly. It's far better to back up master once too often than one too few times!

There is generally no need to back up the model database unless you modify it by changing default database options or add your own objects to it. If you are forced to re-create master, model is automatically rebuilt.

By default, Trunc Log on Checkpoint is true for msdb, so you can only do full and differential backups. You can change this if you want to, but because msdb is not a transactional database there is really no need to. When you schedule jobs, save DTS packages, or configure replication information is saved in msdb, therefore, you may want to make a backup after completing any of these operations. The msdb database is also updated when you run backups and when your scheduled jobs run. If you re-create master, msdb is re-created as well (exactly as it was when you first installed SQL Server), so it's usually good practice to back up msdb and master at the same time.

Recovering from Disasters

When something goes wrong, the first thing you need to do is figure out what the problem is; without that information, you can't determine where to start your recovery efforts. Some failures are obvious: you will generally know whether there has been a hard drive crash or other event such as a fire or flood. Other errors are subtler. You might start Enterprise Manager only to find that a database has been marked suspect or you might run a DBCC and find that a database contains corruption. You might just find that SQL Server refuses to start. The first place you need to look is the SQL Server error log.

Working with the SQL Server Error Log

By default SQL Server keeps its error log in \MSSQL7\LOG in a file named ERRORLOG. There is no extension (file type) on the current error log. You can change this location by modifying the SQL Server startup parameters. A new error log is created each time SQL Server starts. SQL Server maintains six prior versions of the error log and names them ERRORLOG.1, ERRORLOG.2, ERRORLOG.3, ERROR-LOG.4, ERRORLOG.5 and ERRORLOG.6. ERRORLOG.1 is just

prior to the current error log; ERRORLOG.6 is the oldest. If a server
crashes, the reason for the crash may be in ERRORLOG.1. If you have
a suspect database or the server won't start, the cause of the problem
might be in the current error log.

 General Tip

In SQL Server 7.0, it's possible to change the default number of error logs. To do this,
you must locate the following registry entry:

    HKey_Local_Machine\SOFTWARE\Microsoft\MSSQLServer\MSSQLServer

Highlight this key, and choose New DWORD from the Edit menu. Name the new value
NumErrorLogs. Then, choose Modify and specify the number of error logs you want
to retain.

If the server is running, you can view all error logs in Enterprise
Manager, or you can use the ReadErrorLog method of a connected SQL
Server object in a DMO application. There's no way to get to the error
log with Transact-SQL.

If the server isn't running (or even if it is), there are other ways to find
SQL Server error messages. First, most critical messages are also available
in the Windows NT application event log, and you can see them
through NT's Event Viewer. Second, the error logs are just text files
and you can read them easily with Notepad.

If the flight recorder was turned on before the crash (see Chapter 3,
"Server and Client Configuration and Troubleshooting"), there may
be useful information in that report as well.

Rebuilding the Master Database

If the master database is physically damaged, you must rebuild it before
you can do anything else. (If master is corrupt or suspect, you do not
need to rebuild it; you can restore it by performing the following
instructions.) A utility that ships with SQL Server, REBUILDM.EXE,
will do this. It is located in \MSSQL7\BINN. You need access to the
Install CD or its contents (it's fine if it has been copied to a drive somewhere) to run this utility. The utility requires the system administrator
password. Make sure you use the same character set, sort order, and
Unicode collation that you used when you installed SQL Server. The
process takes 5–10 minutes. After it has been done, the master database,
model, and msdb are in exactly the same state they were when you finished installing SQL Server originally.

 General Tip

Run sp_helpsort or sqldiag (see Chapter 3) after you install SQL Server and save
its output. That way you won't have to depend on your memory for character set, sort
order, and Unicode collation.

After master is rebuilt, you restore your backup with the procedures outlined in this section for other databases. When you are restoring master, however, the *SQL Server* must be started in single-user mode. To start the server in single-user mode, use the -m switch. (See Chapter 3 for details on SQL Server startup switches.) After you restore master, restore msdb and any backup you may have made of model. Then proceed to restore each of the application databases following the procedures outlined here.

Restoring Databases

When you understand what has happened, you can begin to plan your recovery. (You must get SQL Server running before you can begin recovering databases.) First, determine what is damaged.

Important!

There cannot be any users in the database while it is being restored. Also, if you are restoring a database to a different server, the character set, sort order, and Unicode collation must be the same as it was on the server where the backup was made.

If only the transaction log is damaged, and there was no activity at the time of the crash, SQL Server opens the database and creates a new transaction log. This log is only 1MB and existing log backups are invalid, so you should expand it to the appropriate size and make a full backup right away. If there were active transactions at the time of the crash, this procedure won't work, and you should follow the database crash procedure.

If the database is damaged, the first thing you want to do is to back up the transaction log *without* removing inactive transactions:

```
BACKUP LOG databasename to DISK = 'filename' WITH NO_TRUNCATE
```

This works only if you do not have Trunc Log on Checkpoint set to true.

Warning

Because of a bug in SQL Server 7.0, you cannot back up the latest log if the primary database file is damaged. See Chapter 4 for instructions on creating a database that increases the probability that you can back up the log when the primary database file is damaged. This bug will be fixed in the next version of SQL Server, currently called SQL Server 2000, but not in any service packs.

After the transaction log backup, you must restore your most recent full database backup.

General Tip

In previous versions of SQL Server, it was necessary to re-create the database before you could restore into it. That's not necessary in SQL Server 7.0; if the database doesn't exist, RESTORE will just create it for you.

What happens after the restore of the full database backup depends on your backup strategy. The following table shows you the steps you need to perform after restoring the full database backup. The steps differ depending on whether the backup of the log succeeded or failed.

Strategy	BACKUP LOG WITH NO_TRUNCATE succeeded	BACKUP LOG WITH NO _TRUNCATE failed
Full database backups	Restore the log backup backup you just made.	None. You lose all changes since the last full database backup.
Full and differential database backups	Restore the latest differential backup. Restore the log backup you just made.	Restore the latest differential. You lose all changes since the last differential.
Full database and transaction log backups	Restore each transaction log backup in sequence, ending with the one you just made.	Restore each of the transaction log backups that you have in sequence. You lose all changes since the last log backup.
Full, differential, and log backups	Restore the latest differential backup. Restore all the log backups since the differential in sequence, ending with the one you just made.	Restore the lastest differential backup. Restore all the transaction logs that you have in sequence. You lose all changes since the last log backup.

In many cases, you will want to restore the entire transaction log. However, it is possible to stop before you reach the end of the log. You need to understand that you are likely to lose something when you do this. Figure 6.6, for example, shows a scenario in which an application that was creating incorrect data in the database began running at noon.

Figure 6.6   Effects of recovering up to a specific point in time.

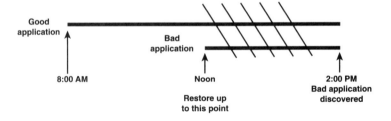

You can stop the bad application, take a transaction log backup at that point (2 p.m.), and then follow the RESTORE procedure. When you apply the 2 p.m. backup of the transaction log, you can tell it to restore only those transactions that completed before noon. This would have the effect of undoing the actions performed by the badly behaved application. However, actions performed by other applications are undone as well.

General Tip

With SQL Server, you cannot browse the transaction log and replay selected transactions. At least one third-party tool provides this capability: the Log Analyzer, originally from Platinum and now available from Computer Associates. It's quite expensive, unfortunately, and does not currently support SQL Server 7.0.

Restoring Databases with Enterprise Manager

If the database is visible in the DATABASES folder, highlight it, right-click, and choose All Tasks, Restore Database. If the database is not visible, highlight the DATABASES folder and choose the same option. The Restore dialog box shown in Figure 6.7 displays.

Figure 6.7   Restore dialog box, General tab.

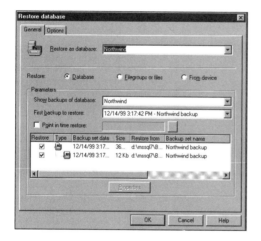

Make sure that the database you want to restore is selected in the Restore as Database drop-down list. All known backups show up in the grid at the bottom of the screen. Notice that both the full database backup and the log backup are shown, and both are checked. SQL Server knows that they should both be applied in order.

If you want to restore to a specific point in time, specify the time in the box above the list of backups.

If you do not want to restore from the backups shown (for example, you are using RESTORE to create a copy of a database), click the From Device button. This screen shown in Figure 6.8 displays.

Figure 6.8   Selecting a different backup.

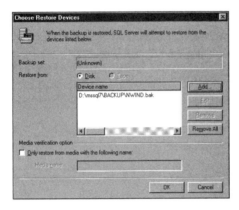

If you click the Add button, you can browse for the backup. Note that if the backup is not on a local drive, you cannot browse to it. Instead, you must type the full name, including the UNC name for the server.

The Options tab shown in Figure 6.9 enables you to place the database files in a new location, as well as to overwrite an existing database.

Figure 6.9   Restore dialog box, Options tab.

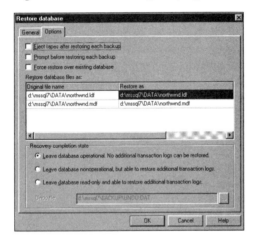

You can change the physical locations of the files on the Restore dialog box, Options screen. You might want to do this if you are using RESTORE to create a copy of a database. If you are restoring the backup to a database with a different name, Enterprise Manager proposes new physical names for the files. You can change these if you want to. It is not possible to change the logical names assigned to each file.

Choose Force Restore over Existing Database when you want to restore a backup of a database with a different name over another database. If you choose Prompt Before Restoring Each Backup, you have the option of not restoring all the backups simultaneously.

Recovery Completion State Option

In most cases, you will just want to restore all the backups, and that's the default setting for this option. On some occasions, however, you may want to restore each backup separately and see what state the database is in. You also need to use this option when you are maintaining a warm standby server (see "Warm Standby Server" later in this chapter). There are three recovery completion state options:

- Leave database operational. No additional transaction logs can be restored (default).
- Leave database non-operational but able to restore additional transaction logs.
- Leave database read-only but able to restore additional transaction logs.

If you choose Leave Database Operational, the backups that were checked on the preceding screen are all restored.

If you choose Leave Database Non-Operational, the only thing that you can do with the database is restore additional transaction logs. You would be most likely to use this option with a standby server. When you select this option and do not restore all the transaction logs, the database is grayed and marked *Loading* in the console tree display.

If you choose Leave Database Read-Only, the database is marked as *dbo use only* in the console tree display. The database owner can read data and determine what state the data is in before making the decision to restore additional logs.

Restoring Database Backups with Transact-SQL

The Transact-SQL restore commands are almost as daunting as the backup commands. The commands for restoring a database and for restoring a transaction log are very similar, as shown in the following:

```
RESTORE DATABASE command
RESTORE DATABASE database_name
[FROM <backup_device> [,...n]]
[WITH [DBO_ONLY]
[[,] FILE = file_number]
[[,] MEDIANAME = media_name]
[[,] MOVE 'logical_file_name' TO
'operating_system_file_name'] [,...n]
[[,] {NORECOVERY ¦ RECOVERY ¦
STANDBY = undo_file_name}]
[[,] {NOUNLOAD ¦ UNLOAD}]
[[,] REPLACE]
[[,] RESTART]
[[,] STATS [= percentage]]]
```

RESTORE LOG *command*

```
RESTORE LOG database_name
[FROM <backup_device> [,...n]]
[WITH
[DBO_ONLY]
[[,] FILE = file_number]
[[,] MEDIANAME = media_name]
[[,] {NORECOVERY ¦ RECOVERY ¦
 STANDBY = undo_file_name}]
[[,] {NOUNLOAD ¦ UNLOAD}]
[[,] RESTART]
[[,] STATS [= percentage]]
[[,] STOPAT = date_time]]
```

If you have only a database backup to restore, the command will look like the following:

```
RESTORE DATABASE Northwind FROM
       DISK = 'D:\Mssql7\Backup\NWIND.bak'
```

If you have a full backup and a differential backup, or a full backup and a series of transaction logs to restore, you must use the WITH NORECOVERY option on all restores but the last. Assume, for example, that you have the following backups to restore:

Backup type	Filename
Full	\MyBackups\NwindFull.bak
Differential	\MyBackups\NwindDiff.bak
Log	\MyBackups\NwindLogNoon.bak
Log	\MyBackups\NwindLog1400.bak

The series of RESTORE commands required should look like this:

```
RESTORE DATABASE Northwind FROM
       DISK = 'c:\MyBackups\NwindFull.bak'
       WITH NORECOVERY
RESTORE DATABASE Northwind FROM
       DISK = 'c:\MyBackups\NwindDiff.bak'
       WITH NORECOVERY
RESTORE LOG Northwind FROM
       DISK = 'c:\MyBackups.NwindLogNoon.bak'
       WITH NORECOVERY
RESTORE LOG Northwind FROM
       DISK = 'c:\MyBackups.NwindLog1400.bak'
```

The WITH options listed in this section enable you to modify the default restore behavior.

DBO_ONLY leaves the database with the DBO Use Only database option set after the restore. You use this option when you want the opportunity to check out the state of the database before allowing users access to it.

FILE = number specifies which file on the backup device should be restored. To find the numbers assigned to the files, use RESTORE HEADERONLY command. In the voluminous output, you will find a column named position, which is the number of the file. If all the backups in the preceding example were on a single device, NWINDBackups, the commands would look like this:

```
RESTORE DATABASE Northwind FROM
        DISK = 'c:\MyBackups\NwindBackups.bak'
        WITH NORECOVERY, FILE = 1
RESTORE DATABASE Northwind FROM
        DISK = 'c:\MyBackups\NwindBackups.bak'
        WITH NORECOVERY, FILE = 2
RESTORE LOG Northwind FROM
        DISK = 'c:\MyBackups.NwindBackups.bak'
        WITH NORECOVERY, FILE = 3
RESTORE LOG Northwind FROM
        DISK = 'c:\MyBackups.NwindBackups.bak'
        WITH FILE = 4
```

If you specify MEDIANAME and provide a media name, the restore operation checks to make sure that the media name you provide matches the one on the backup set. If it does not match, the restore terminates. If you don't provide a media name, no check is performed. It's a good idea to specify a media name when you do the backup, and to check the media name when you restore. That way, you can be certain you are restoring the correct backup.

MOVE enables you to restore the database to different physical files from those that it originally used. You must specify the same number of files as there were when the database was created. Use this if you are moving a database to a different server with BACKUP and RESTORE or if you are creating a copy of the database for testing.

NORECOVERY | RECOVERY | STANDBY = undofile changes the way the restore process works. The default is RECOVERY. When RECOVERY is specified, the restore rolls back any uncommitted transactions. This is the behavior you want when you are restoring all the files in the backup simultaneously, but not the behavior you want when you want to restore individual log backups and then look around or when you are maintaining a standby server. Figure 6.10 illustrates a sample set of transactions and log backups.

Figure 6.10   Transactions spanning log backups.

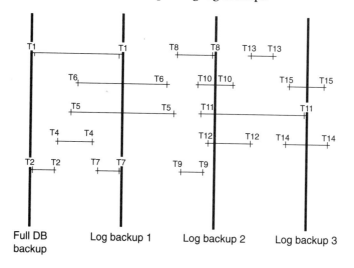

As you can see, two transactions were not committed at the time of log backup 1 (T5 and T6), three transactions were not committed at the time of log backup 2 (T10, T11, and T12), and two transactions were not committed at the end of log backup 3. If you want to restore through log backup 3, only T14 and T15 (which will never complete because the crash happened in the middle of them) should be rolled back. You must use the NORECOVERY option when restoring the full database backup, and log backups 1 and 2. STANDBY is similar to NORECOVERY, but it stores uncommitted transactions in the UNDO file. If another log is restored, it reapplies the uncommitted transactions from the STANDBY file before restoring the log. The STANDBY option is primarily for use with a standby server (as discussed later), where you don't know when the last log backup is coming.

NOUNLOAD | UNLOAD specifies whether a backup tape should be ejected at the end of the restore.

REPLACE specifies that if there is already a database with the name specified in the RESTORE command and either the database name in the backup is not the same as the name in the backup set, or the files differ, a new database will be created and the old database deleted. You can restore a backup of the Northwind database to Northwind, for example, without specifying REPLACE. If you have a database named TestNorthwind on the server, however, and you want to restore a backup of Northwind to TestNorthwind, you must specify REPLACE.

RESTART is used to restart an interrupted RESTORE operation and is only used with multivolume tape backups.

STATS performs the same function as it does in the BACKUP command.

STOPAT applies to restores of the transaction log only. Use it to specify the point in time to which you want to roll the transaction log forward.

 General Tip

If you receive an Error 4306 when trying to restore a transaction log, you did not specify NORECOVERY or STANDBY on the preceding RESTORE operation. You should restart the operation. Use the NORECOVERY or STANDBY option on all but the final step.

If you restored a transaction log with the NORECOVERY or STANDBY options, and now discover that it was actually the last log to be restored, execute the RESTORE DATABASE WITH RECOVERY command so that the database will be available.

Restoring a Database with DMO

 General Tip

Books OnLine has an excellent example of code for restoring databases.

To restore a database using DMO, you must first create a Restore object. Set the Database property to the database name, and then set the Devices property if you are using predefined backup locations or set the Files or Tapes property to the list of files that contains the backup. Set the Action property to one of the following values:

Constant	Description
SQLDMORestore_Database	Restore the database
SQLDMORestore_Log	Restore records from the transaction log

A variety of other properties correspond to the Transact-SQL options previously outlined. The following table lists the Restore object properties and their corresponding Transact-SQL options.

Property	Transact-SQL Option
BackupSetName	None
FileNumber	FILENUMBER
LastRestore	NORECOVERY | RECOVERY
MediaName	MEDIANAME
PercentCompletionNotification	STATS
RelocateFiles	MOVE
ReplaceDatabase	REPLACE
Restart	RESTART
StandbyFiles	STANDBY = undofile
ToPointInTime	STOPAT
UnloadTapeAfter	NOUNLOAD | UNLOAD

The Restore object has several methods. Use the SQLRestore method to restore the backup according to the property settings in the Restore object. Use SQLVerify to verify a backup. Use GenerateSQL to create a script for the restore. Use ReadBackupHeader for a report similar to that produced by the RESTORE HEADERONLY command.

Like the Backup object, the Restore object has Complete, PercentComplete and NextMedia events that you can use in your applications.

Restoring Files and File Groups

You can restore a specific file or file group from either a file or file group backup or from a full database backup. The same cautions apply to restoring part of the database as apply to backing up only a part of it.

When you are restoring files or file groups, you begin with the file group or file backup rather than with the full database backup, and there are no transaction logs to restore. Use the same techniques to restore a file or file group as you use to restore a database or transaction log.

Moving Databases to Different Servers

Sometimes you want to have the same database on more than one server. Perhaps you want to take a copy of a production server to create a test database, or move a database to a client site. In addition, you may need to maintain a warm standby server. You can do this in several ways:

- Using BACKUP and RESTORE
- Using *Data Transformation Services* (DTS)
- Using sp_detach_db and sp_attach_db

Maintaining a warm backup server is a more complicated than just using BACKUP and RESTORE to move a database.

You can use BACKUP and RESTORE or DETACH/ATTACH as long as the SQL Servers have the same character set, sort order, and Unicode attributes. If any of these attributes differ, DTS is the only choice, other than moving data as text and objects as scripts. BACKUP and RESTORE are most appropriate for maintaining standby servers. DETACH/ATTACH are the most useful for servers that are not connected; they are much faster even for connected servers than DTS is.

 General Tip

SQL Server 7.0 backups can be restored to machines with different processors. You can back up a database on an Alpha and restore it to an Intel machine. This wasn't possible in previous versions of SQL Server.

If you move a database with either BACKUP and RESTORE or ATTACH and DETACH, there is a risk of creating "orphaned users." This comes about from the way SQL Server maps database users to SQL Server logins. When a SQL Server login is given access to a database, the login ID (not the login name) is used to map logins into database users. When you move a database from one server to another with either BACKUP and RESTORE or DETACH and ATTACH, it is possible that the internal identifiers map to different logins on the target than they did on the source or do not match any login on the target server. The latter users are "orphaned." A system procedure identifies these orphans and enables you to fix them. The procedure is called sp_change_users_login; although, in fact, it has nothing to do with changing logins at all! You can use this procedure in several ways. Execute the following command:

```
sp_change_users_login 'report'
```

In executing this command, you get a list of all the database users not mapped into *any* login. These are the orphans. Note that it does not list the users who are matched to the wrong login. You need to create logins for the orphaned users. You can do this automatically by issuing the following command:

```
sp_change_users_login 'Auto_Fix', '%'
```

This command matches the specified database user with the closest SQL Server login. There is a risk of a mismatch resulting in a user receiving incorrect permissions, so I recommend not using sp_change_users_login this way.

A third option enables you to give a database username and a login name. The preceding login ID is replaced with the one that corresponds to the new login name, as shown here:

```
sp_change_users_login 'Update_One', username, loginname
```

Username can be any pattern that works with the LIKE operator.

! **Important!**

The sp_change_users_login procedure deals only with SQL Server Authentication, not Windows NT Authentication, logins.

" IMO

I don't think sp_change_users_login is very useful, except where it helps you identify orphaned users. It is far better to manage the users with scripts. If you detach a database from one server and attach it to another where there are the same login names, for example, you would drop all the database users with sp_dropuser or DMO after you attach the database to the target. Then, you would use sp_adduser or DMO to add the users back to the database. When you use scripts, you are ensured the correct login mappings. You have to re-establish object permissions and add the users to roles, as well, when you do this. You need to do the same thing if you are using BACKUP and RESTORE to move a database from one server to another.

It's also possible to use bcp to copy the sysxlogins table on the source server to a file and load it to the sysxlogins table on the target. If you do this, make sure that you don't include the built-in logins such as system administrator in the file. You will also need to use a format file on the source and target servers so that you can exclude the three computed columns (isrpcinmap, ishqoutmap, and selfoutmap). Note that the sysxlogins table is undocumented; the only way to find out what columns it contains is to use sp_help.

Moving a Database with *BACKUP* and *RESTORE*

This simple process requires you to create a backup of a database on the source server and restore it to the target server. This can be done easily with Enterprise Manager, Transact-SQL, or DMO using the techniques previously described. It's not necessary to create the database on the target server; just restore it, modifying physical filenames appropriately.

Moving a Database with Data Transformation Services

Using DTS to move a database is a slow method, but is the only tool you have (other than a "grow your own") if character sets and so on differ between the two servers.

With DTS you can easily move between servers that are connected. You can move all objects and all data, or just objects or just data. It's simple to do this with the Import or Export Wizards. You specify the source server and database. You also specify the target server and target database. If the target database does not exist, you have the opportunity to create it. After you specify the source and target, you see a screen that looks like the one shown in Figure 6.11.

Figure 6.11   Requesting database/object transfer.

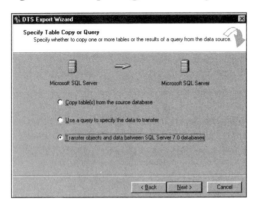

You want to choose the third option as shown in Figure 6.11. After you have done this, the screen shown in Figure 6.12 displays.

Figure 6.12   Choosing what to transfer.

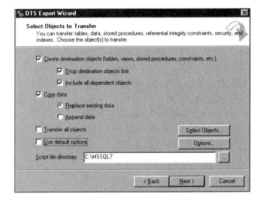

The wording on the screen shown in Figure 6.12 is unclear. The first set of choices gives you the chance to create all the tables, views, and so on at the destination. If you check Drop Destination Objects First, any objects with the same name at the destination are destroyed and replaced with the ones being transferred. The Include All Dependent Objects option needs an explanation. There are dependencies between objects. For example, a view can be created over one or more tables. The view is said to be dependent on the table(s). If you transfer one of the underlying tables, and you have this option checked, the view is also transferred.

You get to choose whether to copy data at all (you may just want to transfer the schema, for example, when moving from test to production) and if so, whether to replace existing data or to append to the data already there.

When you see the Select Objects to Transfer screen, the last two options on the screen are also checked by default. When you uncheck them, the two buttons at the right brighten. The first option enables you to selectively transfer objects. You may have some tables that you used in development, for example, but don't want to move to the new server. If so, you can click the Select Objects button and transfer only those objects that you want to move. The Options button enables you to specify the options used for the transfer. In many cases, you will want to modify these. When you click the Options button, the screen shown in Figure 6.13 displays.

Figure 6.13   Advanced Transfer Options.

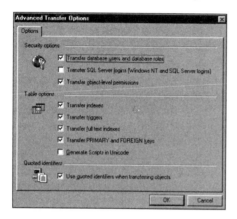

This screen contains some important things to notice. The options shown are the defaults. First of all, it offers to transfer database users and roles (see Chapter 8 for details on users and roles). If you accept the option, the transfer scripts these for you. If you don't have identical SQL Server logins on the target server, however, the users and roles cannot be added to the database. The next choice might seem the obvious solution to the problem. But if you choose the option to transfer logins, they are transferred with null passwords! I don't recommend using either of these options. You should manage logins and database users and roles with scripts, and run those scripts on the target server before doing the transfer. Unfortunately, Enterprise Manager, which supports scripting of many elements of a SQL Server installation, does not provide scripting options for any of these. There are methods for scripting logins, users, and roles in DMO, and Chapter 8 provides a sample of how to script each of them with Transact-SQL.

Unfortunately, if you don't move logins, users, and roles, you cannot leave the third box checked, either, because you have to have users to grant object permissions. Uncheck all three of the security options.

You probably won't want to change the Table options; you will generally want to move indexes, triggers, and constraints. In most cases, you will want to uncheck Use Quoted Identifiers.

Moving a Database with *ATTACH/DETACH*

SQL Server 7.0 includes a very useful feature: the capability to detach a database from the server. After this has been done, the database no longer exists from SQL Server's point of view. The files, however, do exist and can be moved around or even emailed to someone! Or you can just copy the files to a different server and attach them there. You can do this with Transact-SQL or DMO; it's not available in Enterprise Manager.

When you move a database with ATTACH/DETACH, it is possible that the mappings between logins and database users will get messed up; see the discussion at the beginning of the chapter that explains how to fix this problem. You cannot detach a database when users are using it.

Detaching and Attaching Databases with Transact-SQL

To detach a database with Transact-SQL, use the following command:

```
sp_detach_db databasename [, skipchecks]
```

Valid values for the optional argument, skipchecks, are true and false. This argument determines whether optimizer statistics are updated for every index in the database. If you leave the argument off or specify true, the statistics aren't updated. If you specify false, the statistics are updated. If you create a database for read-only media, you should specify false, and get updated statistics. Otherwise, leave the statistics alone.

"   IMO

I think setting the values for skipchecks is very confusing; it's kind of a "double negative." Why should I specify false when I want it to do something? Be sure to remember that the default is to skip updating; then it makes more sense.

Example

Detach a database without updating optimizer statistics, as follows:

```
sp_detach_db MyDB
```

Detach a database and update the optimizer statistics, as follows:

```
sp_detach_db MyDB, FALSE
```

When you copy the files or otherwise get them to the target server, you need to attach them to that server. The syntax for the command to do this follows:

```
sp_attach_db databasename, physicalfile1 [, … physicalfile16]
```

This command creates the database and the file mappings. You must specify at least the primary data file. If any of the other files are in different physical locations than their original location, you must specify the locations for these as well. If the database is comprised of more than 16 files, you must create the database with the FOR ATTACH option instead of using the sp_attach_db command. You should only use this command for databases that were detached with the sp_detach_db command.

If you detach a database that was involved with replication on the source server, you should run the stored procedure, sp_removedbreplication, after you attach the database to the target.

You can use a special version of the sp_attach_db command when the database consists of only one data file. It creates a new transaction log for you and runs the sp_removedbreplication stored procedure. The command is as follows:

```
sp_attach_single_file_db databasename, primarydatafilephysicallocation
```

Examples

```
sp_attach_db MyDB, 'c:\Proddata\MyDB_Data1.mdf',
        'c:\Proddata\MyDB_Data2.ndf' 'd:\ProdLog\MyDB_Log.ldf'
sp_attach_single_file_db Northwind, 'C:\mssql7\data\northwind.mdf'
```

Detaching and Attaching Databases with DMO

A SQLServer object has three methods:

- AttachDB
- DetachDB
- AttachDBWithSingleFile

These methods correspond to sp_attach_db, sp_detach_db, and sp_attach_single_file_db, respectively.

The DetachDB method takes a required string argument, the database name, and an optional Boolean argument, bCheck. If bCheck is true, the statistics are updated before the database is detached; if it is false or omitted, the statistics aren't updated. Note that this is the opposite of the meaning of true and false in Transact-SQL.

The AttachDB method takes a string argument, the database name, and a SQL-DMO multistring argument containing the list of physical filenames. This list must be formatted in the same fashion as the list of files for Transact-SQL. Both arguments are required.

The AttachDBWithSingleFile method has two string arguments: the database name and the physical filename of the primary data file.

Examples

The following examples assume that you already have a connected SQLServer object name oMyServer.

Detaching a Database

```
oMyServer.DetachDB "MyDB" ' statistics are not updated
oMyServer.DetachDB "MyDB", TRUE ' statistics are updated
```

Attaching a Database

```
oMyServer.AttachDB "MyDB","[c:\Proddata\MyDB_Data1.MDF], ⏎
                           [c:\Proddata\MYDB_Data2.NDF] ⏎
                           [d:\Prodlog\MyDB_Log.LDF]"
```

Attaching a Single File Database

```
oMyServer.AttachDBWithSingleFile "Northwind",
"c:\mssql7\data\northwind.mdf"
```

Maintaining a Warm Standby Server

If you require very limited downtime because of hardware problems, you may want to maintain a standby server. This is a SQL Server identical to your primary server. Ideally, even the contents of the system databases such as master and msdb are the same. The servers must have the same character set, sort order, and Unicode collation.

The process of maintaining a standby server requires that you first create a full backup of the database(s) on the primary server. Transfer the backup files to the standby server and restore them. Because you do not know when you will need to use the standby server, use the WITH STANDBY = undofile option on the restore. The databases will be in read-only mode. As you make log backups on the primary server, apply them to the standby server, again using the WITH STANDBY = option. You should use the same undofile for each restore. If the primary server fails, back up the latest transaction log without truncating the active portion, if possible. Apply it to the standby server again using the WITH STANDBY = undofile option. After the last backup has been applied, make the server operational with the following command:

```
RESTORE DATABASE databasename WITH RECOVERY
```

The users are not automatically switched to this server. There are two possibilities:

- Take the former primary server out of the network and give the standby server the same name, and, if appropriate, IP address. In this case, aside from the momentary outage, the change is transparent to the users.

- Tell the users that they should connect to the former standby server.

A high-transaction-volume environment with several databases requires a lot of management to transfer logs, restore backups, and so on. Microsoft has provided a tool to help you with the task of maintaining a warm standby server. Unfortunately, this tool is not part of SQL Server itself. It comes with the BackOffice Resource Kit 4.5 and is called Log Shipping.

General Tip

You can buy the BackOffice Resource Kit, which includes a useful 700-page SQL Server 7.0 Resource Guide document as well as a CD, in most bookstores. The software and online version of this document is included in TechNET and the Microsoft Developer Network Universal subscriptions.

The Log Shipping tool consists of some scripts that you apply on the standby server. These scripts generate some tables and some scheduled jobs that look for transaction log backups on the primary server, copy them, and apply them to the standby. After you have applied the full database backup, these tools take care of all the log backups for you. Because they are Transact-SQL scripts, you can customize them to meet your specific needs.

Under the Covers

Several tables in msdb are used to keep track of backup and restore history:

- **backupset** contains detailed information about each backup, including whether it is a full, log, differential, or file or file group backup, the date on which the backup was made, the position, and so on. The name is a little misleading, I think, because there is an entry for each backup, not an entry for a file or a predefined backup device. This table is related in a one-to-many relationship with the backupfile and backupmediaset tables.
- **backupfile** contains details for each database file backed up during the backup.
- **backupmediaset** keeps track of the media set name and description. It has a one-to-many relationship with the backupmedia family table.
- **backupmediafamily** is used to keep track of tapes that were used in the same physical drive for the same media set.

Three tables keep track of the restore history:

- **restorehistory** contains many records for each row in the backupset table. The data maintained includes the restore date, the destination database, and the name of the user who performed the restore. restore-history has a one-to-many relationship with both the restorefile and restorefilegroup tables.

- **restorefile** contains the file number, physical drive, and physical name of each file that has been restored.

- **restorefilegroup** contains the name of each file group that has been restored.

Over time, these history tables can grow very large. You will probably want to develop purge procedures for them.

7

SQL Mail

SQL Server can send and receive email. In addition, email is also a fundamental part of the job scheduling and alerting facilities covered in Chapter 8, "Jobs and Alerts."

Setting up mail for SQL Server is not difficult and will greatly enhance the power of your SQL Server installation. The next section explains some of the underlying concepts. Then the discussion turns to how to set up mail on your SQL Server. Finally, this chapter shows you how to configure SQL Server and the SQL Agent so that they can use email.

Mail and SQL Server

SQL Server interacts with email in two different ways. First, developers can build applications that use SQL Server's mail stored procedures:

- **sp_processmail** reads mail messages, usually consisting of a single query and uses **xp_sendmail** to return the results to the requester.

- **xp_sendmail** can be used by developers to send a message of any sort. It can include a file attachment.

- **xp_startmail** starts a mail client session, and must be invoked before any other mail stored procedures can be used.

- **xp_stopmail** ends SQL Server's mail session.

These capabilities are referred to as *SQL Mail.*

Second, the SQL Server Agent can use mail to notify users of the success or failure of jobs as well as when error conditions occur in the server. This usage is referred to as *SQL Agent Mail.*

SQL Mail establishes a simple *Messaging Application Programming Interface* (MAPI) connection to a mail host. SQL Agent Mail can establish a simple or an extended MAPI connection to a mail host. Both SQL Mail and SQL Agent Mail can work with Exchange, Windows NT Mail (Windows Messaging), a Post Office Protocol 3 (POP3) server, or any mail server that supports simple MAPI.

 General Tip

If you use Windows Messaging, you should make sure that you have a recent MAPI32.DLL. Otherwise, you may find that messages get stuck in SQL Server's Outbox. This problem should be corrected in Windows NT Service Pack 3. Outlook 97 and Outlook 2000 also include the correct version of MAPI32.

For mail to work, it is essential that the SQL Server and the SQL Agent log in to NT with a domain account that is a local administrator on the SQL Server machine. See Chapter 2, "Installation and Upgrade," for more information about this account.

Setting Up SQL Mail

Before you can use SQL Mail, you need to do the following:

1 Create a mail ID for the SQL Server/SQL Agent Login account on your mail server, and

2 Install the mail client software on the SQL Server computer.

After you have completed these steps, you need to create a profile for the SQL Server and SQL Server Agent logins. The following sections show you how to do this with Exchange, POP3 mail, and Lotus Notes. If you have another mail host, the process will be similar but you will have to consult with your mail software vendor to find out specifics for your mail system.

Setting Up SQL Mail for Exchange

To set up SQL Mail for Exchange, first make sure that you have (or someone has) given the SQL Server Login account an email address in your Exchange Server. If you have not already done so, install the Outlook client software.

General Tip

If you are not using the current version of Exchange, you need to install an Exchange client rather than an Outlook client.

Then, follow these steps:

1 Log in to NT using the SQL Server's login ID and password.

2 In Control Panel, double-click the Mail applet. The wizard that appears leads you through the process of creating a mail profile.

3 You will see three choices:

- Exchange
- Windows Mail
- Internet Mail

Uncheck the Windows Mail and Internet Mail services. You will also need to know the SQL Server's email address and the name of your Exchange Server.

The Wizard asks whether the mail client should be added to the startup group. You should choose to add it.

4 When you finish creating the profile, open the Inbox and send a test message to the SQL Server email address.

5 Right-click the Inbox and choose Properties. Click the Profiles button on the screen that appears next.

6 Record the name assigned to the profile you just created. (It is usually the name of the user or "MS Exchange Settings.")

Now you are ready to configure SQL Server and SQL Agent, so log out
of NT and log back in with your usual login and password.

Setting Up SQL Mail for a POP3 Server

To set up SQL Mail on a POP3 server, you need to install Windows
Messaging on the SQL Server computer if it is not already installed as
well as the MAPI-compliant mail client you are using. Then, follow
these steps:

1 Log in to the SQL Server computer with the SQL Server's login ID
   and password.

2 In Control Panel, double-click the Mail applet. Make sure that you
   select only the Internet Mail service, and that you specify connection
   through the network. You need to specify the name of the mail server
   and an automatic transfer method.

3 Specify the SQL Server's email address.

4 Enter the SQL Server login ID in the Full Name box.

5 In the mailbox name, provide the login name for the mail server. Use
   the default address book and folder settings. You will want to add the
   service to the start-up group.

6 When you finish creating the profile, right-click the Inbox icon and
   choose Properties. Click the Profiles button and record the name of the
   profile you just created.

7 Next, you need to start the mail client you will be using. Create a connection to your mail server, specifying the name of the account, the
   POP3 server name, the SMTP server name, email address, and password
   if there is one. Make sure that the connection is configured to use the
   network.

8 Test the client setup to make sure that mail can be sent and received.

Now you are ready to configure SQL Server and SQL Agent, so log out
of NT and log back in with your usual login and password.

Setting up SQL Mail for Lotus Notes

To set up SQL Mail for Lotus Notes, follow these steps:

1 Log in to NT with the SQL Server login ID and password.

2 First, you must uninstall Notes if it is installed locally, and then you
   must install Windows Messaging and reboot. Install Notes locally, and
   choose Workstation Setup. When setup is complete, start Lotus Notes.

3 Specify ID Was Given to Me in a File, and select the ID file that can be
   found on SQL Server's home share. Next, specify your Notes server.
   Close Lotus Notes.

4 In Control Panel, open the Mail applet.

5 Click Add and choose Lotus Notes Mail. Make sure that this is the only mail service selected, and then click Next.

6 Enter a name for the profile you are creating. Make a note of this name; you will need it later.

7 Enter the password, if the SQL Server account has a Notes password. Click Next to have a personal address book created for the SQL Server. Add any Notes address books you want SQL Server to have access to. If you have added address books, select the one you want to be searched first.

8 When the profile is complete, start Lotus Notes and make sure that you can send and receive mail.

After you have completed the preceding steps, you are ready to configure SQL Server and SQL Agent. Log out of Windows NT and log back in with your usual login and password.

Configuring SQL Mail and SQL Agent Mail

It is easiest to configure SQL Mail and SQL Agent Mail in Enterprise Manager, although it can also be done with DMO. You can't configure SQL Mail or SQL Agent Mail in Transact-SQL.

Configuring SQL Mail

You find SQL Mail in the SUPPORT folder in the console tree. Right-click the SQL Mail icon and choose Properties. A screen that looks like the one shown in Figure 7.1 is displayed.

Figure 7.1   Configuring the SQL Mail profile.

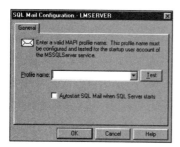

If the profile name you wrote down when you set up mail does not show in the drop-down list, just type it in. Make sure that you spell it correctly or it won't work! Check the Autostart SQL Mail When SQL Server Starts option so that SQL Mail will always be ready to send and receive mail. Click the Test button. After what seems to be an inordinately long time, you should receive a message that says it successfully stopped and started a MAPI session.

If you get a MAPI login failure, SQL Server is likely not logging in with the same account and password as you used when you set up Mail, or that you have incorrectly spelled the profile name. Check the spelling of the profile name, change it if it is incorrect, and retest. If the SQL Server login is incorrect, change it and retest.

Configuring SQL Agent Mail

To configure SQL Agent Mail, open the MANAGEMENT folder, right-click the SQL Agent icon, and choose Properties. The dialog box shown in Figure 7.2 is displayed.

Figure 7.2   Configuring SQL Agent's mail profile.

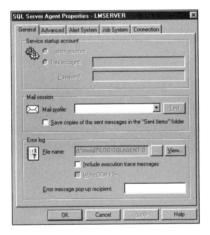

In the middle of the screen, either select the profile from the drop-down list or type it, again making sure to spell it correctly. You probably don't want to save copies of the messages in the Sent Mail folder unless you want to log in as SQL Server and read them. Click the Test button. (It will be much quicker than the test for SQL mail was!) If there are problems, see the discussion under the configuration for SQL Mail.

Troubleshooting Mail

If SQL Mail hangs, which it frequently does if you have a lot of different processes sending mail, the problem is in MAPI, not in SQL Server. Note that the problem is worse on fast machines and multiprocessor machines. You just need to stop and start the SQL Server to clear this problem. SQL Agent Mail is less prone to this problem because it uses extended MAPI rather than simple MAPI.

You can also try a different mail client to see whether this reduces the number of times SQL Mail hangs. Some people have found that Outlook 98 works very well.

The only guaranteed way to get SQL Mail to run with no problems is by single-threading all calls to **xp_sendmail**.

8

Jobs and Alerts

One of the most useful features of SQL Server 7.0 is its capability to automate routine tasks and to notify the administrator when certain conditions occur in the SQL Server environment. It's also possible to define jobs on one server, download them to other servers, and have those servers report success or failure back to the master server whenever the job runs.

This chapter first outlines some of the concepts underlying these features. Then it looks at configuring the SQL Server Agent, and the process of creating and maintaining operators, jobs, and alerts. Finally, the chapter discusses setting up a master-target server architecture.

 General Tip

The Transact-SQL commands and the DMO objects used in this subsystem are quite complicated. I recommend that you start out by working in Enterprise Manager until you are comfortable with all the pieces. Then you can use it to generate SQL scripts and study them so that you can see how everything fits together. You also need an understanding of the underlying Transact-SQL before you can work with these features in DMO.

Understanding Jobs, Operators, and Alerts

This part of SQL Server is controlled by the SQL Server Agent service, and most of the data that supports it is stored in msdb. The SQL Server Agent interacts with the Windows NT event log, SQL Server, and SQL Agent Mail, as shown in Figure 8.1.

Figure 8.1   SQL Server Agent interactions.

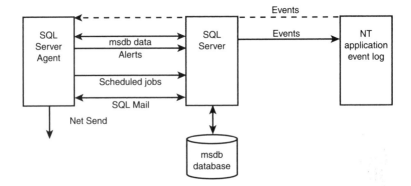

A *job* is just a step or set of steps that runs on a schedule. A job may consist of several steps, and you can define conditional execution of the steps. Suppose, for example, that a job consists of three steps. You can specify that if step 1 fails, step 3 should be executed. If step 1 succeeds, you can execute step 2 and skip step 3. There are several different kinds of steps. This chapter looks at the following:

- **Transact-SQL steps.** Sets of Transact-SQL statements that run in the context of a particular database.

- **CmdExec steps.** Commands issued at the operating system's command-line prompt. These include BAT files and executable programs.

- **Active Script steps.** These steps are written in an ActiveX scripting language such as Visual Basic Script, Java Script or Perl.

A job can be scheduled to run on a recurring basis, a single time, when the SQL Server starts, or when the CPU is idle.

Operators are just email, pager, and/or NET SEND addresses. The jobs and alerts can be set up to send various notifications to operators. If you want to use email, you need to mail-enable both the SQL Server and the SQL Agent. You can find instructions for doing this in Chapter 7, "SQL Mail." To send messages to a pager, the pager must be email capable. Your mail server, a third-party vendor, or the paging network itself may provide this capability. NET SEND can only be used on Windows NT.

Alerts notify you when something happens, and they can execute jobs, perhaps to take corrective action. Alerts are triggered by a SQL Server error message recorded in the Windows NT Application event log or a performance condition.

Jobs, alerts, and operators can be organized into categories, which just classify them and may make your work easier if you use these features often.

Figure 8.2 illustrates some of the possible interactions in this subsystem.

Figure 8.2   Interaction of jobs, alerts, and operators.

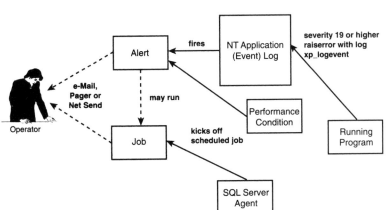

General Tip

If you take advantage of these features, your administrative tasks will be easier. Assume, for example, that you are responsible for ensuring that the backups on several servers, not necessarily all in the same place, run successfully every night. You can define yourself as an operator, schedule the jobs, and set up a notification that will let you know whether anything fails. You can go about your other business, leaving the SQL Server Agent in control. Of course, you'll still be tied to your pager! You need to keep in mind that if the job hangs, or the SQL Server Agent goes down, no modifications will be sent. You may want to notify people that things have succeeded as well as that they failed; in this way if you don't get a report, you'll know that something went wrong.

Configuring the SQL Server Agent

The configuration information for the SQL Server Agent is stored in the Registry under the following:

HKEY_LOCAL_MACHINE\Software\Microsoft\MSSQLServer\SQLServerAgent

You can't configure the SQL Server Agent with Transact-SQL. It is possible to modify some of the alert settings with DMO. The easiest and safest way to configure SQL Server Agent is to do so with Enterprise Manager rather than to edit the Registry. To configure the Agent, open the MANAGEMENT folder, right-click on the SQL Server Agent icon, and choose Properties. The screen shown in Figure 8.3 displays.

Figure 8.3   SQL Server Agent configuration, General tab.

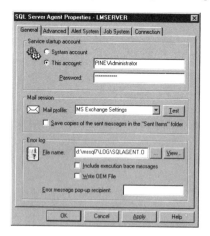

General Properties

On the Properties screen, you can change the NT login ID and password for the SQL Server Agent service. (Chapter 2, "Installation and Upgrade," provides details about this account.) Chapter 7 tells you how to set up the SQL Agent's mail profile.

SQL Server Agent keeps its own error log. The current log and nine previous versions of it are available. By default, the current log is SQLAGENT.OUT, and it is kept in \MSSQL7\LOG. The previous versions are SQLAGENT.1 through SQLAGENT.9. SQLAGENT.1 is the log just before the current one and SQLAGENT.9 is the oldest log. You must stop SQL Server Agent service before you can modify the properties of the error log. Change the name of the error log by typing it or by browsing for the location and file you want. By default, execution trace messages are not logged. Doing so routinely creates a lot of overhead for the Agent. You should turn on this option only when you are experiencing problems with scheduled jobs, alerts, or replication.

If you don't need Unicode in any error messages, you can check the Write OEM file box. This reduces the size of the error log, and is particularly useful if you are including execution trace messages. It also makes the logs easier to read if you are looking at them outside of Enterprise Manager. If your SQL Agent is running on NT, you can specify the network name of someone who should be notified if there are error messages. Messages are sent via NET SEND; you don't need a mail server to use this feature. This capability is not available on Windows 9x.

The Properties screen also enables you to view the current error log. The previous versions are text files; you can view them with Notepad or any tool that can read text files.

Advanced Properties

The Advanced tab enables you to specify whether you want the SQL Server Agent to restart the SQL Server if it stops unexpectedly (see Figure 8.4). Enabling this makes me nervous; if my server stops unexpectedly, I want to know why, so I usually don't check this box. It is, however, enabled by default.

You can also tell the SQL Server Agent to restart itself if it stops unexpectedly. This option is turned off by default. I usually leave it that way. SQL Server Agent uses the xp_sqlagent_monitor extended stored procedure to monitor itself and make sure that it is available to execute scheduled jobs, raise alerts, and notify operators. If the SQL Server Agent service terminates unexpectedly, the procedure can restart the service.

In the middle section of the screen is something called Event Forwarding. You can use this event-forwarding capability to set up an alerts management server. When an error occurs, the SQL Server Agent looks to see whether an alert is associated with the error on the local server. If so, it fires that alert. When you set up event forwarding, the error message can be sent to another server. You can do this for all events (the local alert will still fire) or only for events that aren't handled locally. You can also restrict the error events to a certain severity level.

Figure 8.4   Configuring SQL Server Agent, Advanced tab.

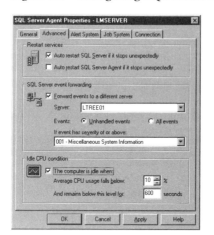

Some advantages accrue when using event forwarding. First of all, you get a centralized view of what is happening on all the servers you are managing. You need to define only operators, alerts, and any associated jobs one time. Some disadvantages also apply, however, including extra load on the alerts management server and increased network traffic. This also creates a single point of failure—if the alerts management server is down, no events are being handled except those that have local handlers.

You shouldn't choose a server used for critical applications as the alert management server, and you must monitor whatever server you do choose to make sure that there isn't congestion because of the alerts. Don't forward events that should be handled locally; for instance, you wouldn't want to forward an error that says a database is out of space. That event would have to be handled on the server on which the database resides.

If you set up event forwarding, you need to monitor the NT Application event log for SQL Server Agent events. If the local alerting system cannot forward the event, it notes that fact in the event log.

It's possible to set or modify the event forwarding part of the configuration with DMO. You use the AlertSystem object, which is part of the JobSystem object of a connected SQL Server. The properties that relate to event forwarding are ForwardingServer, ForwardingSeverity, and ForwardAlways.

You can combine the alerts management function with the master server function (see the discussion of master servers later in this chapter).

The last part of the Advanced Properties screen enables you to define what you consider to be an idle CPU. These rules are used for any jobs scheduled to run when the CPU is idle. You specify a CPU utilization threshold and a duration. You might consider the system to be idle when CPU utilization falls below 10%, for example. (This is the default.) However, you don't want CPU-idle jobs kicking off just because of a momentary dip in utilization; instead, you specify how long the utilization must remain below 10%. By default, it must be below the threshold for 10 minutes. You don't need to specify these values if you don't plan to use CPU-idle jobs.

Alerts System Properties

Figure 8.5 shows the screen you use for configuring the Alerts system. It enables you to define a template to be used for messages sent to pagers (but not regular email messages).

Figure 8.5   Configuring SQL Server Agent, Alert System tab.

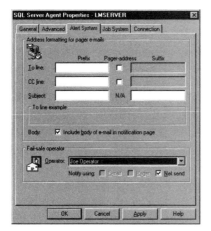

You can choose whether to include the pager address; if you do, you can add a suffix as well. The other thing you can do on this screen is set up a fail-safe operator. Normally, an alert notifies an operator. The fail-safe operator is notified if there is a communication problem reaching the usual operator by email, pager, or NET SEND. If the fail-safe operator doesn't exist, you can get to the operator definition screen from here by choosing New Fail-Safe Operator from the drop-down menu.

You can define or manipulate the template and the fail-safe operator with DMO. Use the AlertSystem object of the JobServer object of a connected SQLServer object. To specify or change the template, use the `PagerToTemplate`, `PagerCCTemplate`, `PagerSubject`, and `PagerToTemplate` properties. To specify or change the fail-safe operator, use the `FailSafeOperator` and `NotificationMethod` properties.

Job System Properties

You can configure some attributes of the job system. Figure 8.6 shows these. SQL Server Agent keeps a history of all the scheduled jobs (by step) in the named sysjobhistory table in msdb. Over time, this table can become quite large, so it is appropriate to limit its size. By default, it has a maximum of 1,000 rows, with a limit of 100 rows for each job. You can modify these values to suit your needs. Keep in mind, however, that job history can quickly become stale. You probably aren't interested in knowing that the full backup of a database ran successfully three years ago. You are allowed to keep an unlimited amount of job history if you want. Doing so increases the size of msdb.

The Clear Log button deletes all the entries in sysjobhistory. I don't recommend doing that. Instead, you should develop a purge procedure that removes older entries or entries for a specific job. You can find a sample one in Appendix D.

 General Tip

Although the table is named sysjobhistory, it is not a system table, and modifications can be made to it without changing the configuration option that allows updates to system tables.

Figure 8.6   Configuring SQL Server Agent, Job System tab.

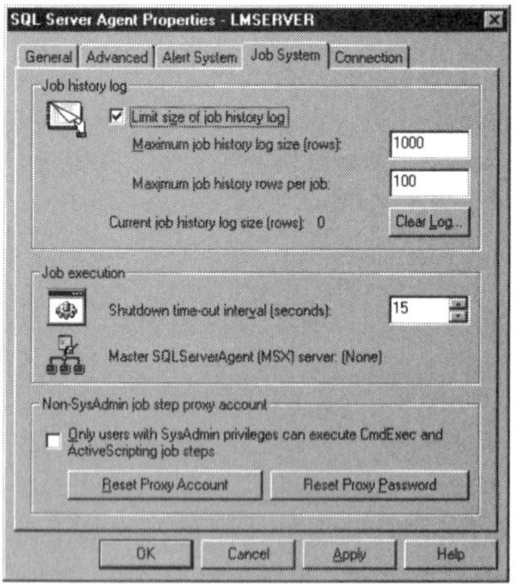

In the Job Execution section of the Job System screen, you specify how long the SQL Server Agent should wait for jobs to finish before it actually shuts down. When the specified time elapses, the SQL Server Agent cancels any jobs in progress, and then shuts down.

If you are configuring the SQL Server Agent on a target server (see the discussion of master-target servers later in this chapter), the name of its master would show on this screen as well.

The last section of the screen deals with something called the *proxy account*. Most jobs are run by a system administrator, and operate in the security context of the SQL Server Agent's NT Login account. This is a highly privileged account. Inside SQL Server, the NT Login account's privileges don't matter because security can be tightly enforced by SQL Server itself. Both CmdExec and Active Script jobs operate outside the SQL Server context, however, and the NT privileges determine what they can do. If a non-system administrator runs a CmdExec or Active Script job, it would run in the SQL Server Agent's security context, not that of the user who was running it. This gives the user power that he shouldn't have, and creates a security hole.

You can choose Prevent Non-System Administrators from Run Jobs, and this is certainly the best thing to do from a security point of view. This makes the system less flexible, however, and isn't appropriate for all organizations. When you installed SQL Server, a special local NT Login account was created for jobs run by non-administrators. This is what the screen means by proxy account. Its name is SQLAgentCmdExec. By default this Login account is an ordinary NT user, and has no special privileges other than those given to "all" users. It provides the security context for CmdExec and Active Script jobs run by people who are not administrators.

You can give the SQLAgentCmdExec Login account any type of permissions needed for the CmdExec and Active Script jobs. If you want to reset the account's permissions to those it had when you first installed SQL Server, use the Reset Proxy Account button. To reset just the password to its initial value, use the Reset Proxy Password button. If the server on which you perform this operation is a *backup domain controller* (BDC), jobs may fail with either an Error 1380 or an Error 1326 until all the BDCs have synchronized their user accounts.

 General Tip

You can force the domain to synchronized with NT's Server Manager or the NLTEST utility that's in the NT Resource Kit.

Connection Properties

The final piece of SQL Server Agent configuration is the connection information shown in Figure 8.7. This specifies how the SQL Server Agent connects to SQL Server. It can either use NT Authentication or SQL Server Authentication. If you use NT Authentication, the SQL Server Agent's NT Login account must be a member of the sysadmins role. Chapter 9, "Security," discusses authentication and roles in more detail.

The *login timeout* is just the number of seconds the SQL Server Agent should wait for a SQL Server connection before giving up.

SQL Server Agent normally communicates with SQL Server by named pipes. If you are not using named pipes, or SQL Server is listening on an alternative pipe, you must specify the alias for the server. Otherwise, you can ignore the SQL Server alias option.

Figure 8.7   Configuring SQL Server Agent, Connection tab.

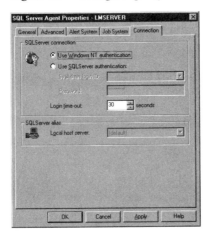

Creating and Maintaining Categories

Categories exist for your convenience. You do not have to use them at all. If you create a lot of jobs, operators, or alerts, however, categories can help you to keep track of what you are doing. You might use categories such as "Backups" or "Nightly Downloads" or "Jobs for the Payroll Database" or "Day Operators" and "Night Operators". As shown in the following list, there are some predefined categories for jobs, but not for operators and alerts:

- **General job categories:**

  [Uncategorized (Local)]. The default category. Jobs are placed in this category unless you request otherwise.

  Database Maintenance. Used for jobs created by the Database Maintenance Planner.

  Full-Text. Used for jobs created by scheduling Full-Text Index population.

  Web Assistant. Used for jobs created by the Web Assistant.

- **Replication categories.** These categories are used for various replication activities:

  REPL-Alert Response

  REPL-Checkup

REPL-Distribution

REPL-Distribution Cleanup

REPL-History Cleanup

REPL-LogReader

REPL-Merge

REPL-Snapshot

REPL-Subscription Cleanup

- **Multiserver categories.** Jobs from MSX. Jobs that have been downloaded from the master server:

  [Uncategorized (Multiserver)]. Default category for multiserver jobs.

If you don't want to define your own categories, you should place your jobs in [Uncategorized (Local)]; you will get easily confused if you put them in another category.

If you create a category, assign jobs to it, and subsequently delete the category, the jobs are placed in the default category for their class. This is either [Uncategorized (Local)] for local jobs or [Uncategorized (Multiserver)] for multiserver jobs.

It's only possible to create and manage job categories with Enterprise Manager. You can create and manage all three types of categories with Transact-SQL and DMO.

Creating and Maintaining Categories with Enterprise Manager

To add, modify, or delete a job category in Enterprise Manager, you must expand the SQL Server Agent, right-click on Jobs, and choose All Tasks, Manage Job Categories. A list of existing categories displays. If you want to delete or modify a category, highlight it in the list and click Delete to delete it or click Properties to change it. When you view the properties of a category, the jobs currently assigned to it display. If you check the Show All Jobs box, all the jobs that you have defined display, together with their current category. You can move the job from its current category to the one you are looking at by checking the box in the Member column. To add a category, click Add, and provide the category name in the dialog box that pops up.

Creating and Maintaining Categories with Transact-SQL

All the commands for maintaining categories are stored procedures in the msdb database. To add a job category with Transact-SQL, you use the command sp_add_category:

```
sp_add_category ['class',] ['type',] 'name'
```

For Operator categories, class should be OPERATOR and type should be NONE. For example:

```
sp_add_category 'OPERATOR', 'NONE',
'Day Operators'
```

The documentation makes it appear that the class and type must be in uppercase, but I tested it on a case-sensitive server and found that the class parameter is not case sensitive, but the type is. Go figure!

For job categories, the class should be JOB and the type must be either LOCAL or MULTI-SERVER. Neither class nor type are case sensitive for job categories. (How Microsoft managed to get it right for jobs and not for operators is a mystery to me!)

Note that both class and type are optional. If you issue the following command, the class will be JOB and the type will be LOCAL:

```
sp_add_category @name = 'MyCategory'
```

For alert categories, the class should be ALERT and type should be NONE. Type is case sensitive as it was for operators.

To change the name of a category, use sp_update_category as shown here:

```
sp_update_category 'class', 'old_name', 'new_name'
```

All three parameters are required.

You can also delete categories. To delete a category, use sp_delete_category:

```
sp_delete_category 'Class', 'Name'
```

If you delete a category that has operators, jobs, or alerts in it, they are placed in the default category, [Uncategorized].

Creating and Maintaining Categories with DMO

To create a category, create a Category object. Set its Name property. Then, set its Type property to one of the following constants:

Constant	Meaning
SQLDMOCategoryType_LocalJob	Category is used to classify jobs that will execute on the SQL Server installation on which the job is stored.

Constant	Meaning
SQLDMOCategoryType_MultiserverJob	Category is used to classify jobs that will execute on one or more TSX target servers.
SQLDMOCategoryType_None	Job is not classified by a category.
SQLDMOCategoryType_Unknown	Category is bad or invalid, or the Category object references a classification used for alerts or operators.

Add your Category object to the OperatorCategories, JobCategories, or AlertsCategory collection of a JobServer object.

To change the name of a category, locate the category in the appropriate collection and modify its Name property. To delete a category, locate the category in the collection and use the Remove method of that collection.

Creating and Maintaining Operators

An *operator* is just an address that can receive notifications. You can create operators with Enterprise Manager, Transact-SQL, or DMO.

 General Tip

If you are sending notifications by email or email-enabled pager, you can notify multiple people by creating a group or mailing list in your email software and using that group as the operator.

Creating and Maintaining Operators with Enterprise Manager

You can create new operators easily by right-clicking on the SQL Server Agent icon in the console pane, and choosing New, Operator. When you do this, the screen shown in Figure 8.8 displays.

Use this screen to provide the email address, the pager email address, and the NET SEND address. The NET SEND address field is not available when the server is running on Windows 9x. If you enter a pager email name, you can specify the hours that the operator is on pager duty. Note that the pager duty schedule is assumed to be the same for all weekdays; it's not possible to specify, for example, hours for Wednesday that differ from those on Tuesday.

Figure 8.8   Operator General tab.

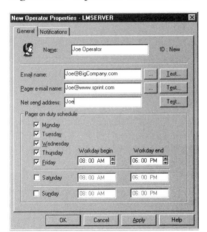

The test buttons to the right enable you to make sure that the addresses are correct; it's a good idea to test them so that you can make sure you don't have a typo or other mistake. In a couple of places in this subsystem, you will find New Operator as an element of an Operator drop-down list. When you click New Operator, the screen shown in Figure 8.8 displays.

Note the Notifications tab. This shows you all the notifications that the operator receives. When you click on Notifications, the screen shown in Figure 8.9 displays.

Figure 8.9   Operator Notification tab.

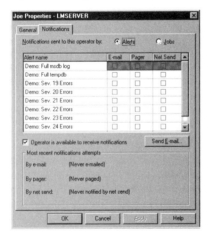

The screen behaves differently for jobs and alerts. When you click the Alerts radio button, you see a list of all the alerts that have been defined. You can request that particular alerts be sent to this operator by checking the appropriate boxes. When you click the Jobs radio button, you see only those jobs that have been set up to notify this operator. If this operator isn't being notified by any job, the Jobs radio button is grayed. When the operator is being notified by a job, you can't make any changes on this screen.

When you add a new operator, you may find it easier to manage alert notifications from the perspective of the operator than from the perspective of an individual alert.

If you uncheck the Operator Is Available to Receive Notifications option, this operator won't receive any notifications until the option is turned on again. The Send Email button enables you to tell the operator of new responsibilities.

The bottom of the screen just shows the most recent attempts to notify this operator.

Creating and Maintaining Operators with Transact-SQL

Creating operators with Transact-SQL is a bit more trouble than creating them with Enterprise Manager. You need to use the `sp_add_operator` command:

```
sp_add_operator 'name' [, enabled]
[,'email_address'] [,'pager_address']
[,weekday_pager_start_time]
[,weekday_pager_end_time]
[, saturday_pager_start_time]
[, saturday_pager_end_time]
[, sunday_pager_start_time]
[, sunday_pager_end_time]
[,pager_days] [,'netsend_address']
[,'category']
```

 General Tip

The `sp_add_operator` stored procedure is in msdb. Either use msdb before issuing the command or specify `msdb..sp_add_operator`.

The meaning of most of the parameters is fairly obvious, particularly if you have used Enterprise Manager to create an operator. There are a few quirks here. If you enter a physical email address or pager address (for example, Joe@BigCompany.com), you must enclose the address in square brackets as shown here:

```
sp_add_operator 'Joe', '[Joe@BigCompany.com]'
```

You don't need to do this if the address is an alias; for example, JoeO would be enclosed in single quotation marks:

```
sp_add_operator 'Joe', 'JoeO'
```

The pager_days parameter is a tinyint and must be specified by adding values taken from the following table.

1	Sunday
2	Monday
4	Tuesday
8	Wednesday
16	Thursday
32	Friday
64	Saturday

If you want to define an operator as being on pager duty on Monday, Wednesday, and Friday, specify the value 42 (2 + 8 + 32) for the pager_days parameter.

Category is the category to which the operator belongs. You don't need to specify this parameter. If you do specify it, it must match the name of a predefined category.

There is also a command—sp_update_operator—that enables you to modify operators. sp_update_operator enables you to change all the attributes of an operator.

Use sp_delete_operator to delete an operator, as shown here:

```
sp_delete_operator 'name' [,'reassign_operator']
```

Name is the name of the operator you want to delete. The optional parameter, reassign_operator, enables you to give all the alerts assigned to the operator that you are deleting to another operator. For example, the following deletes the operator named Joe:

```
sp_delete_operator 'Joe'
```

If Joe had been being notified about any alerts, those alerts now have no one to notify. To delete Joe and give Susie responsibility for alerts originally assigned to Joe, you issue the following command:

```
sp_delete_operator 'Joe', 'Susie'
```

Creating and Maintaining Operators with DMO

To create a new operator using DMO, you must create a new Operator object and set its properties. The following table shows the properties you can use together with their data types.

Property	Data Type
Category	String
EmailAddress	String
Enabled	String
Name	String
NetSendAddress	String
PagerAddress	String

Property	Data Type
PagerDays	Long
SaturdayPagerEndTime	Date
SaturdayPagerStartTime	Date
SundayPagerEndTime	Date
SundayPagerStartTime	Date
WeekdayPagerEndTime	Date
WeekdayPagerStartTime	Date

The following table shows the constants you must use for `PagerDays`.

Constant	Meaning
SQLDMOWeek_Sunday	Operator is paged on Sunday.
SQLDMOWeek_Monday	Operator is paged on Monday.
SQLDMOWeek_Tuesday	Operator is paged on Tuesday.
SQLDMOWeek_Wednesday	Operator is paged on Wednesday.
SQLDMOWeek_Thursday	Operator is paged on Thursday.
SQLDMOWeek_Friday	Operator is paged on Friday.
SQLDMOWeek_Saturday	Operator is paged on Saturday.
SQLDMOWeek_WeekDays	Operator is paged on Monday, Tuesday, Wednesday, Thursday, and Friday.
SQLDMOWeek_WeekEnds	Operator is paged on Saturday and Sunday.
SQLDMOWeek_Unknown	No assignment has been made for the referenced operator.

You set the `PagerDays` property by adding the constants you want. If the operator is on pager duty Monday, Wednesday, and Friday, for example, you set `PagerDays` as shown here:

```
MyOp.PagerDays = SQLDMOWeek_Monday +
                 SQLDMOWeek_Wednesday +
                 SQLDMOWeek_Friday
```

After you have established values for the properties, you can add the Operator object to the Operators collection of the JobServer object of a connected SQL Server.

You also have read-only access to the following properties maintained by SQL Server:

- LastEmailDate
- LastEmailTime
- LastNetSendDate
- LastNetSendTime
- LastPageDate
- LastPageTime

You should not set these properties, but you might want to retrieve them. You can update an operator by finding the appropriate operator in the Operators collection. Use the BeginAlter method before you start changing properties. If you don't do this, each change is sent immediately to SQL Server. After you have changed all the properties you want to change, use the DoAlter method to send the changes to SQL Server.

You can delete an operator by removing it from the Operators collection. There does not appear to be a way to assign alerts to another operator when you use DMO.

If you plan to categorize your operators, you must create the category before you can use it as the value for the Category property of the operator.

Creating and Maintaining Jobs

SQL Server 7.0 jobs are extremely powerful. As mentioned earlier, they are not limited to Transact-SQL. You can create jobs that use command shell commands (CmdExec jobs) as well as jobs that use Active Scripting languages such as VB Script, JScript and PerlScript. You can create jobs that contain only a single step, or you can create jobs that contain multiple steps. Multistep jobs enable you to set up complex sequences of activities that may execute conditionally. You can add as many steps to a job as you want. They need not all be of the same type. You can also mix Transact-SQL, CmdExec, and Active Script steps in the same job. Suppose, for example, that you have a job that backs up the transaction log for a particular database every half hour. However, each night you need to use the bulk copy program to load some data into a table. For performance reasons, you need the bulk load to be non-logged. That requires a change of database option settings and will invalidate your log backup sequence.

You can define a job that has the following steps:

1. Disable the log backup job (Transact-SQL or Active Script step).

2. Manually back up the log (Transact-SQL step or Active Script step).

3. Back up the database (Transact-SQL step or Active Script step).

4. Change the Select Into option (Transact-SQL or Active Script step).

5. Run the bulk copy (CmdExec step).

6. Change the Select Into option (Transact-SQL or Active Script step).

7. Back up the database (Transact-SQL or Active Script step).

8. Enable the log backup job (Transact-SQL or Active Script step).

Then, you can enforce the following rules:

- If steps 1, 2, 3, or 4 fail, quit the job and notify someone of the failure.
- If step 5 succeeds or fails, go on to step 6.

This capability enables you to automate many routine tasks that require conditional execution of certain steps.

 General Tip

When designing steps, you need to remember that the jobs are going to be started by the SQL Server Agent. There won't be a human being around to interact with them, so the steps should not present dialog boxes or require user input.

A job has several parts:

- The job itself
- The steps
- The schedules
- History

A job can have multiple active schedules. All active schedules determine when the jobs run. Jobs can be scheduled to run once, on a recurring schedule, when SQL Server starts, or when the CPU is idle.

 General Tip

Although the job scheduling engine provides a great deal of flexibility in scheduling jobs, there may be some situations in which you need more than one schedule for a job to get it to run exactly when you want. For example, a recurring schedule handles cases where you want to run a job every *n* hours. But it doesn't handle the case in which you want to run a job at 10 a.m., 2 p.m., and 4 p.m. every day. For that, you need two active schedules: one that runs the morning job and one that runs every 4 hours between 10 a.m. until 3 p.m. and one to run at 4 p.m.

Like operators, jobs can be organized into categories to make it easier for you to manage them.

You can create and maintain jobs with Enterprise Manager, Transact-SQL, and DMO. This part of Enterprise Manager is very well designed and helps you to understand how the various pieces fit together. And, even if you are never planning to use Enterprise Manager, I recommend that you read the Enterprise Manager section of this chapter before tackling the Transact-SQL section. If you have created a job in Enterprise Manager or DMO and want to see the underlying Transact-SQL, right-click on the job and choose Script Job.

 IMO

I strongly recommend that you start out with Enterprise Manager, even if you're a die-hard SQL bigot like I am or a die-hard DMO bigot, which I am not.

Creating and Maintaining Jobs with Enterprise Manager

To create a job with Enterprise Manager, either right-click on the SQL Server Agent icon and choose New, Job or right-click on the Jobs icon and choose New Job. Either method takes you to the screen shown in Figure 8.10.

Figure 8.10   Job Definition screen, General tab.

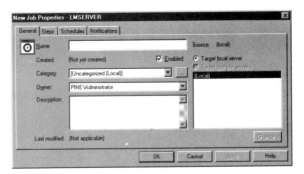

General Job Properties

On the Job Definition screen, you must give the job a name. By default, the job is enabled; you can control whether jobs can run by enabling and disabling them. You can assign the job to a category by selecting the category from the drop-down list. By default, the person who creates the job is its owner. If a member of the sysadmin role (discussed in Chapter 9) creates a job, he or she can assign the job to someone else.

General Tip

It's important to remember that CmdExec and Active Script steps of jobs that aren't owned by the administrator run in the security context of the SQL Agent CmdExec NT Login account and that this Login account must have the necessary NT privileges to perform operations specified in these steps.

The Description field provides documentation for the job. In Figure 8.10, only the Target Local Server option is enabled. If you are creating jobs on a server that has been designated a master server, you need to choose between the Target Local Server and the Target Multiple Server options.

After you specify the general job properties, the next thing you need to do is add one or more steps to the job.

Defining Job Steps

Click on the Steps tab, and click the New button at the bottom of the screen. The New Job Step screen appears (see Figure 8.11).

Figure 8.11   Creating a job: The New Job Step, General tab.

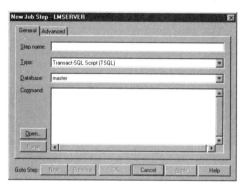

You must give the step a name. Enterprise Manager assumes you are going to create a Transact-SQL step. Transact-SQL steps operate in a specific database, so you need to select the database from the drop-down menu. You can just type the SQL statement or statements that you want to execute in the area labeled Command, or you can use the Open button and read SQL statements from a file. After you have entered a command, you can use the Parse button to check it for correct syntax.

 General Tip

The job can still fail even though SQL parses successfully. Only syntax is checked. If you enter the following statement it parses successfully:

    BACKUP DATABASE pubs to DISK = 'c:\pubsbackups\pubs.bak'

If the folder c:\pubsbackups does not exist, however, you get an error at runtime, not when the statement is parsed.

 General Tip

When you are creating steps that refer to disk drives, it's important to remember that SQL Server or SQL Server Agent will be issuing the command. That means that any drive letters you use must be from the SQL Server's point of view. Don't use the drive letters that you may have mapped them to. Suppose, for example, that the SQL Server machine has a C: drive and a D: drive. You have mapped the SQL Server computer's D: drive to L: on your computer. If you were to define a step with the following command

    BACKUP DATABASE Northwind TO DISK = 'L:\nwind.bak'

the command would fail because SQL Server does not know anything about an L: drive; it only knows about a D: drive.

If you select Operating System Command (CmdExec) from the Type drop-down list, the screen changes. Instead of the database drop-down list, you find a box labeled Process Exit Code of a Successful Command. It contains a zero by default, because that's the normal success exit for a BAT file or other DOS command. If you are running an executable that returns another value for success, you need to supply that value here. Enter your command in the box just as you would a Transact-SQL command. Neither the Open nor the Parse options are available for a CmdExec step.

If you select Active Script from the Type drop-down list, the screen changes again. You receive a choice of Visual Basic Script, JavaScript, and Other. If you choose Other, you need to provide the name of the scripting language (for example, PerlScript). Again, type your command in the box or use the Open button to read it from a file. The scripting language must be installed on your machine before you can parse the script.

When you click on the Advanced tab of the New Job Step screen, a screen similar to the one shown in Figure 8.12 displays.

Figure 8.12   New Job Step, Advanced tab.

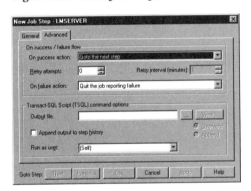

You must specify the action you want to take when the step succeeds and when it fails. When the job has only one step, your choices are as follows:

- Quit the Job Reporting Success
- Quit the Job Reporting Failure
- Go to the Next Step

When the job has multiple steps, you can choose which step to perform next when the step succeeds or when the step fails. You can also specify a number of retry attempts and a retry interval. This may be useful if you are running a step that might encounter deadlock or blocking conditions. Don't retry an infinite number of times; if a condition has not corrected itself in two or three tries, it probably isn't going to. The step is not considered to have failed until it has been retried the specified number of times.

For a Transact-SQL step, you can have the output of the SQL statement directed to a file and/or included in the step history. If you choose the latter, you can see the results of the statement(s) when you view the job history. By default, the Transact-SQL statements run in the selected database under the identity of its owner. If you are a sysadmin, you can specify the name of a user whom you want to impersonate here.

For CmdExec steps, the bottom of the screen differs slightly. You can specify an output file for the results of the command. You could issue the command DIR, for example, and send the result to a file. There is no way to attach the output to the step history. If you have an Active Script step, no options show at the bottom of the screen.

After you have defined the steps, you will probably want to create a schedule for the job.

Defining the Job Schedule

After you save your step, the New Job Properties screen displays again. When you click on the Schedules tab, and click the New button, a screen displays enabling you to enable or disable a schedule and to specify the schedule type. Your choices are as follows:

- Start Automatically When SQL Server Agent Starts
- Start Whenever the CPU Becomes Idle
- One Time
- Recurring

In most environments, the SQL Server Agent is automatically started when Windows NT starts. If you have jobs that need to be run to set up things each time NT is started, that's what you'd choose. If you have a job that is resource intensive that you want to defer until the CPU is idle, you'd make that choice. If this job is only going to run once, choose one time, and specify the date and time at which it should run. Many of your jobs will be recurring, which is the default choice. By default, recurring jobs run once a week on Sunday at 12:00:00 a.m. To specify a different schedule, click the Change button. The screen shown in Figure 8.13 displays.

 General Tip

In many places in Enterprise Manager, you have the opportunity to schedule something. Whenever you click the Change button, the same screen as the one in Figure 8.13 displays.

Figure 8.13   Defining a recurring job schedule.

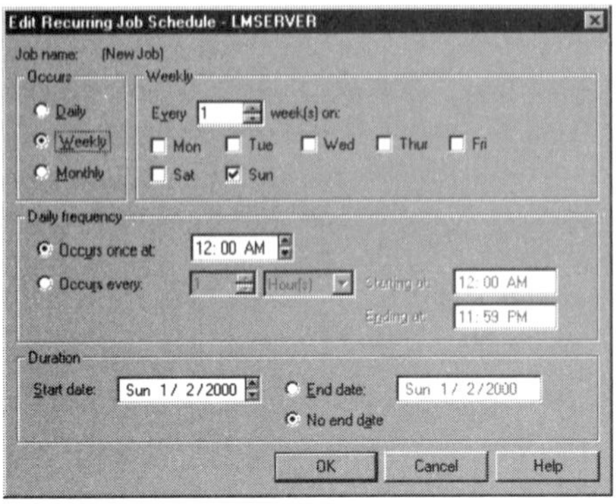

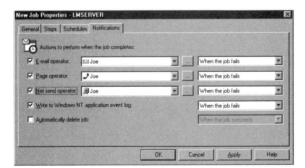

There is a great deal of flexibility in the scheduling engine. You can specify whether the job occurs on a daily, weekly, or monthly basis. Figure 8.13 shows the options for a weekly job; in this screen, you can specify whether it should run every week, every two weeks, and so on, as well as the days on which it should run. If you choose a monthly job, you can specify whether it should run on a particular day (1–31) of all months, a particular day, on every other month, and so on. You can also request that it run on the second Tuesday of each month. A daily job can run every day, every other day, every third day, and so forth.

Regardless of whether you choose Daily, Weekly, or Monthly, you still must specify the daily frequency. This can be once a day at a certain time, or every *n* minutes or hours. If you choose Occurs Every, you can also specify a start time and an end time. You can define a schedule that allows the job to run every day, for example, every 10 minutes between the hours of 9 a.m. and 5 p.m.

The last part of the schedule definition enables you to define the beginning and ending date for this schedule.

Defining the Job Notifications

The last part of the job definition is setting up notifications. When you click on the Notifications tab, the screen shown in Figure 8.14 displays.

Figure 8.14   Defining notifications with the Notifications tab.

The choices you make here depend on the choices you made when defining operators. However, there are two nice "oops" choices built in. If you get here and you forgot all about operators, just choose New Operator from any of the drop-down lists and you can create an operator. If you click one of the Browse buttons (the ones with an ellipsis (...)), you can see and modify operator properties. You can send notifications when the job

- Fails
- Succeeds
- Completes

If you choose When the Job Completes and send email, a page, and a NET SEND, your operator will probably start ignoring your messages. I usually just send notices in the case of failure. After all, success should be routine! Notice that you can also write to the Windows NT Application event log. If you have many jobs writing to the event log, you may have to increase its size and/or set it to automatically overwrite.

❝❝   IMO

At the bottom of the Notifications screen is an option that, when enabled, automatically deletes the job after it succeeds, fails, or cancels. I have never understood the point of this option. If I have gone to all the trouble to create a job, I'm certainly not going to delete it automatically. I may disable it, but I'd be inclined to keep it around in case I need it again, either as itself or as a model for something else. But I am a known packrat, and these habits are clearly why I have to keep buying hard-drive space.

Modifying and Deleting Jobs

If you want to modify a job after you have created it, just right-click on it, and choose Properties. You will see the same screens that you saw when creating it, and can modify it as you see fit.

When you want to delete a job, right-click on it and choose Delete.

Creating and Maintaining Jobs with Transact-SQL

With Transact-SQL, you must create and maintain jobs as their component parts. First, you need to create the job together with the notifications; then you can add the steps and schedules. All the commands that deal with jobs are stored procedures in the msdb database.

General Tip

If you want to have the same job on different machines, it's easiest to create the job with Transact-SQL. You can create a script that defines a job with Enterprise Manager. To do this, right-click on the job in the details pane, and choose All Tasks, Script job. You can also create the script manually using the commands described in this section.

 General Tip

These commands have a lot of parameters. You will probably want to familiarize yourself with invoking stored procedures by using the @name=value form rather than the method of specifying all parameters in sequence if you are not already familiar with it. To make the syntax easier to read, I have not included the @name for each parameter. In many cases, it is the same as the parameter. If you have questions about the @name for a parameter, consult Books OnLine; they're all detailed in the syntax there.

Adding a Job

To add a job, use the command sp_add_job:

```
sp_add_job 'job_name' [,enabled]
[,'description'] [,step_id]
[,'category'] [,category_id]
[,'login'] [,eventlog_level]
[, email_level] [, netsend_level]
[,page_level] [,'email_name']
[, 'netsend_name'] [,'page_name']
[,delete_level] [, job_id OUTPUT]
```

All the parameters except job_name are optional. *job_name* is just the name you want to assign to the job.

enabled specifies whether the job is enabled (runnable). The default is enabled (1). To create a disabled job, specify 0.

description is the description of the job. You can place any documentation you like in this parameter.

step_id specifies the first step to be run in the job. (It's not necessary to start with the first step.) It is 1 by default.

category is the name of the category to which the job belongs. If it is not specified, the default category is used. category_id is the internal identifier assigned to the category. You can provide either the category or the category_id; it's not necessary to provide both.

login is the SQL Server login of the user who owns this job. By default, it is set to the login of the user running sp_add_job.

eventlog_level, email_level, page_level, and netsend_level all specify when the notification should be sent. As shown in the following table, you have four choices.

Value	Description
0	Never
1	On success
2	On failure
3	Always

The default is on failure (2).

email_name, netsend_name, and page_name are the operator's email address, NET SEND address, and pager email address.

delete_level specifies when the job should be deleted. The values are the same as those for event_log_level.

sp_add_job returns the job_id that was assigned. This is a variable of type uniqueidentifier. You can use the ID rather than the name to refer to the job when adding steps and schedules if you want.

Defining Job Steps

To add a step to a job, use sp_add_jobstep:

```
sp_add_jobstep [job_id ¦ 'job_name']
[, step_id] ,'step_name'
[,'subsystem'] [, 'command']
[, 'parameters'] [, code]
[, success_action] [, success_step_id]
[, fail_action] [, fail_step_id]
[,'server'] [, 'database']
[, 'user'] [, retry_attempts]
[, retry_interval] [, run_priority]
[,'file_name'] [,[@flags =] flags]
```

Although it would appear from the parameters that only the job_id or job_name and step_name are required, some internal checking ensures that you have supplied everything you need for the step type. The database parameter is not needed (and should not be supplied) for a CmdExec step, for example, but is required for a Transact-SQL step.

job_id or job_name is either the ID of the job or the name of the job that owns this step. You may provide either the ID or the name, but not both. You must provide one of them.

step_id is the sequential number assigned to this step within the job. If you don't provide a value for step_id, the step is added at the end of the list of job steps. If you provide a value lower than the highest step number plus 1, the procedure automatically renumbers the steps. If the job has four steps and you add a new step with step_id 3, for example, the old step 3 becomes step 4 and the old step 4 becomes step 5. You cannot leave gaps in step numbers. If the job already has a step 1, for example, you cannot add a step 3. You will get an error message if you try.

step_name is just the name of the step. You must provide a step name.

subsystem is the step type. It must be one of the following values.

Subsystem Value	Description
ACTIVESCRIPTING	Active Script
CMDEXEC	Operating system command or executable program
TSQL	Transact-SQL statement

The default is TSQL. The values are not case sensitive.

command is the Transact-SQL, operating system, or Active Script command. A maximum of 3,200 characters applies. It is possible to have some values substituted into the command at runtime by using some specific tokens in the command. These tokens, which are case sensitive, are shown in the following table.

Token	Description
[A-DBN]	When the job is run by an alert, the name of the database in which the alert fired replaces this token.
[A-SVR]	Server name. If the job is run by an alert, the name of the server in which the alert fired replaces this token.
[A-ERR]	If this job is run by an alert, the error number that caused the alert replaces this token.
[A-SEV]	If the job is run by an alert, the severity level that caused the alert replaces this token.
[A-MSG]	If the job is run by an alert, the message text associated with the alert replaces this token.
[DATE]	Current date (in YYYYMMDD format).
[JOBID]	Job ID.
[MACH]	Computer name.
[MSSA]	Master SQL Server Agent name.
[SQLDIR]	The directory in which SQL Server is installed. By default, this value is C:\MSSQL7.
[STEPCT]	A count of the number of times this step has executed (excluding retries). Can be used by the **step** command to force termination of a multistep loop.
[STEPID]	Step ID.
[TIME]	Current time (in HHMMSS format).
[STRTTM]	The time (in HHMMSS format) that the job began executing.
[STRTDT]	The date (in YYYYMMDD format) that the job began executing.

These tokens enable you to make small customizations of the command.

parameters is reserved for future use. Presumably it will allow some additional parameterization of a command.

code is the value that indicates successful execution of a CmdExec step. It defaults to 0.

success_action and fail_action describe what should be done when the step succeeds or fails. The following table lists valid values for these parameters.

Value	Action
1	Quit with success
2	Quit with failure
3	Go to next step
4	Go to step ?

The default for `success_action` is 1. The default for `fail_action` is 2.

`success_step_id` and `fail_step_id` is the step number to go to if the task succeeds or fails when 4 is specified for the action.

`server` is reserved for future use.

`database` is the name of the database in which a Transact-SQL command should execute.

`user` is the database username to use when running a Transact-SQL command. If it is null, the Transact-SQL command runs in the context of the job owner.

`retry_attempts` is the number of times to retry the step. The default is 0.

`retry_interval` is the number of minutes to wait between retries. The default is 0.

`run_priority` is reserved for future use.

General Tip

Interestingly, this parameter is supported in DMO. It's also supported in the code for `sp_add_jobstep`, where it is described as having the following values:

−15 = Idle

−1 = Below normal

0 = Normal

1 = Above normal

15 = Time critical

I have not tested it to see what it does. It may be benign, but I'm biased against using undocumented features.

`file_name` is the name of the output file for Transact-SQL and CmdExec steps. It cannot be used for Active Script steps.

`flags` goes with `file_name` and specifies whether the output should be appended to the file. It also specifies whether the output should be appended to the step history. It can be one of the following values.

Flag Value	Description
0	Overwrite output file and don't append results to step history
2	Append to output file and don't append results to step history
4	Append results to step history and overwrite output file.
6	Append to step history and append to output file
6	Append to step history only

General Tip

The values listed in the preceding table are not what the documentation says. I determined the actual values by configuring the job in different ways and then scripting it to see what was generated. I'm still a little worried about the meaning for 6, but I assume that it is interpreted as append to step history and, *if* there's an output file, append to it too. I also found inside the `sp_add_jobstep` procedure itself a comment that lists a value of 1 for an encrypted command.

Defining Job Schedules

To define a job schedule, use `sp_add_jobschedule`:

```
sp_add_jobschedule {job_id, ¦ 'job_name'},
'name' [, enabled] [, freq_type]
[, freq_interval] [, freq_subday_type]
[, freq_subday_interval]
[, freq_relative_interval]
[, freq_recurrence_factor]
[, active_start_date] [, active_end_date]
[, active_start_time] [, [active_end_time]
```

Either job_id or job_name must be provided, but not both.

name is the name of the schedule, and is required.

enabled specifies whether the schedule is enabled. It defaults to 1 (enabled). Use 0 when the schedule should be disabled.

freq_type specifies when the job should be run. It must be one of the following values.

Value	Description
1	Once
4	Daily
8	Weekly
16	Monthly
32	Monthly, relative to freq interval
64	Run when SQL Server Agent starts
128	Run when the computer is idle

freq_interval interacts with freq_type, as shown in the following table.

freq_type	freq_interval
4 (daily)	Every freq_interval days. If you want a daily job to run every other day, freq_type would be 4 and freq_interval would be 2.
8 (weekly)	freq_interval is one or more of the following (OR'ed together): 1 = Sunday 2 = Monday 4 = Tuesday 8 = Wednesday 16 = Thursday 32 = Friday 64 = Saturday

freq_type	freq_interval
	If you want a weekly job to run on Monday, Wednesday, and Friday, `freq_type` would be 8 and `freq_interval` would be 42 − 2 + 8 + 32. This can be further qualified by `freq_recurrence_factor`.
16 (monthly)	On the `freq_interval` day of the month.
	If you want a monthly job to run on the fifth day of every month, `freq_type` would be 16 and `freq_interval` would be 5. This can be further qualified by `freq_recurrence_factor`.
32 (monthly relative)	`freq_interval` is one of the following: 1 = Sunday 2 = Monday 3 = Tuesday 4 = Wednesday 5 = Thursday 6 = Friday 7 = Saturday 8 = Day 9 = Week day 10 = Weekend day

These don't stand alone; they are further qualified by `freq_recurrence_factor` and `freq_relative_interval`.

`freq_interval` does not apply to jobs that run once, when SQL Server Agent starts or when the CPU is idle.

`freq_recurrence_factor` specifies the number of weeks (for weekly jobs) or months (for monthly jobs) between job executions. It's an integer. It only applies to `freq_types` 8, 16, and 32.

`freq_relative_interval` is used only with `freq_type` 32 (monthly relative) and specifies the relative unit. It can take the following values.

Value	Unit
1	First
2	Second
4	Third
8	Fourth
16	Last

`freq_subday_type` specifies the units for `freq_subday_interval`. It can take the following values.

Value	Unit
1	At the specified time
4	Minutes
8	Hours

General Tip

The documentation implies that these values are to be entered as hexadecimal numbers (for example, 0x1, 0x4, 0x8). However, they are really integers.

`freq_subday_interval` specifies the number of `freq_subday_types` between executions of the job. It is an integer, with a default of 0. If `freq_subday_type` is minutes, `freq_subday_interval` must be between 1 and 1440. If `freq_subday_type` is hours, `freq_subday_interval` must be between 1 and 24. `freq_subday_interval` is irrelevant for At the Specified Time.

Before discussing the rest of the parameters for `sp_add_jobschedule`, I want to take a complicated schedule example and show you how these `freq_` parameters all fit together. I want to schedule a monthly job that runs on the third Tuesday of every other month. When the job runs, I want it to run every 10 minutes. Because I've said third, `freq_type` is 32 (monthly relative), and `freq_relative_interval` is 4 (third). Tuesday gets captured by a `freq_interval` value of 3 (Tuesday). Every other month is reflected in a `freq_recurrence_factor` of 2. Then, on the days when the job executes, I want it to run every 10 minutes. That means that `freq_subday_type` is 4 (minutes) and `freq_subday_interval` is 10. Here's how `sp_add_schedule` command looks:

```
sp_add_jobschedule @job_name = N'Test3',
@name = N'testsched', @enabled = 1,
@freq_type = 32,
@freq_interval = 3,
@freq_relative_interval = 4,
@freq_recurrence_factor = 2,
@freq_subday_type = 4,
@freq_subday_interval = 10
```

“ IMO

Now you see why Microsoft (and I) recommend using Enterprise Manager to define jobs!

The following four more parameters must be dealt with:

- `active_start_time`
- `active_end_time`
- `active_start_date`
- `active_end_date`

`active_start_time` and `active_end_time` specify when the job should start running on its `subday_interval`. The schedule I created previously has it run every 10 minutes all day long. By specifying an `active_start` and `active_end` time, I can constrain the job so that it only runs every 10 minutes between midnight and 5 a.m. Both values must be specified in 24-hour time in the format HHMMSS. If `active_start_time` is not specified, 00:00:00 (midnight) is assumed. If `active_end_time` is not specified, 23:59:59 is assumed.

`active_start_date` and `active_end_date` specify the period during which the job is active. Values for these fields must be in YYYYMMDD format. `active_start_date` cannot be earlier than 19000101. If `active_start_date` is not specified, the creation date for the job is used. If `active_end_date` is not specified, 99991231 is used.

Modifying and Deleting Jobs

If you want to change any of the properties of the job, its steps, or its schedules, you use one of the three following commands:

- `sp_update_job`
- `sp_update_jobstep`
- `sp_update_jobschedule`

`sp_update_job` has all the parameters that `sp_add_job` does, and they have the same meaning. It has one additional parameter, `new_name`, which enables you to change the name of the job. There's also a parameter named `automatic_post` that is listed as reserved and not further described. That parameter does not appear in `sp_add_job`. It will be interesting to find out what it means in the future!

`sp_update_jobstep` has exactly the same parameters as `sp_add_jobstep`, and they have the same meaning. It does not have a `new_name` parameter; use the `name` parameter if you want to change the name of the step.

`sp_update_jobschedule` has all the parameters that `sp_add_job_schedule` has, and they have the same meaning. It has one additional parameter, `new_name`, which enables you to change the name of the schedule.

To delete a job, use the command `sp_delete_job` as shown here:

```
sp_delete_job {job_id ¦ 'job_name'}
```

You must specify either the `job_id` or the `job_name`, but not both. When you delete a job, all its history, steps, and schedules is also deleted.

The documentation shows an `originating_server` parameter, and mentions a `delete_history` parameter. Neither is implemented in this release.

To delete a job step, use the command `sp_delete_jobstep`:

```
sp_delete_jobstep {job_id, ¦ 'job_name'}, step_id
```

You must provide either a `job_id` or a `job_name`, but not both. If `step_id` is 0, all steps for the job are deleted. When you delete a step from a multistep job, `sp_delete_jobstep` renumbers the steps for you. You need to be careful when you delete a step. Suppose, for example, that you had step 3 going to step 4 on success and step 5 on failure. When you delete step 4, step 3 has nowhere to go on success. From reading the stored procedure, it looks to me like step 3 will be told to go to step 3 on success, which is not going to work very well!

To delete a job schedule, use the command `sp_delete_jobschedule` as shown here:

```
sp_delete_jobschedule {job_id, ¦ 'job_name'},
'sched_job_name'
```

You must provide either a `job_id` or a `job_name`, but not both. Remember that you can disable a schedule with `sp_update_jobschedule` and later re-enable it. Delete only schedules you are certain you no longer need.

Creating and Maintaining Jobs with DMO

You can create and maintain jobs with DMO. I advise you to read the Transact-SQL section if you are going to create a job with DMO. It gives you a fuller understanding of the various properties than I provide here. In most cases, the names of the properties are identical to, or very similar to, the names of the parameters presented in the Transact-SQL section.

Defining a Job

To define a job, create a Job object. Modify its properties, and add the Job object to the Jobs collection of a JobServer object. The following table shows the job properties that you can modify.

Property	Description
Category	Category name.
DeleteLevel	When job should be deleted. Values for this property are taken from the list of level constants.
Description	Documentation for the job.
EmailLevel	When operator should be emailed. Values for this property are taken from the list of level constants.
Enabled	True if job is enabled, false otherwise.
EventLogLevel	When message should be written to event log. Values for this property are taken from the list of level constants.
Name	Name of job.
NetSendLevel	When operator should receive NET SEND message. Values for this property are taken from the list of level constants.
OperatorToEmail	Name of an operator.
OperatorToNetSend	Name of an operator.
OperatorToPage	Name of an operator.
Owner	Job owner.
PageLevel	When operator should be paged. Values for this property are taken from the list of level constants.
StartStepID	Step at which to start.
Type	Local or multiserver job. Values for this property are taken from the list of type constants.

Level Constants

Constant	Meaning
SQLDMOComp_All	Same as SQLDMOComp_Always.
SQLDMOComp_Always	Send message or write to event log regardless of success or failure.
SQLDMOComp_Failure	Send message or write to event log when the job fails.
SQLDMOComp_None	Do not send any messages or write to the event log.
SQLDMOComp_Success	Send message or write to the event log when the job succeeds.

Type Constants

Constant	Description
SQLDMOJob_Local	Job will execute on the SQL Server installation on which the job is stored.
SQLDMOJob_MultiServer	Job will execute on one or more TSX target servers.
SQLDMOJob_Unknown	Job is bad or invalid.

Some additional properties are available to you after the job has been created. These are read-only properties. The properties that start with the word Current are available while the job is running. The following table describes these read-only properties.

Property	Description
CurrentRunRetryAttempt	Number of times the job has executed without success.
CurrentRunStatus	Executing state of a job.
CurrentRunStep	Step number and name of the currently executing step.
DateCreated	Date job was created.
DateLastModified	Date job was last modified.
HasSchedule	True if the job has a schedule.
HasServer	True if the job has a target server (multiserver jobs).
HasStep	True if the job has a step.
JobID	ID assigned to job when it was created.
LastRunDate	Last run date.
LastRunOutcome	Status of last run.
LastRunTime	Time the job last ran.
NextRunDate	Next date the job will run.
NextRunScheduleID	Schedule that determines next run.

continues ▶

continued ▶

Property	Description
NextRunTime	Next runtime.
OriginatingServer	Server job originated from (multiserver jobs).
VersionNumber	System-maintained versioning.

Defining a Job Step

To define a job step, create a JobStep object. Set its properties and add it to the JobSteps collection of a Job object. The following table lists the properties of a JobStep object.

Property	Description
AdditionalParameters	Reserved for future use.
CmdExecSuccessCode	Value that indicates successful completion of a CmdExec step.
Command	The command to be executed.
DatabaseName	The database in which a Transact-SQL command executes.
DatabaseUserName	The database username that should be used to execute a Transact-SQL command.
Flags	According to the documentation, this property is reserved for future use, and no constants are supplied for it. Because this is available in Transact-SQL and Enterprise Manager, which uses DMO and allows entry of choices reflected in Flags, however, it is probably possible to use the values for the parameter to sp_add_job_step for this property. The property is visible in the JobStep object.
Name	Step name.
OnFailAction	Action to take when step fails. Values for this property are taken from the list of action constants.
OnFailStep	Step to go to when Go to step action is requested for failure.
OnSuccessAction	Action to take when step succeeds. Values for this property are taken from the list of action constants.
OnSuccessStep	Step to go to when Go to step action is requested for success.
OSRunPriority	Controls execution-thread priority for the step. Note that this property is fully documented, and constants exist for it. Because it is listed as reserved in Transact-SQL, it likely doesn't accomplish anything.
OutputFileName	Name of the output file, if any.
RetryAttempts	Number of times to retry the step.

Property	Description
RetryInterval	Delay between retries.
Server	Reserved for future use.
StepID	Step ID.
SubSystem	Subsystem name (TSQL, CMDEXEC, ACTIVESCRIPTING).

Action Constants

Constant	Description
SQLDMOJobStepAction_GotoStep	Continue execution at the next identified step.
SQLDMOJobStepAction_GotoNextStep	Continue execution at the next sequential step.
SQLDMOJobStepAction_QuitWithFailure	Terminate job execution, reporting failure.
SQLDMOJobStepAction_QuitWithSuccess	Terminate job execution, reporting success.
SQLDMOJobStepAction_Unknown	Job step logic is unassigned for the referenced job step.

Some read-only properties are also available to you after the step has completed. These include the following.

Property	Description
LastRunDate	Date step last ran
LastRunDuration	Duration of last run
LastRunOutcome	Outcome of last run
LastRunRetries	Number of retries on last run
LastRunTime	Time step last ran

Defining a Job Schedule

To define a schedule, create a Schedule object. Set its properties and add it to the JobSchedules collection of a Job object. The following table shows the properties of a Schedule object.

Property	Description
DateCreated	Date JobSchedule was created.
Enabled	True if JobSchedule is enabled, false otherwise.
Name	Schedule name.
ScheduleID	Internal identifier assigned to the JobSchedule.

If you have read the Transact-SQL section or played with scheduling in Enterprise Manager, you probably can't believe it's that simple. And, in fact, it isn't. You must deal with another object. After you have created a JobSchedule object, you must get the Schedule object from the

JobSchedule object. Then you must set its properties. You should use the `BeginAlter` method when you start manipulating the properties, and the `DoAlter` method when you are done. This prevents each individual property value change from being sent to the SQL Server. The following table shows the properties of the Schedule object.

Property	Description
ActiveEndDate	Date this schedule ends.
ActiveEndTimeOfDay	Time that the frequency subday interval ends.
ActiveStartDay	Date this schedule starts.
ActiveStartTimeOfDay	Time that the frequency subday interval begins.
FrequencyInterval	How often the job runs. This property is specified with the `FrequencyInterval` constants listed in the following section.
FrequencyRecurrenceFactor	Every *n* (days, months, weeks).
FrequencyRelativeInterval	First, second, third, and so on.
FrequencySubDay	Hour, minute, and so on. This property is specified with the `FrequencySubDay` constants listed in the following section.
FrequencySubDayInterval	Hours or minutes.
FrequencyType	Daily, monthly, weekly. This property is specified with the `FrequencyType` constants listed in the following section.

Frequency Interval Constants

Constant	Description
SQLDMOFreqSub_Hour	Schedule reflects an activity scheduled using an hour as the unit.
SQLDMOFreqSub_Minute	Schedule reflects an activity scheduled using a minute as the unit.
SQLDMOFreqSub_Once	Schedule reflects an activity that occurs once on a scheduled day.
SQLDMOFreqSub_Unknown	Subunits are invalid for the scheduled activity.

Frequency Type Constants

Constant	Description
SQLDMOFreq_Autostart	Scheduled activity is launched when SQL Server Agent starts.
SQLDMOFreq_Daily	Activity is scheduled to occur every `FrequencyRecurrenceFactor` days.
SQLDMOFreq_Monthly	Activity is scheduled to occur every `FrequencyRecurrenceFactor` months.

Constant	Description
SQLDMOFreq_MonthlyRelative	Activity is scheduled to occur every FrequencyRecurrenceFactor months on a day relative to the first day of the month.
SQLDMOFreq_OneTime	Activity is scheduled to occur one time.
SQLDMOFreq_OnIdle	Activity is scheduled to occur whenever SQL Server Agent is idle.
SQLDMOFreq_Unknown	Activity is not scheduled.
SQLDMOFreq_Weekly	Activity is scheduled to occur every FrequencyRecurrenceFactor weeks.

Frequency Interval Constants

Settings for the FrequencyInterval property depend on the values used for FrequencyType. FrequencyInterval has no meaning for run once, run at SQL Server Agent start, or CPU idle steps. The following table shows the meaning of FrequencyInterval for the different FrequencyType values.

FrequencyType	FrequencyInterval
SQLDMOFreq_Daily	Long integer. If FrequencyInterval is 4, the job runs every four days.
SQLDMOFreq_Monthly	Long integer representing the day of the month on which the job runs. If the frequency interval is 5, the job runs on the fifth day of every month.
SQLDMOFreq_MonthlyRelative	Activity is scheduled to occur every n months on a day relative to the first day of the month.
SQLDMOFreq_Weekly	Bit-packed long integer. Specify the days with the following constants: SQLDMOWeek_Sunday SQLDMOWeek_Monday SQLDMOWeek_Tuesday SQLDMOWeek_Wednesday SQLDMOWeek_Thursday SQLDMOWeek_Friday SQLDMOWeek_Saturday SQLDMOWeek_WeekDays SQLDMOWeek_WeekEnds For a job that runs weekly on Tuesday and Thursday, use the following: SQLDMOWeek_Tuesday + SQLDMOWeek_Thursday

Frequency Relative Interval Constants

Constant	Meaning
SQLDMOMonth_Day	Scheduled activity occurs on an occurrence of a day (such as the first day of the month).
SQLDMOMonth_Friday	Scheduled activity occurs on a Friday.
SQLDMOMonth_MaxValid	SQLDMOMonth_WeekEndDay.
SQLDMOMonth_MinValid	SQLDMOMonth_Sunday
SQLDMOMonth_Monday	Scheduled activity occurs on a Monday.
SQLDMOMonth_Saturday	Scheduled activity occurs on a Saturday.
SQLDMOMonth_Sunday	Scheduled activity occurs on a Sunday.
SQLDMOMonth_Thursday	Scheduled activity occurs on a Thursday.
SQLDMOMonth_Tuesday	Scheduled activity occurs on a Tuesday.
SQLDMOMonth_Unknown	Bad or invalid value.
SQLDMOMonth_Wednesday	Scheduled activity occurs on a Wednesday.
SQLDMOMonth_WeekDay	Scheduled activity occurs on a weekday (Monday through Friday).
SQLDMOMonth_WeekEndDay	Scheduled activity occurs on a weekend day (Saturday or Sunday).

Modifying and Deleting Jobs with DMO

To modify a job, locate the appropriate object in the Jobs collection of a JobServer object and change its properties. To modify a job step, locate the appropriate object in the JobSteps collection of a Job object and change its properties. To modify a job schedule, locate the appropriate object in the JobSchedules collection. Modify the properties of the JobSchedule object as well as any properties of its Schedule object.

To delete a job, use the Remove method of the Jobs collection of a JobServer object. To delete a job step, use the Remove method of the JobSteps collection of a Job object. To delete a job schedule, use the Remove method of the JobSchedules collection of a Job Object.

Testing a Job

After you have gone through the process of creating a job, you need not wait until it's scheduled runtime to see whether it works correctly. In fact, I recommend that you test and debug it after right after you create it. After all, you don't want to discover tomorrow morning that your backup command had a syntax error!

You can test jobs with Enterprise Manager, Transact-SQL, and DMO.

Testing a Job with Enterprise Manager

To test a job with Enterprise Manager, click on the Jobs icon. Select the job in the right pane, right-click, and choose Start Job. If it's a multistep job, you can select the step you want to start with. You will not see any evidence that the job is running. Right-click on the job, and choose Refresh Job. You then see changes in the Status column. After the job completes, you can determine whether it was successful.

 General Tip

It's a big pain to have to do all this refreshing in Enterprise Manager. It's necessary, however, because Enterprise Manager isn't constantly polling to see what is happening. If it did so, it would put extra demands on the SQL Server Agent and the SQL Server itself.

Testing a Job with Transact-SQL

To test a job with Transact-SQL, use the command `sp_start_job`:

```
sp_start_job {'job_name' | job_id}
[, error_flag] [, 'server_name']
[, 'step_name'] [, output_flag]
```

You must provide either a `job_name` or a `job_id`, but not both.

`server_name` is only applicable to multiserver jobs. It specifies the name of the server on which you want to run the job. The server must be one of the targeted servers.

Specify a `step_name` if you want to start at a step other than the first.

`error_flag` and `output_flag` are reserved for future use.

The `sp_start_job` stored procedure is in msdb.

Unfortunately, testing a job this way is not very gratifying. The only message you get is Job XXX Started Successfully. There is no indication of success or failure. To find out what happened, you either need to view the job history with Transact-SQL (see "Viewing Job History") or return to Enterprise Manager and look at it there.

Testing a Job with DMO

To test a job with DMO, locate the appropriate Job object in the JobServer object's Jobs collection, and use the Job's `Start` method. The method takes an optional argument, `step_name`, which you can use if you want to start at a step other than the first. You can use various properties of the Job and JobStep objects to interrogate the job's status and success or failure.

Viewing Job History

Job history is maintained at the job level and at the job step level. You can view this most easily with Enterprise Manager, but it is also possible to view it with Transact-SQL and DMO.

Viewing Job History with Enterprise Manager

To view job history in Enterprise Manager, you just right-click on the job in the right pane and choose View Job History. The default display shows the job level history only. To see step details, check the Show Step Details box at the top of the screen. You can also use this dialog box to delete all history for the job by clicking the Clear button.

Viewing Job History with Transact-SQL

If you want to view the job history with Transact-SQL, use the sp_help_job_history command, as shown here:

```
sp_help_jobhistory [{job_id ¦ 'job_name'}]
[, step_id] [, sql_message_id]
[, sql_severity] [, start_run_date]
[, end_run_date] [, start_run_time]
[, end_run_time] [, minimum_run_duration]
[, run_status] [, minimum_retries]
[, oldest_first] [, 'server']
[, 'mode']
```

 General Tip

If you look at the documentation for sp_help_job_history command, you will see that it appears to deal only with multiserver jobs. However, it works perfectly well with local jobs as well.

If you do not specify either job_id or job_name, you will see all jobs.

If you do not specify a step_id, you will see all the steps. If you want to see only a specific step, provide its step_id.

sql_message_id enables you to restrict the history display to a specific SQL Server error number. It must be an integer taken from the list of available SQL Server error numbers (including user-defined errors). This applies to Transact-SQL steps only.

sql_severity enables you to restrict the history display to a particular SQL Server severity level. It is an int and must be between 1 and 25. This applies to Transact-SQL steps only.

start_run_date and end_run_date enable you to restrict the history display to a particular start and/or end date. These dates must be entered in the form YYYYMMDD.

start_run_time and end_run_time enable you to restrict the history display to a particular start and/or end time. These times must be entered in the form HHMMSS.

minimum_run_duration enables you to view history for only those jobs that ran for at least a specific amount of time. You must enter the duration in the form HHMMSS.

run_status enables you to restrict the history display to jobs that completed with a specific status. The following table lists the valid values for run_status.

Value	Description
0	Failed
1	Succeeded
2	Retry (step only)
3	Canceled
4	In-progress message
5	Unknown

`minimum_retries` enables you to see only those jobs where a retry was attempted at least a certain number of times.

General Tip

The documentation says that this is the minimum number of times a job should retry (specified when the step was created), but in fact, the procedure compares the number of actual attempted retries to `minimum_retries`.

Use a value of 1 for `oldest_first` to request that the jobs be listed with the oldest first. By default, the jobs list with the newest first.

`server` enables you to restrict the history display to a specific server.

`mode` determines what columns appear in the output. Use FULL to get the most detailed information. Use SUMMARY to get a simpler report. SUMMARY is the default. The values for mode are not case sensitive.

To delete the job history for a specific job, use the command `sp_purge_jobhistory`:

```
sp_purge_jobhistory {'job_name' ¦ job_id}
```

You must provide a `job_name` or a `job_id`, but not both.

The `sp_help_jobhistory` and `sp_purge_jobhistory` stored procedures are in msdb.

General Tip

Note that this purges all history for the job. You may want to purge only part of the history. See Appendix D for sample code for purging history tables.

Viewing Job History with DMO

To view a job's history with DMO, you use the EnumHistory method of the Job object. This returns a QueryResults object that contains the history. This is equivalent to the FULL mode of `sp_help_jobhistory`. All jobs are included in the report.

To restrict the report, you need to modify the JobServer's JobHistoryFilter object before you invoke the EnumHistory method. You do not need to create this object; the JobServer object exposes it. The following table shows the properties of a JobHistoryFilter object.

Property	Description
EndRunDate	Restrict output to jobs with a specific EndRunDate. Long integer with a value in the form YYYYMMDD. If this property is 0, EndRunDate is ignored.
EndRunTime	Restrict output to jobs with a specific EndRunTime. Long integer with a value in the form HHMMSS. If this property is 0, EndRunTime is ignored.
JobID	Restrict output to a specific JobID.
JobName	Restrict output to a specific JobName.
MinimumRetries	Restrict output to jobs with attempted retries that meet or exceed the specified number.
MinimumRunDuration	Restrict output to jobs with a duration that meets or exceeds the specified number.
OldestFirst	True if you want the oldest jobs listed first, otherwise false.
OutcomeTypes	Restrict the output to a specific OutcomeType (see OutcomeTypes constants in the following section).
SQLMessageID	Restrict output to a specific SQL Server error number.
SQLSeverity	Restrict output to a specific SQL Server severity.
StartRunDate	Restrict output to jobs with a specific StartRunDate. Long integer with a value in the form YYYYMMDD. If this property is 0, StartRunDate is ignored.
StartRunTime	Restrict output to jobs with a specific StartRunTime. Long integer with a value in the form HHMMSS. If this property is 0, StartRunTime is ignored.

OutcomeTypes *Constants*

Constant	Description
SQLDMOJobOutcome_Cancelled	Restrict output to jobs cancelled by a user.
SQLDMOJobOutcome_Failed	Restrict output to jobs that failed.
SQLDMOJobOutcome_InProgress	Restrict output to jobs currently running.
SQLDMOJobOutcome_Succeeded	Restrict output to jobs that succeeded.
SQLDMOJobOutcome_Unknown	Do not restrict output by OutcomeType.

To remove the job history for all jobs, use the PurgeJobHistory method of the JobServer object. To remove the job history for a specific job, provide its ID or name in the JobHistoryFilter object before invoking the PurgeJobHistory method.

Alerts

You can define and maintain alerts with Enterprise Manager, Transact-SQL, and DMO. Again, I recommend starting with Enterprise Manager. If you create an alert in Enterprise Manager, and you want to see the underlying Transact-SQL, right-click on the alert in the details pane of Enterprise Manager and choose All Tasks, Script Alert.

SQL Server ships with some demo alerts; you may find it useful to study these alerts and see how they work.

Alerts can respond to SQL Server error messages. You can connect an alert to any of the SQL Server error conditions. You can also create your own error messages, and set up alerts that respond to these messages.

Be aware, however, that you are not allowed to define alerts for one SQL Server error: Error 1204, which occurs when SQL Server has run out of locks. The list of non-alert errors is stored in the Registry under the following key:

```
HKEY_LocalMachine\Software\MSSQLServ70\SQLServerAgent
```

You can add other alerts to this list, but do not remove Error 1204. It generates recursive alerts. You would add other alerts to this list only if you are finding that the alerting system is creating a performance problem because the number of alerts is higher than SQL Server Agent's alert processing rate. Even then, it's a last-resort solution. It is better to either increase the delay between alert responses, clear the NT Application event log, or correct the problem causing the alert to fire.

 General Tip
You may also see Error 4002 in the list in the Registry. This is not a valid error in SQL Server 7.0, but was the error raised for a login failure in previous versions.

Alerts can also respond to performance conditions. These alerts are based on the same objects and counters available in Performance Monitor. (Chapter 10, "Performance Tuning," contains more information on Performance Monitor.) There are 16 objects, but only 10 of them are available for performance condition alerts. It's not possible to create alerts on the replication objects or on the BackupDevice object. The available objects and counters are described in Books Online, and are discussed in more detail in Chapter 10. Many of the counters are not really something you would want to be notified about; rather, they are statistics that you would track over time as part of a performance-monitoring plan. For example, it's probably not useful to receive an email telling you that the cache hit ratio has just fallen below 80%. Chances are that it will go back up again once the data for the current query is all in the cache. You are, of course, free to define alerts for any or all of them. The following tables show the counters that I think are most useful. I've organized the tables by object.

SQL Server: Databases Object

The following counters are maintained for each database. You can specify which database instance you want to use when you define the alert.

Counter	Description
Data File(s) Size (KB)	Cumulative size (in kilobytes) of all the data files in the database, including any automatic growth. If you know that there is limited disk space, you can set up an alert that notifies you before the database runs out of space.
Log Growths	Total number of times the transaction log for the database has been expanded. If you are experiencing a high rate of log growths, the initial allocation for the log was possibly too small, or the amount added each time may be too small. You can set up an alert that notifies you of a high number of growths, and then add files or change the increment for the transaction log.
Percent Log Used	Percentage of space in the log in use. If you have not set your log up to autogrow, you could use this counter to notify you when a certain percentage of the log is used. You could then expand the log or back it up to free space before the users start encountering errors.

SQL Server: General Statistics Object

Counter	Description
User Connections	If you know that your server can handle a certain number of connections, you can create an alert that notifies you when the anticipated number is being exceeded.

SQL Server: User Settable Object

This is a very useful object, because it enables you to define up to 10 different measures. You can tie alerts to these measures. You can also see the measures in Performance Monitor. The counters are named User Counter 1 through User Counter 10. To use these counters, you must use stored procedures named sp_user_counter1 through sp_user_counter10. The procedure named sp_user_counter1 provides a value for User Counter 1; the one named sp_user_counter2 provides a value for User Counter 2, and so forth. The procedures take a single input parameter that must be an integer. These procedures are not automatically executed. You must execute the stored procedure through an application. (You could set up a job that runs them at a particular interval, for example, or use triggers to update them when conditions in a particular table change.) With these counters, you can tie alerts to conditions such as the number of rows in a table. To store the count of the number of rows in Northwind's Order Details table in User Counter 1, you would write Transact-SQL as follows:

```
declare @NumRows int
SELECT count(*) from [Order Details]
exec sp_user_counter1 @NumRows
```

You can also insert your code directly into the sp_user_counterx procedures, and then execute them.

Message Management

You can use SQL Server's message management capabilities without using alerts at all, but the topic fits in very nicely here. After that, I describe the process of creating and maintaining alerts.

A table named sysmessages in the master database contains SQL Server's error messages. A message has an error number, a severity, and a description. A message can also have an optional language ID; this enables you to use the same error number and severity but provide messages in different languages.

Error numbers for user-defined messages must be 50000 or higher.

Severity levels in SQL Server range from 0 to 25. Messages with severity levels 10 and below are informational. Levels 11 to 16 are errors that can be corrected by the user. Level 17 is used for insufficient resource conditions. Severity levels 18 and 19 indicate a non-fatal internal error. Severity levels 20–25 are serious, fatal errors and almost always mean your SQL Server or some database is about to crash.

When you define a message, you can request that it always be written to the NT Application event Log. Some messages issued by SQL Server are already defined that way. You can also change the predefined messages so that they are written to the event log. Any message written to the NT log are also written to the SQL Server error log. It's also possible to request that the message be logged at the time the error occurs.

You can manage messages with Enterprise Manager or Transact-SQL. You cannot manage messages with DMO.

Managing Messages with Enterprise Manager

To get to the message management features in Enterprise Manager, highlight a server in the console pane and choose Manage SQL Server Messages from the Tools menu. The search screen shown in Figure 8.15 displays.

Figure 8.15   Message Search screen.

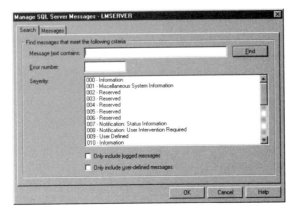

You can search for messages based on one of the severities shown in the drop-down list, or a specific error number, or a part of the message. You can restrict the results to only show you logged messages or only user-defined messages. These criteria can be combined. When you have entered the criteria, click the Find button. The Messages screen shown in Figure 8.16 displays.

General Tip

You would think that you could just click on the Messages tab without filling in criteria and see all messages. However, all you will see is an empty screen. To see all messages, you must click the Find button.

Figure 8.16   Message results screen.

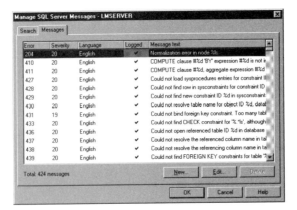

This screen lists all the messages that matched your criteria. You can use this screen to edit existing messages, create new messages, and delete messages. Note that you can't delete SQL Server messages. To create a new message, just click New. To edit an existing message, highlight the message in the list and click Edit. The screen shown in Figure 8.17 displays.

Figure 8.17   Message Entry and Edit screen.

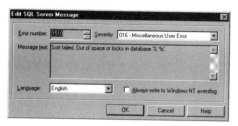

You are not allowed to edit the text of a SQL Server message. However, you can change the flag that causes it to be written to the event log. This is important if you want to define an alert for a message that isn't normally logged.

    General Tip

If SQL Server has defined the message as logged, you cannot change it so that it isn't logged.

Managing Messages with Transact-SQL

Transact-SQL doesn't provide a nice search facility like Enterprise Manager does. You can locate messages by issuing queries against the sysmessages table, but that's about it. The sysmessages table does not contain a clear indication that messages are logged. When you add a logged message, the column named dlevel is set to 128. However, other logged messages do not have values of 128 for dlevel. The algorithm for determining whether a system message is logged is not documented.

To add a message to sysmessages, or to modify its text and/or severity level, use the command sp_add_message:

```
sp_addmessage msg_id, severity, 'msg'
[, 'language'] [, 'with_log']
[, 'replace']
```

msg_id is the number assigned to the message. severity is its severity level.

msg is the message itself. The message can contain placeholders similar to those used in C's printf. These placeholders can be replaced with actual values when the message is raised.

language is the name of the language that the message goes with. It must be a language installed on your server. If you don't specify language, it defaults to the language of the connection that issues the command. Language is part of the key for messages, and must be supplied if you are replacing message text and have the same message for multiple languages.

with_log must be TRUE if you want the message to be written to the NT event Log. If you do not specify with_log, it defaults to FALSE.

Use replace when you want to change the severity level or text of an existing message. You must use the value REPLACE for this parameter. Note that if you change the severity level of a message that has language US English, severity level is changed for messages in all languages for that message_id.

If you want to change the logged nature of a message, use sp_alter_message:

```
sp_altermessage message_number, 'WITH_LOG',
    'value'
```

Value is either TRUE or FALSE.

General Tip

If you use REPLACE on all your sp_addmessage commands, you don't have to worry about whether the message exists. If the message isn't there, it is added. If it is there, it is modified.

To delete a message, use sp_dropmessage as shown here:

```
sp_dropmessage message_number [, 'language']
```

message_number is the number of the message to be dropped. It must be 50000 or higher. If you have the same message_number in multiple languages, specify a language to drop only one. Use All as the value for language to drop all messages with the same number.

Creating and Maintaining Alerts with Enterprise Manager

To create an alert with Enterprise Manager, right-click the SQL Server Agent and choose New, Alert. The screen shown in Figure 8.18 displays.

This screen is used for defining alerts that respond to SQL Server errors. You must give the alert a name. The alert is enabled by default; you can disable it by unchecking the enabled box. If you want to respond to a specific error number, click the option button next to error number. If you know the number, you can just type it. If you click the Browse button, you will see the message search screen discussed previously. Your alert does not have to respond to a specific number; you can have it respond to all messages with a given security level by clicking the option button next to Severity and choosing the level from the drop-down list. You can restrict the alert to a specific database, or you can have it respond when the error or severity level occurs in any database. You can restrict the alert to a specific text string that appears in the error messages. This string will be used in a LIKE comparison, so you can include wild cards.

Figure 8.18   Event alert definition screen.

 General Tip

Be certain that what you put in the Error Message Contains This Text Box actually appears in the error message. The alert won't fire if the string doesn't match exactly.

If you want to create a performance condition alert, select SQL Server Performance Condition Alert from the Type drop-down list. The screen changes to the one shown in Figure 8.19.

Figure 8.19   Performance Condition Alert screen.

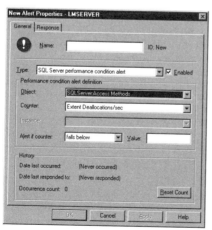

You select the object and counter from the drop-down lists. If the counter has different instances, such as a database, you can select the instance from the drop-down list as well. These alerts are threshold alerts. You can have the alert fire when the counter falls below some value, becomes equal to some value, or rises above some value.

The second part of the alert is the response. You define responses on the screen shown in Figure 8.20.

Figure 8.20   Alert Response screen.

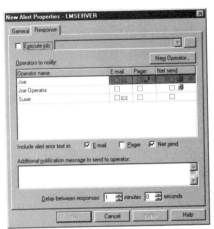

It's possible to run a job in response to an alert. To do this, check the Execute Job box. You can then select the job from the list of available jobs. If you have not already created the job, choose New Job, which takes you to the Job Creation screen (shown in Figure 8.10). The Browse button enables you to see the properties of the job. All the operators you have defined show in the Operator list. If you haven't created the operator, the New Operator button takes you to the Operator Creation screen (as shown in Figure 8.8). You must check the boxes beneath the type of notification or no notices will be sent. If you want Joe to be notified by email, pager, and NET SEND, for example, you must check all three boxes. You can include the error text in the messages by checking the appropriate boxes. You can also supply additional text that will be sent to the operator. This is free form; you can put whatever you want in this notification.

At the bottom of the screen is a place to delay between responses. It's important to use this field. It takes some time for the operator to resolve the problem; and, particularly with performance condition alerts, the situation will continue to happen. If you set up an alert on total database size, for example, after the database reaches that size, it's likely to stay there or increase. If you didn't delay between responses, the operator's inbox or pager would be flooded with notifications.

General Tip

If you have not installed SQL Server Service Pack 1, the delay between responses does not work for performance condition alerts. The response is sent every 20 seconds no matter what you specify for the delay. This bug is fixed in SP1.

To modify an alert, just right-click on it in the details pane and choose Properties. To delete an alert, right-click on it and choose Delete.

Creating and Maintaining Alerts with Transact-SQL

All the commands that deal with alerts are stored procedures in msdb. Alerts have two parts: the alert itself and its notifications. To add an alert, use the command `sp_add_alert`:

```
sp_add_alert 'name'
[, {message_id | severity}]
[, enabled] [, delay_between_responses]
[, 'notification_message']
[, include_event_description_in]
[, 'database']
[, [ 'event_description_keyword_pattern']
[, {job_id | 'job_name'}]
[, raise_snmp_trap]
[, [ 'performance_condition']
[, 'category']
```

`name` is required.

`message_ID` is the error number. It defaults to 0. It must be 0 if severity is provided.

`severity` is the severity level that the alert responds to. It must be a value from 1 to 25. If `message_id` is provided, it must be 0.

The default for `enabled` is 1 (true). Use 0 to disable an alert.

`delay_between_responses` is the number of seconds to wait before sending notifications.

`notification_message` is the additional message to be sent to the operator. It can be up to 512 Unicode characters. It defaults to null.

`include_event_description_in` specifies what types of notifications should have the error message included. Values must be taken from the following table.

Value	Description
0	None
1	Email
2	Pager
4	NET SEND

The values are added together to specify multiple types. The default is 5: email and NET SEND (1 + 4). To include the description in all notifications, use 7 (1 + 2 + 4).

`database` contains the name of a database, if the alert is associated with a specific database. It should be null when the alert applies to all databases.

`event_description_keyword_pattern` is a definition of a string that must be found in the error message for the alert to fire. It is used in a LIKE comparison, and the LIKE wildcards (%, _) can be used. The pattern is `nvarchar(100)`.

If the alert is to execute a job, provide either the `job_id` or the `job_name`, but not both.

`raise_snmp_trap` takes a value of 0 (no) or 1. The default is 0. SQL Server 7.0 alerts cannot raise SNMP traps.

`performance_condition` is the name of the condition to which the alert is tied. This name must be provided in the form shown here:

```
object¦counter¦instance¦comparator¦value
```

`comparator` is <, >, or =. `value` is a number. The names of the object and counter must match those in the table sysperfinfo, which is in master. `instance` may be omitted, but the vertical bars must still be there.

```
SQLServer:General Statistics¦ User Connections¦¦>¦300
```

Appendix B, "Performance Condition Alert Objects, Counters, and Instances," contains a table of the valid object, counter, and instance (other than database name) values.

`category` is the name of the category to which this alert belongs. You must have already defined the category before you can use it here.

After you have created the alert, you must use the command `sp_add_notification` to add each operator who should be notified when the alert fires:

```
sp_add_notification 'alert', 'operator',
notification_method
```

`alert` is the name of the alert.

`operator` is the name of the operator.

`notification_method` is taken from the following table.

Value	Description
1	Email
2	Pager
4	NET SEND

The values must be added together if you want the operator to be notified by multiple methods. To notify the operator by email and NET SEND, for example, use the value 5.

To modify an alert, use `sp_update_alert` as shown here:

```
sp_updatealert 'name' [,'new_name']
[, enabled]
[, {message_id ¦ severity}]
[, delay_between_responses]
[, 'notification_message']
```

```
[, include_event_description_in]
[, 'database_name']
[, 'event_description_keyword']
[, {job_id ¦ 'job_name'}]
[, occurrence_count] [, count_reset_date]
[, count_reset_time]
[, last_occurrence_date]
[, last_occurrence_time]
[, last_response_date]
[, last_response _time]
[, raise_snmp_trap]
[,'performance_condition']
[, [@category_name =] 'category']
```

You must be in the msdb database to issue this command; exec
msdb..sp_update_alert does not work.

Most of the parameters are the same as those for adding an alert. You
must provide the name of the alert. Use the new_name parameter if you
want to change the name of the alert.

SQL Server keeps track of the number of times the alert has occurred
as well as the date and time it happened last and the date and time it
was last responded to. You can modify these fields, and you should
modify them when you change characteristics of the alert because they
no longer contain meaningful information. occurrence_count,
last_occurrence_date, last_occurrence_time, last_response_date, and
last_response_time can only be set to 0. No other value is permitted.
When you set the occurrence_count to 0, SQL Server does not set the
count_reset_date or time fields. If you modify the occurrence_count,
you should set those fields. count_reset_date must be in the form
YYYYMMDD, and count_reset_time must be in the form HHMMSS.

To modify a notification, use sp_update_notification. You must run this
command from the msdb database. The parameters for this command
are identical to the ones for sp_add_notification.

To delete an alert, use sp_delete_alert. It takes a single parameter: the
name of the alert. You must run this command from the msdb database.
When you delete an alert, all notifications for that alert are also deleted.

To delete a notification, use sp_delete_notification. It takes two
parameters: the name of the alert and the name of the operator. Neither
the alert nor the operator is affected when you delete a notification;
only the notification is deleted. You must run this command from the
msdb database.

Creating and Maintaining Alerts with DMO

When you want to add an alert using DMO, you create an Alert object.
Specify its properties, and add it to the Alerts collection of a JobServer
object. Note that an alert is not active until you have added at least one
notification to it using the AddNotification method of either an Alert
object or an Operator object. The following table describes the
properties of an Alert object.

Property	Description
Category	The name of a category.
CountResetDate	Date the occurrence count was reset.
CountResetTime	Time the occurrence count was reset.
DatabaseName	Name of the database the alert is restricted to, if any.
DelayBetweenResponses	Number of seconds to wait before responding again to the same alert.
Enabled	True if the alert is enabled, false otherwise.
EventCategoryID	Reserved for future use.
EventDescriptionKeyword	Pattern to search for in the error message string; comparison is with LIKE.
EventID	Reserved for future use.
EventSource	Reserved for future use.
HasNotification	Total number of operators who may be notified of this alert (read-only).
ID	Internal identifier.
IncludeEventDescription	Specifies whether the error message should be included in responses. Values for this property must be taken from the table of IncludeEventDescription constants that is given in the following section.
JobID	ID of job to run when the alert fires. Note that in DMO you must provide the ID. The name property is read-only.
JobName	Name of the job.
LastOccurrenceDate	Date the alert last fired.
LastOccurrenceTime	Time the alert last fired.
LastResponseDate	Date the alert last sent a response to an operator.
LastResponseTime	Time the alert last sent a response to an operator.
MessageID	Error number. You cannot specify both a MessageID and a Severity.
Name	Name of the alert.
NotificationMessage	Additional message text to send to the operator.
OccurrenceCount	Number of times the alert has fired.
PerformanceCondition	String that specifies an object, counter, instance, comparator, and value. See the discussion of how this must be formatted in the Transact-SQL section.

Property	Description
Severity	Long integer with a value from 1–25. You cannot specify Severity if you specified a MessageID.
Type	Alert type. Values for this property must be take from the table of type constants shown in the following section.

IncludeEventDescription *Constants*

Constant	Description
SQLDMONotify_All	Always include the alert error text regardless of the notification method used.
SQLDMONotify_Email	Include the alert error text when notifying by email.
SQLDMONotify_NetSend	Include the alert error text when notifying by NET SEND.
SQLDMONotify_None	Do not include alert error text in any notification attempt.
SQLDMONotify_Pager	Include the alert error text when notifying by pager.

These constants can be combined. If you want to include the description in email and NET SEND, you set the IncludeEventDescription property to the following:

```
SQLDMONotify_Email + SQLDMONotify_NetSend
```

Type Constants

Constant	Description
SQLDMOAlert_NonSQLServer Event	Alert is raised by an event not defined for SQL Server.
SQLDMOAlert_SQLServerEvent	Alert is raised when a specified SQL Server error condition, or any error condition of a specified severity, occurs.
SQLDMOAlert_SQLServer PerformanceCondition	Alert is raised when a performance condition rises above, falls below, or equals a threshold.

The first of these constants is interesting, because there is currently no way to use this alerting mechanism outside of SQL Server. I have often speculated that it was likely to appear in a broader context at some point. I wonder if the first constant bears that out.

To make the alert active, you must add at least one notification. To add a notification, use the AddNotification method of the Alert object. It has two arguments. The first is the operator name. The second is the notification type, which is a long integer. The following table shows the constants for this argument.

NotificationType Constant	Description
SQLDMONotify_All	Always include the alert error text regardless of the notification method used.
SQLDMONotify_Email	Include the alert error text when notifying by email.
SQLDMONotify_NetSend	Include the alert error text when notifying by NET SEND.
SQLDMONotify_None	Do not include alert error text in any notification attempt.
SQLDMONotify_Pager	Include the alert error text when notifying by pager.

These constants can be combined. If you want to notify the operator by email and NET SEND, pass the following as the `NotificationType` argument:

```
SQLDMONotify_Email + SQLDMONotify_NetSend
```

To modify an alert, find the appropriate Alert object in the Alerts collection of a JobServer object. Use the `BeginAlter` method, and then modify its properties. Because any alert history is no longer meaningful, use the `ResetOccurrenceCount` method to set the occurrence count and related dates and times to 0. The method updates the `CountResetDate` and `CountResetTime` properties for you. Use the `DoAlter` method to send the changes to SQL Server.

To modify a notification, use the `UpdateNotification` method. It has the same arguments as the `AddNotification` method.

When you want to delete an alert, locate the appropriate alert in the Alerts collection of a JobServer, and use the Alerts collection's `Remove` method. All notifications for that alert will be deleted. To delete a single notification, use the `DeleteNotification` method of an Alert object.

Multiserver Jobs

SQL Server 7.0 enables you to define a server as a *master* server. You can define jobs on the master server and download them to many *target* servers. Although the process is referred to as downloading, in fact, the target servers must poll the master periodically and pull down jobs to themselves. These target servers run the jobs and report the results back to the master server. This provides you with centralized monitoring and management. The target servers need not be connected to the master at the time the jobs run. Only SQL Servers running on Windows NT can be master or target servers.

Target servers are described as enlisting with the master and defecting from the master. A master server is referred to as an *MSX*; a target server is referred to as a *TSX*. A target server can enlist with only one MSX. If the TSX wants to enlist with a different MSX, it must first defect.

Target servers must log in to NT with a domain account (see Chapter 2 for more details on this). It is not possible to enlist a target server that is logged in as LocalSystem. The TSX NT login does not have to be the same as the MSX login.

A special operator must be named MSXOperator. This operator is created on the master and target servers and is the only operator that can receive notifications from the jobs that run on a target server.

If you are planning to use a SQL Server as a master server, you should choose one that is not heavily used. If you are using the alert-forwarding feature, you might want to make a master server the alert-forwarding server for all its targets. In that way, you have a central point for managing the servers.

᠎᠎ IMO

I do not recommend attempting to set up a master-target server architecture with Transact-SQL or DMO. The support is incomplete, and some of the setup operations are done with direct INSERT statements into tables in msdb. Use Enterprise Manager to set up master and target servers.

Setting up a Master-Target Architecture with Enterprise Manager

Servers that will be targets must be registered with Enterprise Manager. Although you can, and normally would, register servers so that a prompt for password is issued when someone tries to connect, that won't work for setting up target servers. You must change the option and specify the password explicitly. You can register the servers in advance, or during the process of making a master server.

You must be able to connect to all the target servers during the setup process, which means that they must be running and connected to the network.

You must enlist at least one target when you create a master server. After that, individual servers can enlist themselves or you can enlist them.

To set up an MSX, right-click on the SQL Server Agent icon in the console tree, and then choose Multi Server Administration, Make This a Master. The Make Master Server Wizard appears. It is extremely simple to use. The first thing you need to do is to provide email, pager, and/or NET SEND addresses for the MSXOperator. Because you, as the administrator, will no doubt have responsibility for managing this, you can use your own email address or that of the person whom you want to receive notifications.

After the MSX operator is created, a list of potential target servers displays. Check the ones you want. If there are targets you want that aren't listed, use the Register Server button and register them. After you have selected targets, a screen that lists the targets displays. You can enter a description for each target on this screen if you want to. A description is not required, but could be helpful in showing you and others where the machines are located. After you enter the descriptions, click Next, and then click Finish on the following screen to begin the process.

After you have configured the server as an MSX, you will see that the SQL Server Agent now shows (MSX) next to it in the console pane. An operator named MSXOperator shows in the list of operators. If you expand the Jobs icon, you will see that you now have two types of jobs: Local and MultiServer. A login has also been created for each target server. These logins have names in the form TSXname_msx_probe and allow the target servers to log in to the MSX.

Managing Target Servers

The purpose of target servers is to run jobs downloaded to them. Creating a multiserver job is almost the same as creating a local job. On the General Job Properties screen, click the Target Multiple Servers button. (If you right-click on MultiServer Jobs and choose New, Target Multiple Servers is already selected.) To specify the servers the job should be sent to, click the Change button. The screen shown in Figure 8.21 displays.

Figure 8.21   Selecting target servers.

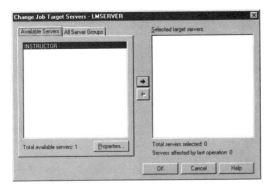

 General Tip

When you are designing jobs for target servers, you need to keep in mind that they run in the target server's NT context. If you are creating a backup job that writes a backup to F:\MYBACKUPS\NWIND.BAK, for example, you have to make sure that *all* the targets have a directory named F:\MYBACKUPS.

Available target servers are shown on the left. Select one, and then click the arrow to move it to the right-hand window. This is a really annoying interface. There is no multiple selection in either window. You must select each target individually.

You will notice that there is a tab labeled All Server Groups. There is clearly a concept of grouping target servers, but this does not seem to be implemented fully in this release. There are references to it in Transact-SQL and in DMO, but Enterprise Manager does not seem to provide a way to specify groups.

After you have selected the target servers, continue with the job definition as described previously.

When the job is completed, you can wait for the targets to connect and download the job, or you can force them to poll. The latter, as well as other multiserver administrative tasks including monitoring status of downloads, is accomplished with the Manage Target Servers function. Right-click on the SQL Server Agent and choose Multi Server Administration, Manage Target Servers. The screen shown in Figure 8.22 displays.

Figure 8.22   Target server status.

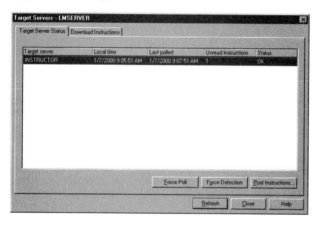

This screen shows you all the target servers with the time they last polled the master. It also shows you whether there are unread instructions and the status. This screen contains three buttons that perform different functions:

- Force Poll makes the highlighted target server(s) poll the MSX immediately.
- Post Instructions sends a message to the target server telling it to defect. This is the best way to get a target to defect.
- If the target is inaccessible or damaged, use the Force Defection button to remove it from the list of target servers.

You can also monitor the download status for a particular target server or all target servers. When you click on the Download Instructions tab, the screen shown in Figure 8.23 displays.

Figure 8.23   Download Status screen.

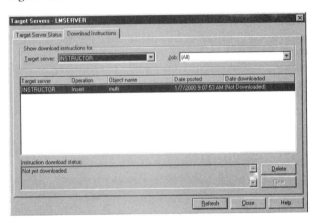

You can view status for a specific target and a specific job.

Under the Covers

The SQL Server Agent subsystem operates entirely with tables in msdb. Fourteen tables are used for jobs, operators, and alerts. (Others are used for replication and database maintenance plans, but I do not discuss those here.) Following are the tables that are used:

- **syscategories** stores the job, alert, and operator categories.

- **sysalerts** contains the basic information about alerts: name, message, and so on.

- **sysnotifications** maintains the relationship between sysalerts and sysoperators. It contains the `alert_id`, the `operator_id`, and the `notification` method.

- **sysoperators** stores information about operators.

- **sysjobs** contains the job definition and notification information. It is related in a one-to-many relationship with sysjobhistory, sysjobschedules, sysjobsteps, sysjobservers, and systaskids.

- **sysjobhistory** contains both job and step history for every job that has run. The size of this table depends on how you configure the SQL Server Agent and whether you periodically clear the job history, either with built-in tools or your own custom routines.

- **sysjobschedules** contains all the schedules for every job.

- **sysjobsteps** contains the detailed steps for every job.

- **systaskids** is used when tasks from earlier versions of SQL Server are upgraded to SQL Server 7.0 jobs. It contains a mapping of the old `taskid` into the new `jobid`.

- **sysjobservers** maintains the relationship between jobs and target servers, and stores outcome information for the last execution of the job on the specific target.

- **systargetservers** contains the description of each TSX. It is related to sysdownloadlist in a one-to-many relationship.

- **sysdownloadlist** contains instructions to be downloaded to the target server. These include jobs and the instruction that tells the target server to defect.

- **systargetservergroups** defines target server groups and is related in a one-to-many relationship with systargetservers and systargetservergroupmembers. I don't understand this; it seems that group membership is reflected twice. But as I mentioned earlier, I don't think target server groups are fully implemented in this release.

 General Tip

If you have the SQL Server 7.0 System Table Map that MSDN published, you will find that some of the definitions of these tables are incomplete. Some columns are missing. If you check out the documentation in Books OnLine, you will sometimes find that it is inaccurate, as well. For example, the documentation for sysdownloadlist doesn't mention the class of instructions that tell a server to defect, but `sp_post_msx_operation` clearly places these instructions there.

9

Security

One of your most important tasks is to manage the security of the SQL Servers you are responsible for. The first section of this chapter outlines some of the underlying concepts of SQL Server security as well as some of the things you need to think about when designing your security plan. After that, this chapter explains how to implement the various levels of security that SQL Server provides. This chapter also provides some information on how to use views to enforce security.

Concepts

This section first presents SQL Server's security model. Then, the discussion turns to the details of each level of security available in SQL Server. This section ends with a discussion about how to design your security plan.

Security Model

SQL Server provides security at several levels:

- **Login.** Anyone who is to log in to SQL Server must be authorized to do so by an administrator.
- **Database.** Anyone who is allowed to access a database must be given permission to do so.
- **Object.** An administrator must give any database user permission to see or change data in tables, to use views, and to execute stored procedures.
- **Statement.** Some statements require permission before a user can issue them. These include the statements that create objects and those that back up databases and transaction logs.

The following subsections describe each of these levels.

Login Security

Every SQL Server user must have a SQL Server login. There are two types of logins:

- SQL Server Authentication logins
- NT Authentication logins

It is possible to use both types of logins on any SQL Server.

General Tip
You may want to use NT Authentication on new applications or new servers. After all, Microsoft may drop support for SQL Server Authentication in some future release.

SQL Server Authentication

When you use SQL Server Authentication, each user has a unique login ID and password. The login is specific to SQL Server and has nothing to do with the user's login to NT. The user logs in to NT with his or her NT login ID and password, and then logs in to SQL Server using his or her SQL Server login and password. I use this all the time—I log in to NT with my NT login, Sharon, and then log in to SQL Server as sa with my sa password.

NT Authentication

When you use NT Authentication, the user logs in to NT with his or her password. When the user connects to SQL Server, SQL Server checks to see whether the network name of the user (the NT login) has been authorized to use the SQL Server. If so, the user is allowed in; if not, the user cannot access the SQL Server. It's also possible to deny access to a particular NT login. NT groups can also be granted access to SQL Server, and you will probably find it easiest to manage complex security schemes by using NT groups. I talk more about this later.

General Tip
NT Authentication is sometimes called *integrated security* or *trusted connections.*

IMO
Those of you who struggled with integrated security in previous versions of SQL Server will be pleased to know that it is much easier to manage in SQL Server 7.0. The standalone Security Manager tool is gone. NT Authentication logins are managed just like SQL Server logins.

General Tip
All the SQL Server 7.0 netlibs (except Banyan VINES and AppleTalk) support NT
Authentication.

Fixed Server Roles

Each login, regardless of how it is authenticated, can be a member of
one or more server roles. Server roles are predefined, and you can't
create new ones. These roles enable you to delegate a portion of the
administrator's tasks. A login has the sum of the privileges of all the roles
in which it is a member. If Joe is a member of the dbcreator role and
the securityadmin role, for example, he can perform the activities
associated with both roles. The roles, and the privileges associated with
them, are listed here:

- **sysadmin.** This is the most powerful role in SQL Server. It is the
  equivalent of the sa login in previous versions of SQL Server. Members
  of the sysadmin role can perform any activity in SQL Server. The sa
  login, which is maintained for backward compatibility, is always a
  member or this role and cannot be removed from it.

 IMO
The sa account has no password when SQL Server is installed. You should password
protect it, but not use it. Instead, define logins (either NT Authentication or SQL
Server Authentication) and make them members of the sysadmin role. In previous
versions of SQL Server, you could only have multiple SQL Server administrators by
sharing the sa password. With the sysadmin role, you can have more than one person
authorized to perform administrative functions, but each will have his or her own
login and password. If you set the server up so that it uses only NT Authentication,
you don't need to worry about the sa password.

 Warning
By default, the NT Administrators group on the SQL Server computer is a member of
the sysadmin role. You can remove the BUILTIN\Administrators group from the
sysadmin role if you don't want the NT Administrators to be able to administer your
SQL Server. If you remove this login from the sysadmins role using a Transact-SQL
command, you must be sure to specify BUILTIN in all caps.

- **serveradmin.** Members of this role can set systemwide configuration
  options and stop the SQL Server.
- **setupadmin.** Members of this role can configure linked servers and
  mark a stored procedure as a startup procedure.
  A startup stored procedure runs whenever the SQL Server is started.
- **securityadmin.** Members of this role can add and delete logins, and
  grant Create Database permissions.

Although the securityadmin role can create logins, it cannot change passwords after the login has been created. Only the user itself or a member of the sysadmin role can change a user's password.

- **processadmin.** Members of this role can kill processes.
- **dbcreator.** Members of the dbcreator role can create databases.

A member of the dbcreator role does not need to be a user in the master database. Granting Create Database statement privileges also enables someone to create databases, but you must first make the login a user in the master database.

- **diskadmin.** Members of the diskadmin role can manage disk files.

The diskadmin role actually can do only one thing relevant to SQL Server 7.0: create a backup device. All the other permissions given to this role are for commands that existed in previous versions of SQL Server. Many of the commands have been removed or have limited support.

To see a complete listing of all the commands that can be issued by a fixed server role, use the following command:

```
sp_srvrolepermission rolename
```

General Tip

It's not possible to change the permissions given to the server roles.

Database Security

When you create a SQL Server login, it has very limited rights. It will be able to access some stored procedures in master, and work with the Northwind and pubs sample databases. It can do this because those databases have a guest user. Any other database access must be explicitly given to the login.

After a login has been given access to a database, the login can be made a member of one or more database roles. Fixed database roles with specific permissions exist in each database; you can define additional roles that will help you manage your security scheme.

General Tip

Previous versions of SQL Server had something called a *group* that could be used to manage permissions. Roles are similar in concept but much more powerful because a user can be a member of more than one role and receives the cumulative set of permissions given to those roles. In previous versions, a user could be a member of only a single group.

Database Users

Before a login can access a database, it must be made a user of the database. It is possible for any login to have a name in the database that differs from his or her SQL Server login name. This is most visible when the user owns the database. In that case, the user loses his or her login identity and is known just as *dbo*.

❝ IMO

I don't recommend giving users database names that differ from their login names. It's confusing, and adds no value.

Some useful functions provide information about user identities; the following table shows these functions.

Function	Description
SUSER_SNAME(*securityid*)	This function returns a login name. If the security ID is given, the name associated with that SQL Server SID is returned. If the function is invoked without a security ID; such as SUSER_SNAME(), the function returns the login name of the current user.
SYSTEM_USER	This niladic function is provided for ANSI compliance. It is identical to SUSER_SNAME().
USER_NAME(*database_user_id*)	This function returns the database username. If the database_user_id is given, the name associated with that database_user_id is returned. If the function is invoked without a database_user_id, such as USER_NAME(), the function returns the database name of the current user.
CURRENT_USER, SESSION_USER, USER	These ANSI-compliant niladic functions are identical to USER_NAME(). Note that USER is provided for backward compatibility with earlier versions of the ANSI standard.

If you are maintaining audit trails or marking records with the name of the person who inserted or changed them, you should always use SUSER_SNAME. The login name is invariant; it doesn't matter what the user's name in the database is. For example, I log in to NT as SHARON. I'm the owner of a database named TEST. In TEST, SELECT suser_sname() would return SHARON, whereas SELECT user_name() would return dbo.

> **⚠ Warning**
>
> SUSER_SNAME ( ) returns NT Authentication login names in uppercase. This caused a problem for me when I was comparing it to some application-specific tables that stored the login name for use in views implementing row-level security. My server was case sensitive. (Views and row-level security are discussed in more detail later in this chapter.)

The Guest User

It is possible to add a user named guest to any database. When a database has a guest user, any login can access the database. You can assign privileges to the guest user just as you would any other user. There is always a guest user in master and tempdb; you must not delete it because all users must be able to access these databases. When you install SQL Server, a guest user is created in the sample databases Northwind and pubs. This allows all logins to access these databases.

> **❝❝ IMO**
>
> It's a good idea to leave the guest user in the sample databases so that people can use them for practice. If you remove it, you will have to authorize users and grant them permissions. You likely have better things to do with your time.

The dbo User

Each database has a "special" user named dbo. The login that creates the database is its owner. The dbo has full power over the database. dbo operates outside the permissions scheme for the database, just as members of the sysadmin role operate outside the permission scheme for the whole server. It is possible to change database ownership with Transact-SQL or DMO; it cannot be done in Enterprise Manager. Only members of the sysadmin role or the database owner can change database ownership.

Changing Database Ownership with Transact-SQL

To change the database owner in Transact-SQL, use the sp_changedbowner command:

```
sp_changedbowner newownerlogin, remapaliases
```

You must use the database whose owner is to be changed. The login must not already be a user in the database. remapaliases specifies whether aliased users should be mapped to the new owner. (See the section "Aliases" later in this chapter.) If you specify true or omit the parameter, the aliases will be mapped to the new owner. If you specify false, existing aliases are dropped.

Changing Database Ownership with DMO

To change database ownership with DMO, use the SetOwner method of a Database object. As shown in the following table, the SetOwner method has three arguments:

Argument	Description
Login	The login name of the new owner.
TransferAliases	If this argument is true, users who were aliased to the previous owner are remapped to the new owner. If it is false, the aliases are dropped.
SetOverrideIfAlreadyUser	If this argument is true, and LoginName is currently a user in the database, the login is dropped and then made the database owner. If this argument is false, and LoginName is already a user in the database, the method fails and returns an error message.

Aliases

Previous versions of SQL Server enabled you to alias one database user to another. This was most often used to allow several people to share the dbo function. This capability is provided in SQL Server 7.0 only for backward compatibility. The documentation states that "Microsoft SQL Server version 7.0 provides roles and the ability to grant permissions to roles as an alternative to using aliases." However, the roles that are provided do not provide the flexibility of the old alias feature.

 Warning

If you use aliases in 7.0, they will work. Support for this feature may go away in future versions of SQL Server, however, so use aliases with caution. Hopefully, Microsoft will sort out the db_owner role before it takes away aliases.

Fixed Database Roles

Each database has a set of predefined database roles. These have specific permissions, and the permissions cannot be changed. The following list describes each of the roles:

- **db_owner.** According to the documentation, this role has all permissions in the database, and it would seem to be logically equivalent to dbo, which is a member of the db_owner role. However, some differences exist:

1 If a member of the db_owner role creates an object, the user, not dbo, owns the object. If Mary is a member of the db_owner role and creates a table named Test, for example, the table will be named

```
Mary.Test
```

Mary must issue the CREATE statement with the owner prefix dbo as shown here:

```
CREATE TABLE dbo.Test
```

It is important to have production objects owned by dbo. (See the section titled "Ownership Chains" later in this chapter.)

Note that it is not possible to specify an owner prefix when creating tables with the graphical tools in Enterprise Manager. If you have non-dbo members of the db_owner role, those users should only create tables with Transact-SQL.

2 The dbo can create database users with either the sp_adduser (old command maintained for backward compatibility) or the new sp_grantdbaccess command. A member of the db_owner role can only use the sp_grantdbaccess command.

- **db_accessadmin.** Members of this role can add users to the database with the sp_grantdbaccess command, but not with the sp_adduser command.

- **db_securityadmin.** Members of this role can grant object permissions on any object in the database. They can also add and delete roles, and add users to, or remove users from, roles.

General Tip

The documentation states that members of the db_securityadmin role can change object ownership. The permission to execute sp_changeobject owner shows when you list the permissions for this role. However, the actual code of the stored procedure requires that the person issuing the command to change ownership must be either a sysadmin or a member of both the db_securityadmin and db_ddladmin roles.

- **db_ddladmin.** Members of this role can create and delete objects. However, they cannot grant, revoke, or deny permissions on objects other than those they own.

General Tip

The db_ddladmin role is a fairly powerful. Members of this role can create their own objects. They can also alter and drop objects owned by others, including those owned by dbo.

- **db_backupoperator.** Members of this role can back up databases and transaction logs and run the DBCC commands that check internal database consistency (for example, DBCC CHECKDB).

- **db_datareader.** Members of this role have read permission on all tables and views in the database.

- **db_datawriter.** Members of this role have insert, update, and delete privileges on all tables and views in the database.

- **db_denydatareader.** Members of this role are not allowed to read data from any table or view.
- **db_denydatawriter.** Members of this role are not allowed to insert, update, or delete from any table in the database.

 General Tip

Books Online states that the db_denydatareader role has permission to deny or revoke select privileges on any table, and that the db_denydatawriter role has permission to deny insert, update, and delete privileges on any table. This is incorrect.

- **public.** The public role is special. Every user is always a member of the public role. You cannot explicitly add users to this role, nor can you remove them from this role. Any permissions given to the public role apply to all users of the database.

To see a complete list of the commands that can be issued by each of the fixed database roles, issue the following command:

```
sp_dbfixedrolepermission rolename
```

 General Tip

Like the server roles, the permissions for the fixed database roles cannot be changed.

User-Defined Database Roles

Members of the db_owner and db_accessadmin roles can create new database roles and make users members of these roles. If you are implementing a complex security scheme, you will probably want to define roles. It's often most useful if these roles correspond to levels in your organization or privilege levels within the database. You may have one set of users who have read access to some tables, for example, and delete access to others. Another set of users has access to a different set of tables. If you create roles with the appropriate privileges, you can easily move a user from one role to another if his or her organizational function changes.

 IMO

It's possible to make one user-defined database role a member of another user-defined role. I don't recommend doing this, however. It will make it much harder to manage your security scheme. Suppose, for instance, that you have created role1, and role1 has a defined set of permissions. If you then create role2, and make role1 a member of it, you will have to keep track of the fact that role2 includes role1.

If you create NT groups and roles that correspond to these groups, and if you use NT Authentication, you can manage many security schemes through NT alone. To do this, follow these steps:

1   Define NT groups in User Manager for Domains.

2   Authorize those groups to log in to SQL Server.

3 Create roles in the target database.

4 Add the NT group as a database user.

5 Make the NT group a member of the appropriate role.

After you have set this up, you can add new users to the appropriate NT group. They automatically acquire the correct SQL Server privileges. As people change function, just use User Manager for Domains to move them to a different NT group. The SQL Server privileges are automatically correct.

 General Tip

If you manage security with NT Authentication, changes on the NT side may cause problems on the SQL Server side. If you rename an NT user, for example, the user can no longer access SQL Server under that login because SQL Server doesn't recognize the new name. If you delete an NT user and add the same NT user, it gets a new NT SID. This won't match SQL Server either. If you delete an NT login, the corresponding login will not be deleted from SQL Server. In all three cases, the SQL Server login is said to be "orphaned." You can use the command sp_validatelogins to identify orphaned logins. After you have identified them, you can delete them. You need to add new logins for NT logins that have been renamed or that have different SIDs from their original SIDs.

 General Tip

If you have a very complex security scheme involving views or internal database security that you build yourself, you will not be able to manage everything through NT.

Application Roles

Application roles make it possible for you to allow a user to perform certain activities only when running a particular application. Suppose, for example, that you want a user to be able to perform selects, inserts, updates, and deletes when running the application, but only to be able to issue SELECT statements when running Query Analyzer or Microsoft Excel. You would give the user a login, make the user a user of the database, and grant select privileges on the tables the user is allowed to see. Then you would create an application role, and grant select, insert, update, and delete privileges on the tables the application is allowed to manipulate. When the user runs the application, the application connects to SQL Server with the user's name and password. Then it activates the application role. From that point on, the user has the privileges associated with the application role. When the user closes the application, the connection is broken and, if the user logs in to SQL Server with some other tool, he or she has only select privileges.

General Tip
In the past, many developers have set up internal security through which the user logs in to the application. The application validates the user (perhaps against a database table) and connects to SQL Server with a special application login. Although this works, there is no way to audit changes. The only login visible to SQL Server is the application login. There is no way to track who did what and when it was done, unless the application manages this.

Application roles differ from other user-defined roles in that they have a password and in that you do not make users members of them.

The application role is activated by the application. After it connects to SQL Server on the user's behalf, it uses the command sp_setapprole to provide the password:

```
sp_setapprole 'role' ,
  {{Encrypt N 'password'} | 'password' }
  ['encrypt_style']
```

The syntax for this command is very confusing. There are two ways to issue the command: with password encryption and without. To activate the application role test with no encryption, for example, you issue the following command:

```
sp_setapprole 'test', 'secret'
```

If you want to pass the password with encryption, your command looks like this:

```
sp_setapprole 'test', {encrypt N'secret'}, odbc
```

The braces are required, and the password must be a Unicode constant (hence, the N at the beginning of the quoted string). The encryption is done with the ODBC Encrypt function. Note that it is not possible to encrypt passwords with clients using DBLibrary.

A typical ADO application that wants to use an application role would have the following steps:

1 Instantiate a connection object.

2 Connect to SQL Server with the user's login name and password.

3 Instantiate a command object and execute the sp_setapprole stored procedure.

4 From this point on, the user has the privileges associated with the application role rather than the privileges associated with his or her login.

 General Tip
If an application role has been activated for a user, access to any other database is limited. The user accesses any other database as guest; if there is no guest user, access is denied.

General Tip

If a user creates objects while connected through an application role, the application owns the objects.

 General Tip

The client application must know the application role password. The password could just be hard-coded in the application, but then, of course, there is the risk of it being easily discovered. It could also be stored in an encrypted form in the Registry. The application could retrieve it from the Registry, decrypt it, and pass it on to SQL Server with the sp_setapprole command.

Object and Statement Security

SQL Server enables you to control who can issue certain statements. It also gives you complete control over who can select data, update data, insert data, and delete data. Select and update privileges can be managed at the column level.

You can grant, revoke, or deny statement or object permissions. To give someone the permission, you grant it. To take a previously granted permission away, you revoke it. A user has the cumulative sum of all privileges granted to it individually and to all roles of which it is a member, including public. If the public role is granted select permission on a table, for example, all users can select from it. To prevent a user from having a permission no matter where else he or she is granted it, use a DENY statement. The following table illustrates a sample security setup.

	Table1	Table2	Table3
Public	SELECT	SELECT	SELECT
Role1	INSERT	INSERT	INSERT
Role2	UPDATE	UPDATE	DELETE
Role3	DENY SELECT		

User1 is a member of Role1. User2 is a member of Role1 and Role2. User3 is a member of Role3. All users are members of the public role. The following table shows what each user can do.

	Table1	Table2	Table3
User1	SELECT, INSERT	SELECT, INSERT	SELECT, INSERT
User2	SELECT, INSERT, UPDATE	SELECT, INSERT, UPDATE	SELECT, INSERT, UPDATE
User3	No access	SELECT	SELECT

Even though User3 receives select access to Table1, 2, and 3 through membership in the public role, the DENY statement overrides this for Table1.

Statement Security

The ability to give users permission to execute certain statements overlaps to some extent with the fixed server and database roles. You can give permission to issue the following statements:

- **CREATE DATABASE.** This permission can be granted only to users in master. Note that you can make a login a member of the db_creator role without making it a database user in master. Members of the db_creator role have this statement permission.

- **CREATE DEFAULT.** This permission allows the user to create and modify default objects. This capability is automatically available to members of the db_ddladmin and db_owner roles.

- **CREATE PROCEDURE.** This permission allows the user to create and drop procedures. This capability is automatically available to members of the db_ddladmin and db_owner roles.

- **CREATE RULE.** This permission allows the user to create and modify rule objects. This capability is automatically available to members of the db_ddladmin and db_owner roles.

- **CREATE TABLE.** This permission allows the user to create and drop tables. This capability is automatically available to members of the db_ddladmin and db_owner roles.

- **CREATE VIEW.** This permission allows the user to create and drop views. This capability is automatically available to members of the db_ddladmin and db_owner roles.

- **BACKUP DATABASE; BACKUP LOG.** This permission allows the person to back up (but not restore) the database or transaction log. This capability is automatically available to members of the db_backupoperator and db_owner roles.

The db_ddladmin has permission to create and manage all objects. However, you may want to use statement permissions instead of using this role. For example, you may want to give the developers permission to create views and stored procedures. If you create a role and give it only those permissions, that is all members of the role can do. If you make them members of the db_ddladmin, they can also create and modify tables.

---

66 IMO

I think you should restrict the ability to create tables to the dbo and members of the db_owner role. Otherwise, you will lose control over the structure of the database. I usually allow developers to create views and procedures. They are not allowed to put these into general availability, however, until I have reviewed them for conformance to standards and performance criteria.

Object Security

Objects can be granted the following permissions:

- **Select.** This permission allows the user to read data. It can be given to all columns in the row, or only to certain columns.
- **Update.** This permission allows the user to modify data. It can be given to all columns or only to certain columns.
- **Insert.** This permission allows the user to insert rows.
- **Delete.** This permission allows the user to delete rows.
- **References.** This permission allows a user to validate a foreign key against a table's primary key. Assume, for example, that TableB contains a foreign key constraint that references TableA. If a user is to be able to insert a row into TableB, that user must have either select privileges on TableA's primary key or references privileges on TableA so that the foreign key constraint can be checked.

The following table summarizes the types of permissions that can be given to each database object.

Object	Select	Select Columns	Update	Update Columns	Insert	Delete	References	Execute
Table	Yes	Yes	Yes	Yes	Yes	Yes	Yes	No
View	Yes	Yes	Yes	Yes	Yes	Yes	No	No
Stored Procedure	No	No	No	No	No	No	No	Yes

 General Tip

A user can be given the ability to execute a stored procedure without being given the rights to do what the stored procedure does. Many organizations require that all modifications be done through stored procedures so that users do not need insert, delete, or update privileges on the tables.

 Warning

If you use EXEC or sp_executesql inside a stored procedure, users of that stored procedure will have to have any of the permissions needed to run the dynamic SQL statement. These statements run outside the security context of the stored procedure.

Object Ownership

The person who creates an object becomes its owner. An object's owner has full rights to the object, and no other users have any access to it unless the owner grants them permission.

When a user asks for an object without specifying the name of its owner, SQL Server first checks to see whether there is an object with the same name that the user owns. If so, the user sees that object. If the user does not own an object with the same name, SQL Server looks to see whether there is an object owned by dbo with the same name. If there is, and the user has permissions on the object, the user sees the object.

In all other cases, the object reference must be qualified by the owner name, such as this:

```
SELECT * FROM username.tablename
```

It is possible to change object ownership with Transact-SQL or DMO; it can't be done with Enterprise Manager. You may want to change object ownership if you want to drop a user that owns objects, or if members of the db_owner role have created objects using the graphical tools in Enterprise Manager.

 General Tip
The ability to change object owners is new in SQL Server 7.0.

Changing Object Ownership with Transact-SQL

To change object ownership with Transact-SQL, use the following command:

```
sp_changeobjectowner 'object', 'newowner'
```

To make Mary the owner of the table Test that is currently owned by Fred, for example, you would issue the following command:

```
sp_changeobjectowner 'Test', 'Mary'
```

Changing Object Ownership with DMO

To change the owner of a table, view, or stored procedure, just modify the object's Owner property.

Ownership Chains

Many objects depend on other objects. For example, views depend on tables. Stored procedures reference tables and views. These dependencies create an ownership chain. If the same owner owns all the dependent objects, the user needs permission only on the top-level object. For example, look at the following procedures:

```
CREATE PROCEDURE ProcA
AS
        SELECT * from Table1
        Exec ProcB
        Select * from View2 /* View2 selects from
                               Table3 and Table4 */
        Update Table5 …
CREATE PROCEDURE ProcB
AS
        DELETE from Table2
```

These procedures reference, directly or indirectly, Table1, Table2, Table3, Table4, and Table5. If the same person owns ProcA, ProcB, View2, Table1, Table2, Table3, Table4, and Table5, a user needs to be given only permission to execute ProcA.

If the owners differ, however, the user needs additional permissions. Consider the following procedures:

```
CREATE PROCEDURE dbo.ProcA
AS
        SELECT * from Joe.Table1
        Exec dbo.ProcB
        Select * from Sue.View2 /* View2 selects
        from Tom.Table3 and
        Mary.Table4 */
        Update dbo.Table5 …
CREATE PROCEDURE dbo.ProcB
AS
        DELETE from Fred.Table2
```

The user who wants to run ProcA needs the following:

- Select permission on Joe.Table1
- Select permission on Sue.View2
- Select permission on Tom.Table3
- Select permission on Mary.Table4
- Delete permission on Fred.Table2

When multiple owners are in the chain, the ownership chain is said to be broken. It doesn't matter that some of the owners may be the same; permission must be checked at every break. Suppose, for example, that Fred creates a view that selects from another view owned by Mary. Mary's view selects from a table owned by Fred. There are two breaks in this chain: from Fred to Mary, and from Mary to Fred. Even though Fred owns the table, permission on it must be checked because of the intermediate object owned by Mary.

 General Tip

I strongly recommend having dbo own all production objects. Permission administration is much easier when you do that.

Using Views as a Security Mechanism

Security in SQL Server goes as low as the column level. It does not, however, provide for row-level security (sometimes referred to as context-based security). In many applications, a level of security beyond that provided by SQL Server is required.

 General Tip

It's possible to implement column security with views. Suppose, for example, that you have a table that contains FirstName, LastName, Address, and Salary. You might give some users select permission on the FirstName, LastName, and Address columns. If a user issues a SELECT * against the table, he or she will get a message because there's no permission on the Salary column. If you create a view with just the columns the user is allowed to see, the user can issue SELECT * with no problems

Some of these requirements are quite simple; for example, a user can see average salary, but not individual salaries. You can create a view for that user that looks like this:

```
CREATE VIEW SalaryView
AS
    SELECT AVG(Salary) FROM Employees
```

Grant the user permission to select from SalaryView, and don't grant permission on the Salary column in the Employees table.

Other security requirements that can be handled by views may be more complex. For example, you may have a database that stores information about customers. Each customer is allowed to see data about its orders, products shipped to it, and so forth. But no customer can see data about other customers. You could implement this security requirement by adding a LoginID column to every row of every table that this restriction applies to. The Orders table might look like this:

```
CREATE TABLE OrdersTable
(
  OrderID int identity
CONSTRAINT pk_Orders PRIMARY KEY,
  OrderDate datetime not null,
  RequiredDate datetime not null,
  ShipDate datetime not null,
  CustomerID int not null
      CONSTRAINT fk_CustomerID REFERENCES
  Customers(CustomerID)
  CustomerLoginName sysname not null)
)
```

Then you would create a view that looks like this:

```
CREATE VIEW Orders
AS
    SELECT * from OrdersTable
    WHERE CustomerLoginName = SUSER_SNAME()
```

Refer back to the description of the SUSER_SNAME() function earlier in this chapter. This allows the customer to only see order information that belongs to it.

For some complex row-level security requirements, you may find that you also need to develop some internal tables to maintain relationships between users and data and use these tables in your views.

Designing a Security Plan

I cannot tell you exactly how your security plan should be set up any more than I can tell you what your backup strategy should be. Security requirements vary by organization and by organizational function. It is possible to have some databases (or even tables in a single database) that require little security and others that require maximum security within the same organization. Employee office phone numbers are likely to be available to everyone, for example, whereas employee salaries are visible to few. A small shop may need only minimal security, whereas a large shop may need a complex permission structure that models the organization. Your organization may have trade secrets that need protection. Government and military organizations often have very stringent security requirements.

You need to determine how closely you want to tie SQL Server security to NT security. If you choose NT Authentication, you need to decide whether you will use NT groups to manage the users or manage the users entirely within SQL Server.

 General Tip

NT Authentication is much cleaner in SQL Server 7.0 than it was in previous versions, and I recommend using it. If you are using products such as Internet Information Server that also support NT Authentication, using NT Authentication in SQL Server makes the most sense. IIS can pass the logon information through to SQL Server as long as it is set up to use NT Challenge and Response, and is running on the same machine as SQL Server.

For each database, you should analyze the roles you need and determine what users or roles are allowed to access each object. In some cases, for example, a read-only database that serves as a resource for everyone, the decision will be as simple as adding a guest user and giving it select privileges on all tables and views. In others, there will be a variety of roles with varying privileges to different objects. You should also decide whether you need application roles and views to meet the security requirements.

 General Tip

It's often helpful to make a matrix of users and objects that shows what access each user has to each object. This can often guide you in developing NT groups and SQL Server roles.

General Tip

If you have complex security requirements, it is important that the security scheme be put into place early in the application development cycle. Many applications work just fine when the application logs in as sa or the dbo, and then fail terribly when the security scheme is in place.

Choosing an Authentication Mode

You can set your SQL Server so that it supports only NT Authentication or supports a combination of NT and SQL Server Authentication. It is also possible to set SQL Server so that only SQL Server Authentication is used. This is for backward compatibility only. You can manage Authentication mode with Enterprise Manager or DMO. There's no way to manage Authentication mode in Transact-SQL.

 General Tip

I recommend using Windows NT Authentication. However, it's sometimes easier to manage SQL Server Agent activities with SQL Server Authentication, and this may lead you to use the combination of SQL Server and NT Authentication so that the Agent can connect to SQL Server as sa.

You can also specify whether logins are audited. If you choose to audit logins, successful and/or failed logins will be recorded in NT's Application event log.

 IMO

If you audit logins, I recommend logging only failed logins. People who have SQL Server logins should be successful, and the fact that they were is not interesting. Logging all logins will fill up the event log quite quickly.

Choosing an Authentication Mode with Enterprise Manager

When you want to specify an Authentication mode, right-click the server in the console pane and choose Properties, and then click the Security tab. The screen shown in Figure 9.1 displays.

By default, SQL Server allows both NT and SQL Server Authentication. If you want only NT Authentication, choose Windows NT only.

You can also specify what level of login auditing you want on this screen.

Figure 9.1   Setting Authentication mode.

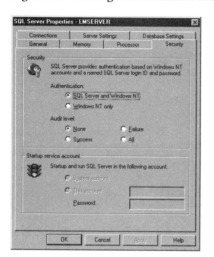

Choosing an Authentication Mode with DMO

Authentication mode and audit level are both controlled with the
IntegratedSecurity object. You need a connected SQLServer object
before you can manipulate the properties of the IntegratedSecurity
object. Authentication mode is specified in the SecurityMode property.
It must be one of the following constants:

Constant	Meaning
SQLDMOSecurity_Integrated	Allow Windows NT Authentication only
SQLDMOSecurity_Mixed	Allow Windows NT and SQL Server Authentication
SQLDMOSecurity_Normal	Allow SQL Server Authentication only

To specify the audit level, set the AuditLevel property to one of the
following constants.

Constant	Meaning
SQLDMOAudit_All	Log all logins regardless of success or failure
SQLDMOAudit_Failure	Log failed logins
SQLDMOAudit_None	Do not log
SQLDMOAudit_Success	Log successful logins

Setting Up Logins

Every user who connects to SQL Server must have a login. You can create and maintain logins with Enterprise Manager, Transact-SQL, and DMO.

Setting Up Logins with Enterprise Manager

To set up either a SQL Server or NT Authentication login with Enterprise Manager, open the Security folder, right-click the Logins icon, and choose New Login. The screen shown in Figure 9.2 displays.

Figure 9.2   Enterprise Manager New Login screen.

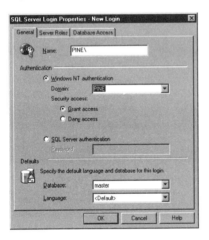

On this screen, you must provide the login name. If you're creating an NT Authentication login, it's easiest if you select the domain from the drop-down list first. The domain name and domain separator appear in the Name box, as shown in Figure 9.2. You must type the login name. Remember that an NT Authentication login can be either a user or a group. You can also use this screen to deny all SQL Server access to an NT user or group.

 General Tip

If your SQL Server is case-sensitive SQL Server, you have to enter the domain\user ID so that it exactly matches the case used in the NT login. Even though NT domains\user IDs are not case sensitive themselves, SQL Server will do a case-sensitive comparison.

IMO

It's a mystery to me why Microsoft didn't give us a Browse button so that we could select from available domain users!

For a SQL Server Authentication login, just click the radio button next to SQL Server Authentication, type the SQL Server login name in the Name box, and provide a password.

At the bottom of the New Login screen, you can specify the login's default database and language.

To change the password for a SQL Server Authentication login, right-click the login in the details pane and choose Properties. Type the new password in the Password box and click OK. You will be asked to confirm the new password.

To delete either a SQL Server or NT Authentication login, right-click the login in the details pane and choose Delete. Note that you cannot delete a login that owns objects in any database.

I discuss the Server Roles and Database Access tabs in the sections "Using Server Roles" and "Managing Database Users" of this chapter.

Setting Up Logins with Transact-SQL

The techniques for creating and modifying logins with Transact-SQL are different for SQL Server Authentication logins and NT Authentication logins. Managing each type of login is described in the following sections.

Managing SQL Server Authentication Logins

To create a SQL Server Authentication login with Transact-SQL, use the following sp_addlogin command:

```
sp_addlogin 'login' [, 'password'] [, 'database']
[, 'language'] [, 'sid']
[, 'encryption_option']
```

database is the login's default database; *language* is the login's default language.

sid is the internal SQL Server security ID. You might want to specify the SID when you want the same login to have the same SID on different servers. This would help you avoid orphaned users (Chapter 6, "Backup and Recovery," contains details about orphaned users.)

General Tip

Note that the SID is varbinary(85), not varbinary(16) as stated in Books OnLine.

By default, SQL Server Authentication passwords are encrypted. It is possible to override this with the encryption_option parameter. This parameter can take the following values.

Value	Meaning
NULL	The password is encrypted. This is the default.
skip_encryption	The password is not encrypted.
skip_encryption_old	The password is not encrypted. The supplied password was encrypted by an earlier version of SQL Server. This option is provided for upgrade purposes only.

General Tip

You should always encrypt passwords. If you do not encrypt them, any member of the sysadmin role can see them in plain text in the sysxlogins table. Do not use skip_encryption_old; it's for the Upgrade Wizard.

To change a password, use the command sp_password, as shown here:

```
sp_password 'old_password', 'new_password'}
[, 'login']
```

Users can change their own passwords as long as they know the old password. If Mary wants to change her password, for example, her command would look like this:

```
sp_password 'secret', 'private'
```

Members of the sysadmin role can change anyone's password. If the user has forgotten his or her password, the sysadmin can use NULL and assign a new password. Assume, for example, that Jerry has forgotten his password. A sysadmin can issue the following command to give Jerry a new password:

```
sp_password NULL, 'abcdef7', 'Jerry'
```

To delete a login, use the command sp_droplogin, as shown here:

```
sp_droplogin 'login'
```

You cannot drop a login that is

- A user in any database
- A database owner
- An owner of a job
- Currently logged in

Creating NT Authentication Logins

To create an NT Authentication login in Transact-SQL, use the command sp_grantlogin:

```
sp_grantlogin 'login'
```

The login parameter must include the domain name and the domain separator as shown here:

```
sp_grantlogin 'PINE\Sharon'
sp_grantlogin '[Pine\Developers]
```

To delete an NT Authentication login, use the command sp_revokelogin:

```
sp_revokelogin 'login'
```

Note that if you revoke a user's login, but that user is a member of a group that also has login privileges, the user can still log in.

To deny access to an NT user or group, use the command sp_denylogin:

```
sp_denylogin 'login'
```

General Tip

Previous versions of SQL Server had two commands—xp_grantlogin and xp_revokelogin—that were used to manage NT Authentication logins. These commands are supported for backward compatibility. You should use the sp_grantlogin and sp_revokelogin rather than the earlier commands.

Setting Up Logins with DMO

To create either a SQL Server or NT Authentication login with DMO, you must follow these steps:

1 Instantiate a Login object.

2 Set the Login object's Name and Type properties. You may also set the Database, Language, LanguageAlias, and DenyNTLogin properties (see the discussion of these properties later in this chapter).

3 Add the Login object to the Logins collection of a connected SQLServer object.

The Name property is a string that must contain either the SQL Server Authentication login name or the NT login name including the domain and domain separator (for example, 'Pine\Sharon').

The Type property specifies the Authentication mode to be used for the login. If specified, it must be one of the following constants.

Constant	Meaning
SQLDMOLogin_NTGroup	Login is the name of a Microsoft Windows NT group.
SQLDMOLogin_NTUser	Login is the name of a Windows NT user.
SQLDMOLogin_Standard	Login is used for SQL Server Authentication. Login name and password may be required when a client connects using the login.

The Database property contains the name of the login's default database. The Language property can be set to the SQL Server internal name of the login's default language. Language alias is the friendly name of the default language.

To deny an NT user or group access to the SQL Server, set the DenyNTLogin property to true.

To set or change the password for a SQL Server Authentication login, use the SetPassword method of the appropriate Login object. This method takes two arguments: OldPassword and NewPassword. The OldPassword argument is not required.

To delete a login, locate the appropriate login in the Logins collection of a connected SQLServer object, and use the Logins collection's Remove method.

Using Server Roles

I described the various server roles earlier in this chapter. It is easy to add logins to the server roles with Enterprise Manager, Transact-SQL, or DMO.

Managing Server Roles with Enterprise Manager

You make a login a member of one or more server roles by right-clicking the login in the details pane, choosing Properties, and clicking the Server Roles tab. The screen shown in Figure 9.3 displays.

Figure 9.3   Enterprise Manager Server Roles screen.

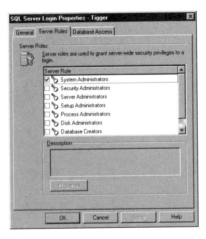

To make a login a member of one or more server roles, just check the box. To remove a login from a role, uncheck the box.

Managing Server Roles with Transact-SQL

To make a login a member of a server role with Transact-SQL, use the command sp_addsrvrolemember:

```
sp_addsrvrolemember 'login', 'role'
```

To remove a login from a server role, use the command sp_dropsrvrolemember:

```
sp_dropsrvrolemember 'login', 'role'
```

For both of these commands, role must be one of the following values:

- sysadmin
- securityadmin
- serveradmin
- setupadmin
- processadmin
- diskadmin
- dbcreator

Managing Server Roles with DMO

To add a login to a server role with DMO, locate the appropriate ServerRole object in the ServerRoles collection of a connected SQL Server. You can identify the role by its Name property, which will be one of the following values:

- sysadmin
- securityadmin
- serveradmin
- setupadmin
- processadmin
- diskadmin
- dbcreator

Use the AddMember method of the ServerRole object to make a login a member of the role; use the DropMember method to remove a login from a role. Both methods take a single string argument: the login name of the user who is to be added or removed.

Managing Database Users

You can manage database users with Enterprise Manager, Transact-SQL, or DMO.

Managing Database Users with Enterprise Manager

Enterprise Manager provides two ways to manage database users. You can look at the login, and grant database access from that perspective, or you can look at the database and authorize users from the database point of view. The end result of both approaches is the same. You will most likely work from the login perspective when you are adding a new login and from the database perspective when you have created a new database.

Managing Database Access from the Login Point of View

To grant access to databases for a login, right-click the login in the details pane, choose Properties, and click the Database Access tab. The screen shown in Figure 9.4 displays.

Figure 9.4   Database Access screen.

Just check the databases to which the login should have access. After you have granted access to a database, you can specify any database roles to which the user should be made a member. To remove a login from either a database or a database role, just uncheck the database or role. If you want to give the user a database username that differs from the login name, just type it.

Managing Database Access from the Database Point of View

To grant a login access to a database, expand the database, right-click the Users folder, and choose New User. The screen shown in Figure 9.5 displays.

Figure 9.5   New Database User screen.

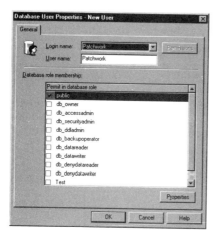

Select the login name from the drop-down list. If you want to change the user's name in the database, enter it in the User Name box. You can make the user a member of database roles by just checking the appropriate boxes.

 General Tip

If you select an NT Authentication user, Enterprise Manager proposes that the username be the NT login without the domain qualifier. Suppose, for example, that the NT login PINE\SHARON has been granted access to SQL Server. Enterprise Manager will propose that the database username be just SHARON. If you have users from multiple domains, you may want to override Enterprise Manager's suggestion so that you know exactly which user is which.

Modify a user's database roles by right-clicking the user in the details pane and choosing Properties. Delete a user from a database by right-clicking the user in the details pane and choosing Delete.

Managing Database Users with Transact-SQL

To add a user to a database with Transact-SQL, use the `sp_grantdbaccess` command. You must issue this command in the database to which the user is to be added, as shown here:

```
sp_grantdbaccess 'login' [, 'name_in_db' [OUTPUT]]
```

It is not necessary to specify a value for name_in_db. If you do not provide a value, the login name is used.

IMO

For some reason, it's possible to get the value of name_in_db as an output parameter. For example, you could issue the following commands:

```
declare @name sysname

exec sp_grantdbaccess Zebra, @name output

select @name
```

The final select statement would show you the database name that had been assigned. Because it is either the name you specify or the login name, both of which you would know before you issue the sp_grantdbaccess command, it's not clear to me what this is useful for.

General Tip

Previous versions of SQL Server used the command sp_adduser to grant logins access to a database. This command is still available for backward compatibility, but you should use sp_grantdbaccess.

To remove a user from a database, use the command sp_revokedbaccess, as follows:

```
sp_revokedbaccess 'name'
```

The name parameter is the user's name in the database.

The sp_revokedbaccess stored procedure cannot remove the following:

- A user who owns objects
- The public role
- The dbo user
- The INFORMATION_SCHEMA user
- The fixed database roles
- The guest user in the master and tempdb databases
- A Windows NT user when access has been granted to a Windows NT group

General Tip

Previous versions of SQL Server used the sp_dropuser command to remove a user from the database. This command is still provided for backward compatibility. However, you should use the sp_revokedbaccess command.

Managing Database Users with DMO

To add a user to the database with DMO, follow these steps:

1 Create a User object.

2 Assign the login name to the User object's Login property.

3 Optionally, assign the database user name to the User object's Name property. (If no value is provided, the login name is used.)

4 Optionally, specify the name of a database role that the user will be a member of. If you do not supply a role name, the user will be a member of the public role.

5 Add the User object to the Users collection of a connected SQL Server Database object.

To remove a user from a database, locate the appropriate user in the Users collection and use the Users collection's Remove method.

Defining Database Roles

You can create database roles with Enterprise Manager, Transact-SQL, or DMO.

Defining Database Roles with Enterprise Manager

To create a new database role in Enterprise Manager, expand the database, right-click the Roles folder, and choose New Role. The screen shown in Figure 9.6 displays.

Figure 9.6   New Role screen.

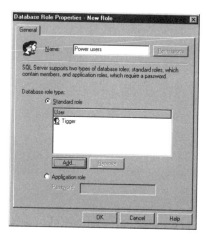

Just give the role a name. If you want to add users to the role at the time you create it, click the Add button. A list of database users displays. From this list, you can select one or more users to add to the role. If you want to create an application role rather than a standard role, click the Application Role button and supply a password.

To modify the list of database users who are members of the role, right-click the role in the details pane and choose Properties.

To remove a database role, right-click the role in the details pane and choose Delete. You cannot remove the fixed database roles. Removing a role does not remove its members from the database.

Defining Database Roles with Transact-SQL

To create a new standard database role with Transact-SQL, use the sp_addrole command:

    sp_addrole 'role' [, 'owner']

By default, the owner of the role is its creator.

To create an application role with Transact-SQL, use the command sp_addapprole:

    sp_addapprole 'role', 'password'

To drop a standard role, use the sp_droprole command:

    sp_droprole 'role'

You cannot drop the predefined database roles. Dropping a role does not remove its members from the database.

To drop an application role, use the command sp_dropapprole:

    sp_dropapprole 'role'

Defining Database Roles with DMO

To create a new database role with DMO, follow these steps:

1 Instantiate a DatabaseRole object.

2 Set its Name property.

3 If it is an application role, set the AppRole property to true, and provide a value for the Password property.

4 Add the DatabaseRole object to the DatabaseRoles collection of a Database object.

To remove a database role, locate the appropriate DatabaseRole object in the DatabaseRoles collection, and use the Remove method of the DatabaseRoles collection.

Using User-Defined and Predefined Database Roles

You can manage the membership of both user-defined and predefined database roles with Enterprise Manager, Transact-SQL, or DMO.

Assigning Users to Database Roles with Enterprise Manager

You can assign a user to database roles at the time you grant access to the database or at the time you create the role. See the sections titled "Managing Database Access from the Login Point of View", "Managing Database Access from the Database Point of View," and "Defining Database Roles with Enterprise Manager" earlier in this chapter.

Assigning Users to Database Roles with Transact-SQL

To assign a database user to a role with Transact-SQL, use the command sp_addrolemember:

```
sp_addrolemember 'role', 'name_in_db'
```

You must use the user's name in the database, which might not be the same as the login name. If you are adding a user to a predefined database role, the role name must be one of the following:

- db_owner
- db_accessadmin
- db_securityadmin
- db_ddladmin
- db_backupoperator
- db_datareader
- db_datawriter
- db_denydatareader
- db_denydatawriter

To remove a user from a role, use the command sp_droprolemember:

```
sp_droprolemember 'role', 'name_in_db'
```

Removing a user from a role does not remove the user from the database. You cannot remove a user from the public role. You cannot remove dbo from any role.

To find out whether a user is a member of a particular role, use the IS_MEMBER function, as shown here:

```
SELECT IS_MEMBER('Developers')
```

The IS_MEMBER function returns 1 if the current user is a member of the role, 0 if the current user is not.

Assigning Users to Database Roles with DMO

To make a user a member of a role, use the AddMember method of the appropriate DatabaseRole object. To remove a user from a role, use the DropMember method of the appropriate DatabaseRole object. Both methods take a single string argument: the database name of the user.

Managing Permissions

As described earlier, you can grant, revoke, and deny permission at the statement and the object level. Both types of permissions can be managed with Enterprise Manager, Transact-SQL, and DMO. Statement and object permissions can be granted to users and to roles. I recommend that you use roles, and grant permissions only to roles. It is much easier to manage permissions if you do it this way.

Managing Statement Permissions with Enterprise Manager

Statement permissions are an attribute of a database. To manage them, right-click the database in the console pane and choose Properties. Click the Permissions tab. The screen shown in Figure 9.7 displays.

General Tip

The Permissions and Options tabs do not appear when you first create a database. They become visible after the database has been created.

Figure 9.7　Statement Permissions screen.

User/Role	Create Table	Create View	Create SP	Create Default	Create Rul
Power users	☑	☐	☐	☐	☐
public	☐	☐	☐	☐	☐
Test	☐	☒	☐	☐	☐
guest	☐	☐	☐	☐	☐
Tank	☐	☐	☐	☐	☐
Tigger	☐	☐	☐	☐	☐

Northwind Properties

General | Transaction Log | Options | Permissions

OK　Cancel　Apply　Help

Roles are identified with a key; users are identified with a head. Just check the permissions you want to grant; uncheck to revoke permissions.

 General Tip

Be very careful when you are trying to revoke. Clicking once on a box grants the permission, and you will see a check mark. Clicking once on a box that is checked places a big red X in the box, as shown for the Test role in Figure 9.7. This means the permission is denied. Remember that a deny is very powerful and prevents a user from having permission no matter where else the permission is granted. You need to click a second time if you just want to revoke the permission.

 General Tip

More statement permissions appear to the right of what is shown on this screen. You need to use the scrollbar to get to them. This screen is very annoying for that reason. It cannot be maximized.

Managing Statement Permissions with Transact-SQL

To manage statement permissions in Transact-SQL, use the GRANT, REVOKE, and DENY statements, as shown here:

```
GRANT {ALL ¦ statement[,...n]}
TO {name_in_db ¦ rolename} [,...n]

REVOKE {ALL ¦ statement[,...n]}
FROM {name_in_db ¦ rolename [,...n]

DENY{ALL ¦ statement[,...n]}
TO {name_in_db ¦ rolename} [,...n]
```

If you use the keyword ALL, all statement privileges are granted to, revoked from, or denied to the users named in the list. If you want to grant, revoke, or deny specific statement privileges, select the privileges from the following list:

- CREATE DATABASE
- CREATE DEFAULT
- CREATE PROCEDURE
- CREATE RULE
- CREATE TABLE
- CREATE VIEW
- BACKUP DATABASE
- BACKUP LOG

Note that CREATE DATABASE privilege can only be granted in master, and anyone to whom it is granted must be a user in the master database.

Managing Statement Permissions with DMO

Statement permissions in DMO are granted, revoked, or denied with the Grant, Revoke, and Deny methods of the Database object. These methods take two arguments: Privilege and GranteeNames.

Privilege is a long integer containing a value from the following table.

Constant	Meaning
SQLDMOPriv_AllDatabasePrivs	Grant/Revoke/Deny all statement privileges to the users or roles listed.
SQLDMOPriv_CreateDatabase	Grant/Revoke/Deny permission to execute the CREATE DATABASE statement.
SQLDMOPriv_CreateDefault	Grant/Revoke/Deny permission to execute the CREATE DEFAULT statement.
SQLDMOPriv_CreateProcedure	Grant/Revoke/Deny permission to execute the CREATE PROCEDURE statement.
SQLDMOPriv_CreateRule	Grant/Revoke/Deny permission to execute the CREATE RULE statement.
SQLDMOPriv_CreateTable	Grant/Revoke/Deny permission to execute the CREATE TABLE statement.
SQLDMOPriv_CreateView	Grant/Revoke/Deny permission to execute the CREATE VIEW statement.
SQLDMOPriv_DumpDatabase	Grant/Revoke/Deny permission to back up database.
SQLDMOPriv_DumpTransaction	Grant permission to back up the database transaction log.

If you want to grant more than one statement permission, you must add the constants together. If you want to grant, revoke, or deny permission to issue CREATE VIEW and CREATE PROCEDURE statements, for example, you use the following:

```
Dim lPrivileges as Long
lPrivileges = SQLDMOPriv_CreateView + _
SQLDMOPriv_CreateProcedure
```

Granteenames is a SQLDMO multistring containing a list of users and/or roles.

Managing Object Permissions with Enterprise Manager

Object permissions in Enterprise Manager can be managed from the point of view of the user, the role, or an object. You will probably want to work from the role perspective when you create a new role and the object perspective when you create a new object.

Managing Object Permissions from the Role or User Perspective

To manage permissions from either the role or the user perspective, right-click the user or role in the details pane and choose Properties. Click Permissions. The screen shown in Figure 9.8 displays.

Figure 9.8   Role-Perspective Object Permissions screen.

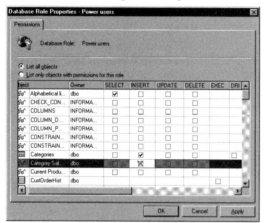

Object permissions are granted by checking a box, and revoked by unchecking a box. The little icons at the left side of the display show what kind of object it is. Glasses represent a view, the thing that looks like a spreadsheet represents a table, and the box with the wavy lines in it represents a stored procedure.

 IMO

Note that there is no way to grant column permissions in Enterprise Manager. It was possible in the 6.5 Enterprise Manager, but that capability was lost in 7.0. Perhaps it will be added in the next release.

DRI stands for *Declarative Referential Integrity*. If you check DRI, you are granting the references privilege described earlier in this chapter.

✔ **General Tip**

This dialog box works like the one for granting statement permissions: Clicking once on a box that is checked means that the permission is *denied*.

Managing Object Permissions from the Object Perspective

To manage permissions from an object perspective, right-click a table, view, or procedure in the details pane. Choose All Tasks, Manage Permissions. The screen shown in Figure 9.9 displays.

Figure 9.9 Object Permissions screen.

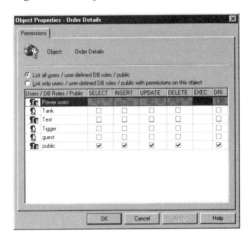

This screen works in exactly the same way as the Role/User
Permissions screen and the same warnings apply. Roles are illustrated
with two heads; users are illustrated with one head.

Managing Object Permissions with Transact-SQL

Object permissions are granted, revoked, or denied with the GRANT,
REVOKE, and DENY Transact-SQL statements, as shown, here:

```
GRANT {ALL [PRIVILEGES] ¦ permission [,...n]}
{[(column [,...n])] ON {table ¦ view}
 ¦ ON {table ¦ view}[(column [,...n])]
 ¦ ON {stored_procedure ¦ extended_procedure}
}
TO {name_in_db ¦ rolename} [,...n]
[WITH GRANT OPTION]
[AS role]

REVOKE [GRANT OPTION FOR]
{ALL [PRIVILEGES] ¦ permission [,...n]}
{[(column [,...n])] ON {table ¦ view}
 ¦ ON {table ¦ view}[(column [,...n])]
 ¦ {stored_procedure ¦ extended_procedure}
}
{TO ¦ FROM} {name_in_db ¦ rolename} [,...n]
[CASCADE]
[AS role]

DENY {ALL [PRIVILEGES] ¦ permission[,...n]}
{[(column [,...n])] ON {table ¦ view}
 ¦ ON {table ¦ view}[(column [,...n])]
 ¦ ON {stored_procedure ¦ extended_procedure}
}
TO {name_in_db ¦ rolename}[,...n]
[CASCADE]
```

`permission` is one of the following:

- `SELECT`
- `INSERT`
- `UPDATE`
- `DELETE`
- `REFERENCES`
- `EXEC`

A column list can be provided only for select and update permissions. Note that there are two ways to specify column privileges:

```
GRANT SELECT (CategoryName, Description)
      ON Categories
      TO …
```

or

```
GRANT SELECT ON Categories(CategoryName,
Description) TO …
```

Both forms accomplish the same thing. The first example conforms to the ANSI standard.

The following several clauses in the GRANT, REVOKE, and DENY statements require explanation:

- `WITH GRANT OPTION`   If a privilege is granted with this option, the user or role that was granted the permission can grant it to others. It is possible to subsequently revoke the ability to grant permissions, and the permission itself.

- `CASCADE`   This is used with REVOKE or DENY to revoke or deny permissions that were granted by a user or role through the `WITH GRANT` option.

Suppose, for example, that you granted Joe select privileges on the Categories table and used the `WITH GRANT` option. Joe uses his ability to grant select on Categories to Mary, Tom, and Susan. If you want to revoke Joe's ability to grant permissions, and remove the permissions from Mary, Tom, and Susan as well, you issue the following statement:

```
REVOKE GRANT OPTION FOR SELECT FROM Joe CASCADE
```

After this statement is executed, Joe still has select privileges on Categories, but can no longer grant it. Mary, Tom, and Susan do not have select privileges.

- `AS role`   `AS` is used when permissions on an object are granted to a role, and members of that role must grant the permissions to others who are not members of the role. Because only a user, rather than a group or role, can execute a GRANT statement, a specific member of the group or role grants permissions on the object under the authority of the group or role.

Suppose, for example, that Jennifer owns a table named Accounts. She grants select on Accounts WITH GRANT OPTION to the Developer role. Timothy is a member of the Developer role. If he wants to grant select on Accounts to Polly, a member of the public role, he would issue the following statement:

```
GRANT SELECT ON ACCOUNTS TO Polly
AS Developer
```

&&   IMO

I do not use WITH GRANT OPTION or AS. I want more control over the permission scheme. I do not want people to grant permissions willy-nilly. If I have a database with no security requirements, I just grant all privileges to the public role and create a guest user. If you look at Northwind or pubs, you will see that this is exactly how they are managed. In most databases, security is important and should not be treated lightly. If multiple people need to grant permissions, make them members of the db_owner or db_securityadmin role.

You can find out which statement permissions are given to the current user or which permissions the user has on a specific object by using the PERMISSIONS function, as follows:

```
PERMISSIONS ([object_id [, 'column']])
```

This function returns a 32-bit bitmap. The lower 16 bits show the permissions the user has; the upper 16 show the permission the user can grant to others.

If you issue the command without an object ID, the bitmap will show statement permissions. If you specify an object ID, you will see object permissions. If you also specify a column name, you'll see the permissions for the current user for the specific column. For details about decoding the bitmap, see the Books Online.

Managing Object Permissions with DMO

Object permissions are managed in DMO with the Grant, Revoke, and Deny methods of the Table, View, and Stored Procedure objects. The Grant and Revoke methods have the following five arguments; the Deny method has the first five:

- **Privilege**   This argument is a long integer specifying one or more table permissions. Values for privilege are taken from the following table.

Constant	Meaning
SQLDMOPriv_AllObjectPrivs	Grant/Revoke/Deny all applicable privileges.
SQLDMOPriv_Delete	Grant/Revoke/Deny permission to execute the DELETE statement for a table or view.
SQLDMOPriv_Insert	Grant/Revoke/Deny permission to execute the INSERT statement for a table or view.

Constant	Meaning
SQLDMOPriv_References	Grant/Revoke/Deny permission to reference the table in declarative referential integrity constraints established on other tables' references permission.
SQLDMOPriv_Select	Grant/Revoke/Deny permission to execute the SELECT statement for a table or view.
SQLDMOPriv_Update	Grant/Revoke/Deny permission to execute the UPDATE statement for a table or view.
SQLDMOPriv_Execute	Grant execute permission on a stored procedure.

If multiple permissions are to be granted, revoked, or denied, you must add the constants. The following example shows how to grant, select, and insert privileges:

```
dim lPrivilege AS Long
lPrivilege = SQLDMOPriv_Insert + SQLDMOPriv_Select
```

- **GranteeNames**   This argument is a SQL-DMO multistring listing users or roles.

- **ColumnNames**   This is a SQL-DMO multistring listing column names within the table or view. When used, the specified privilege is extended only to the columns named. This can be used only with select and update permissions.

- **GrantGrant**   When using the Grant method, if this is true, the right to grant the permission to others is also granted. When using the Revoke method, if this is true, the right to revoke the privileges named from others is given. When using the Deny method, if this option is true, the right to deny the privilege to others is given.

- **AsRole**   This is a string identifying a role to which the connected user belongs. See the example in the preceding section.

The Revoke method has one additional argument:

- **RevokeGrantOption**   When true, the ability to grant permission to others is revoked. When false (default), no change is made to the ability to extend permission.

Under the Covers

The Authentication mode and audit level are stored in the Registry under HKEY_LOCAL_MACHINE\SOFTWARE\MICROSOFT\ MSSQLSERVER\MSSQLSERVER. Login mode is 0 when the server allows NT and SQL Server Authentication; it is 1 when only NT Authentication is allowed. AuditLevel ranges from 0 to 3 with the following meanings.

AuditLevel	Meaning
0	None
1	Sucessful logins
2	Failed logins
3	All logins

Other security information is stored in several different system tables:

- **sysxlogins.** This table is in the master database, and contains the login name, default database, default language, encrypted password, and information about whether the login is an NT user or an NT group.

 General Tip

In previous versions of SQL Server, login information was stored in a table named syslogins. In SQL Server 7.0, syslogins is a view over sysxlogins that presents information in the same structure as the old syslogins table.

- **sysusers.** This table is in every database. It is used to store both users and roles. The public role always has internal identifier 0. Other roles have internal identifiers 16384 and higher. Users are assigned identifiers less than 16384. The dbo is always user 1. There is a mapping between the user and the login SID stored in this table.

 General Tip

You may find individual user entries in sysusers even though you have only authorized NT groups access to the database. When a user who is a member of a group creates an object, SQL Server generates an entry in sysusers for the user's NT login. If you look at database users in Enterprise Manager, you will see the individual login with the phrase "Via Group Membership" describing it. The object will be owned by the individual, not the group.

- **sysmembers.** This table is also in every database. It stores the mapping of database IDs to roles.
- **sysprotects.** This table is also in every database. It contains a list of permissions that have been granted or denied to users. The list includes both object and statement permissions. The name of the grantor is included.

 IMO

sysprotects used to keep track of permissions that had been revoked. This capability disappeared with version 6.0. I am sorry it is gone. I personally think that there is a difference between someone having never had a permission and someone having had a permission revoked. There's usually a reason for the latter, and we have no way to track this anymore.

- **syspermissions.** This table contains information about the grantor and the grantee of permissions. Most of the fields in this table are documented as "for internal use," and it is not clear to me what the actual function of this table is.

10

Performance Tuning

The most significant factor in the performance of any SQL Server database is the design of the database itself. You cannot turn any knobs that will make a badly designed database perform well. Hardware-knob tuning can help a bit (maybe 10%), but that is not enough for most needs. The topic of high-performance database design would be a book in itself, and I'm not going to try to cover that topic here. What I will do is show you how to analyze performance, using the tools supplied in SQL Server 7.0. This chapter starts out by talking about the Query Processor (also called the Query Engine or Relational Engine). Then, this chapter shows you how to use SQL Profiler, a valuable tool for monitoring various performance problems. This chapter also discusses the Index Tuning Wizard, a tool that helps you determine what indexes are useful for improving the performance of queries. This chapter also shows you how to use SQL Performance Monitor and describes some of the counters that you want to keep your eye on. Finally, the chapter ends by discussing some of the configuration options related to performance.

 General Tip

This section uses the terms clustered index and non-clustered index a lot. These two types of indexes available in SQL Server are described in Chapter 4, "Storage Management."

The Query Processor

The Query Processor (also referred to as the Query Optimizer) is responsible for taking every statement sent to SQL Server and figuring out how to get the requested data or perform the requested operation. When your SQL statement arrives at the server, the Query Processor must perform the following steps (sometimes referred to as compilation):

1 Checks that the syntax is correct. Missing commas, misspelled keywords, and so on get removed here. If the statement is syntactically correct, the Query Processor goes on to the next step.

2 Parses the statement. The processor breaks the statements down into its component parts, identifies joins, where clauses, and so on. The output of this step is a *sequence tree*, an internal structure that represents the SQL statement.

3 Normalizes the sequence tree. In this step, the Query Processor verifies that the table and columns mentioned in the statement actually exist. (If they don't, an error message is sent back to the client.) It also inserts conversion functions to handle implicit data conversion and may perform some syntax optimizations. The output of this step is a *query graph*, which is a structure that makes it easier for the next step to work on the query.

4 Optimizes the query. In this step, the Query Processor analyzes potential *query plans*—ways of executing the statement. The SQL Server Query Optimizer is a cost-based optimizer. This means that it evaluates the cost of various plans, and ultimately selects the plan with the lowest cost.

5 Executes the plan. In this step, the Query Processor uses the plan developed in step 4 to retrieve the requested data or carry out the requested operation.

The important part of this process, from this chapter's point of view, is step 4. The decisions that the Query Optimizer makes in selecting a plan determine how good (or bad) the performance of that query will be. The Optimizer has a variety of techniques to select from when developing query plans. These include methods for retrieving data and methods for joining data.

Retrieval Techniques

Depending on the query, the Optimizer selects one or more of the following retrieval techniques:

- **Bookmark lookup.** This technique uses the record pointer (either the clustering key or the rowid) in a non clustered index to find the desired rows.

- **Clustered index scan.** This technique scans the clustered index looking for the rows that meet the criteria. This may be used in preference to a table scan when the data must be returned in the order of the clustering key. If ordering is not required, the index is scanned in an optimal manner, and the order of the output is unpredictable.

- **Clustered index seek.** This technique uses the clustered index to find the row or rows.

- **Index scan.** This technique scans the non-clustered index to find the desired row or rows. This may be used when the index covers the query (all the fields in the select list and the where clause are in the index).

- **Index seek.** This technique uses the non-clustered index to identify the desired row or rows. This technique is followed by a bookmark lookup to actually retrieve the data.

- **Table scan.** This technique scans the entire table from beginning to end looking for the desired row or rows.

The Optimizer uses several factors to determine which technique should be used for each table in the query:

- The query itself. Are there any *Search Arguments* (SARGs) that would allow an index seek to be used? A SARG is a where clause condition in the form <column> <operator> <constant>.

General Tip

In SQL Server 7.0, the Optimizer can use multiple indexes on the same table; this capability didn't exist in prior versions of SQL Server.

- Statistics maintained for each index (see the statistic's section later in this chapter).
- The number of rows that will be returned by the query.

Because of the third factor, a different plan may be developed for two queries that appear, on the surface, to be the same. Consider, for example, a table that has 10,000 rows. Column1 contains values ranging from 1 to 10000, and these two queries:

```
SELECT * from Table where Column1 < 10
SELECT * from Table where Column1 < 9000
```

The first query returns only 9 rows; the second returns 8999 rows. It is likely that some type of index seek would be a lower-cost plan for the first query and some type of scan would be a lower-cost plan for the second.

Join Techniques

The Optimizer has three different join techniques at its disposal:

- Hash match
- Merge join
- Nested loops

Join strategies are not as simple as retrieval strategies, so each of these techniques is briefly described in the following sections. The statistics and number of rows to be joined influence the Optimizer's choice of join technique.

Hash Joins

Hash joins can be used on any join that uses equality as the join operator.

 General Tip

Joins that use other operators, such as <, >, ≥, ≤, or <>, will not be able to use a hash join technique. Hash joins are only effective for equality queries; for other queries, hash joins will not be used.

With a hash join, the keys in one of the two tables are divided into *hash buckets*. An algorithm that will distribute data relatively evenly between the buckets is used to do this. SQL Server uses the smaller of the two tables, called the build table, to drive the hash join process. Assume, for example, that we are trying to join the Orders and Order Details tables in the Northwind database. Both tables have a column named OrderID, and there are fewer rows in Orders than in Order Details. Some sample data is shown in the following Orders list.

OrderID

10

11

12

13

14

15

An easily understood hashing algorithm (although not the one SQL Server uses) is division-remainder. With this algorithm, the key value is divided by a number (usually a prime number) and the key is placed in the bucket that corresponds to the remainder. This sample data contains only a few rows, so I will use 3 as the divisor. That means that we will have 3 "buckets": 0, for the keys that 3 divides evenly; 1, for the keys that have a remainder of 1 when divided by 3; and 2 for the ones that have a remainder of 2, as shown in the following hash buckets table.

Bucket 0	Bucket 1	Bucket 2
12	10	11
15	13	14

General Tip

A paper by Goetz Graefe, principal architect of the Query Engine, describes SQL Server's hashing algorithm as "based on a repeatable randomizing function."

After the build table has been divided into the hash buckets, the second table, called the Probe Input table, is inspected. The following list illustrates some of the data in Order Details (each order may have many related details).

OrderID

11

11

11

12

14

14

15

15

SQL Server takes the first OrderID from Order Details, divides it by 3, and looks for a match in the appropriate bucket. It repeats this process for every row in the Probe Input table. The end result of this process, for our sample data, would be a listing of Orders and Order Details for OrderIDs 11, 12, 14, and 15. Orders 10 and 13 don't have any matching Order Details.

Merge Joins

A merge join also requires an equality operator in the join clause. Merge joins require that both inputs be sorted on the values being matched. It reads from one input, and then compares a value from that input to the second input. Because both are sorted, it is possible to determine whether a match can be found quickly. If no match is found, the next record from the first input is read. Assume, for example, that we have the same Orders and Order Details lists used in the previous example, as shown in the lists in the following sections.

Orders List

OrderID

10

11

12

13

14

15

Order Details

OrderID

11

11

11

12

14

14

15

15

The process reads the first entry from the Orders list. Because the first entry in the Order Details list is greater than 10, there is no match. So the next record from Orders (order 11) is read. This is matched against the first three records in the Order Details list. The process continues until all the records in the first list have been processed.

This technique is likely to be used when both lists have indexes on the fields in the join clause. In some cases, the Optimizer decides to sort an unsorted input stream to take advantage of the merge join technique.

Nested Loops

The nested loops (also called *nested iteration*) technique can be used for any type of join, not just equality joins. A nested loops join does not require that the inputs be in any particular order. In a nested loops join, the first input is processed row-by-row, just as it is in a merge join. Because the second table is not in order, however, the entire second table must be searched for matches. Indexes can be used to reduce the volume of records that must be searched. A *naive nested loops join* scans an entire table or index. An *index nested loops join* uses an index to locate matching records instead of scanning the entire table or index. Sometimes, the Optimizer builds a temporary index for use in a nested loops join. In this case, the join technique is called a *temporary index nested loops join*.

General Tip

Although it sounds like a nested loops join must do a lot more work than either a hash join or a merge join, it is, in fact, the most efficient strategy in many cases. In small transactions in which the outer table is small and there is an appropriate index on the inner table, the nested loops join is faster than either the hash join or the merge join. It is not efficient when the query involves two large tables.

Statistics

I mentioned previously that the Optimizer uses statistics in making its decisions about how a query should be processed. Each index has a statistics entry that contains information about the distribution of keys and the selectivity of the index. The selectivity of an index often determines whether the Optimizer uses it for a particular query.

General Tip

Selectivity describes how unique the index is. A unique index always has a selectivity of 1, meaning that only one row is returned in response to an equality query. If the index has many duplicate values, the selectivity is low.

General Tip

In SQL Server 7.0, the distribution statistics can be spread over more than one page. The statistics are stored as a long string of bits spread across multiple pages just as image data is. The column named statblob in the sysindexes table points to the distribution statistics.

By default, index statistics in SQL Server 7.0 are maintained automatically. You can change this behavior (as noted later in this chapter). The Query Optimizer determines whether the statistics are up-to-date, and recomputes them if necessary. The Optimizer makes this determination by interrogating the column rowmodctr in the sysindexes table. This column tracks the number of modifications (inserts, changes to indexed columns, and deletes) made to the table since the last time the statistics were updated. It compares this column to a threshold to determine whether the statistics should be updated. SQL Server uses the following rules to determine when statistics should be automatically updated:

1 If a table in tempdb has 6 or fewer rows, statistics are updated after 6 modifications to the table.

2 If any table has 500 or fewer rows, statistics are updated after 500 modifications to the table.

3 If any table has more than 500 rows, statistics are automatically updated after 500 + 20% of the rows have been modified. If a table has 10,000 rows, for example, statistics are updated after there have been 2,500 modifications to the table.

These rules recognize that it takes a lot more modifications to a big table to make the distribution statistics inaccurate than it does for a small table.

 General Tip

Previous versions of SQL Server did not automatically maintain the statistics; updating them was a part of routine maintenance.

Usually, except for small (less than 8MB) tables, statistics are computed by a sampling technique. This avoids the cost of scanning the entire table. If you do not want the statistics to be managed automatically, you can set the database option, Auto update statistics, to false. You can also turn off automatic update for a specific table or index.

It is also possible to have statistics on a nonindexed column. The Optimizer automatically creates column statistics when there isn't an appropriate index. If you don't want the Optimizer to compute these statistics, you can set the database option, Auto create statistics, to false.

 General Tip

If you issue the sp_helpindex command on a table, you may see "indexes" that have names starting with _WA_Sys_. These are actually column statistics computed by the Optimizer.

Automatic statistics management can be a blessing or a curse, and in some cases you will want to turn it off. It can interfere with performance by doing repeated updates of the statistics or interrupting production queries for statistics maintenance. Because statistics maintenance is fairly resource intensive, it can take a long time.

General Tip

I recommend leaving the Auto update statistics option set to true. If you don't want particular tables to have automatic statistics update performed because it interferes with other work, use sp_autostats to set the option to false only for those tables.

 General Tip

You may want to monitor when statistics updating is going to happen and disable it if the system is in a peak period. The following pseudo-code shows you the basic algorithm for doing this:

```
if (sysindexes.rows > 500)
    if (sysindexes.rows * 0.20 >= sysindexes.rowmodctr
and it is production hours)
        begin
            disable autostats
            log autostats disable
        end
    else
        begin
            stats ok
        end
    else
        if (sysindexes.rowmodctr >= 425) -- 75 change leeway
        begin
            disable autostats
            log autostats disable
        end
```

Managing Statistics with Transact-SQL

Several commands deal with statistic management:

- **The UPDATE STATISTICS command.** This command computes statistics for all indexes on a table or for a specific index. This command also enables you to turn off automatic statistics update for a table or index.

- **The sp_updatestats command.** This command computes statistics on all indexes on all tables in a database.

- **The CREATE STATISTICS command.** This command computes statistics for a particular column. This command also enables you to turn off automatic statistics maintenance for a particular column.

- **The sp_createstats command.** This command computes statistics for all columns, except text, ntext, image, and computed columns, in all tables in the database.

- **The sp_autostats command.** This command shows you whether automatic statistics updating is turned on or off for a table or an index, and enables you to change whether statistics are updated automatically.

- **The DBCC SHOWSTATISTICS command.** This command shows you the current distribution statistics for an index or a column.

The following sections describe each of these commands.

UPDATE STATISTICS

The UPDATE STATISTICS command has the following syntax:

```
UPDATE STATISTICS table
[index ¦ (statistics_name[,...n])]
[WITH [FULLSCAN ¦
SAMPLE number {PERCENT ¦ ROWS}]
[[,] ALL ¦ COLUMNS ¦ INDEX]
[[,] NORECOMPUTE]]
```

table is the name of the table for which statistics are to be updated. You can specify a particular index or a list of statistics_names. A statistics_name is the name given to column statistics when they were computed. If you don't specify an index, all indexes on the table are updated.

FULLSCAN tells the UPDATE STATISTICS command to do a full scan of the table when computing the statistics. By default, it does a sample of enough rows (SQL Server determines what number is required) to get meaningful statistics. If you specify SAMPLE PERCENT ¦ ROWS, you can tell it how many rows or what percentage to scan. If the number you specify is too small to give meaningful statistics, SQL Server adjusts the number.

 General Tip

If your data is badly skewed (for example, it has lots of entries that start with the letter A, lots that start with the letter M, and few entries that start with any other letter), the sampling techniques may not produce useful statistics. In this case, you may get better results with a FULLSCAN.

If you use the ALL option, all indexes and column statistics are updated. If you use the COLUMNS option, only column statistics are updated. If you use the INDEX option, only index statistics are updated.

When you specify NORECOMPUTE, you turn off automatic updates of statistics until you update them again without this option or until you modify the option with sp_autostats.

sp_updatestats

The sp_updatestats command updates all statistics on all tables in the database. Because this could be a time-consuming activity, even with sampling, I don't recommend using this command.

CREATE STATISTICS

The CREATE STATISTICS command is used to create statistics on columns that aren't indexed. Its syntax is as follows:

```
CREATE STATISTICS statistics_name
ON table (column [,...n])
WITH [[ FULLSCAN| SAMPLE number PERCENT ]]
[[,] NORECOMPUTE]]
```

statistics_name is required. You can compute statistics on multiple columns; the statistics are computed as they would be for an index on multiple columns. One set of statistics are computed for the combination of the columns.

The FULLSCAN, SAMPLE PERCENT, and NORECOMPUTE options have the same meaning that they have for UPDATE STATISTICS. Note that it is not possible to specify a number of rows to sample for column statistics.

You cannot create statistics on text, ntext, image, or computed columns.

When you create column statistics, there will be an entry for statistics_name added to the sysindexes table.

You can delete statistics created with the CREATE STATISTICS command by using the DROP STATISTICS statement, as follows:

```
DROP STATISTICS table.statistics_name [,...n]
```

sp_createstats

The sp_createstats command creates statistics on every eligible column in every table in the database. Statistics are not created for columns that already have statistics—the first column in any index and columns with explicitly created statistics. Explicitly created statistics include those created by the Optimizer and those created by the CREATE STATISICS command. Columns of type text, ntext, and image are ineligible, as are computed columns. The syntax for this command is as follows:

```
sp_createstats ['indexonly'] [, 'fullscan']
[, 'norecompute']
```

If you specify indexonly, statistics are computed only for columns that are indexed. If you omit this keyword, statistics are computed on all eligible columns. If you specify fullscan, column statistics are computed by a full scan of the tables. If you omit this keyword, statistics are computed by sampling. If you specify norecompute, automatic updating of the computed column statistics are turned off.

I don't recommend using this command. It has a very global effect and may be very time consuming.

sp_autostats

The sp_autostats command enables you to turn automatic updating of statistics on or off. The syntax for this command is as follows:

```
sp_autostats 'table_name'[, 'stats_flag']
[, 'index_name']
```

If you issue the `sp_autostats` command with just a table name, as shown in the following, you will see the setting for all indexes and column statistics for the table:

```
sp_autostats [Order Details]
```

The report also shows you the date the statistics were last updated.

`stats_flag` can have a value of ON or OFF. The following command turns off updating of all index and column statistics for the Order Details table:

```
sp_autostats [Order Details], 'OFF'
```

 General Tip

You must enclose the word ON or OFF in single quotation marks. The keyword is not case sensitive.

To specify whether statistics should be automatically maintained for an index or a set of column statistics, supply either the index name or the statistics name, as shown here:

```
sp_autostats [Order Details], 'ON',
PK_ORDERDETAILS
```

DBCC SHOWSTATISTICS

If you want to see the statistics for an index or a column, you issue the `DBCC SHOW_STATISTICS` command:

```
DBCC SHOW_STATISTICS (table, target)
```

`table` is the name of the table. `target` is the index name or statistics name.

When you issue this command, you will get the following report:

```
Statistics for INDEX 'PK_Order_Details'.
Updated               Rows          Rows Sampled Steps
--------------------  -----------   ------------ ----------
Oct 13 1999  3:08PM   2155          2155         270
Density       Average key length
------------  -------------
1.1922787E-3  7.9999347

All density         Columns
1.2048193E-3        OrderID
4.6403712E-4        OrderID, ProductID

Steps
-----------
10248
10251
10253
10256
10259
10262
10264
.
.
.
```

The most interesting part of this report is the column labeled Density. Density is the inverse of selectivity; the lower the density, the higher the selectivity is. A perfect value for density is 0, meaning that there are no duplicates. In this particular example (and in every run of DBCC I have seen), the overall density computation is inexact. The index PK_Order_Details implements the primary key for the Order Details table and there cannot be any duplicates. However, the density is .0011922787, so there seems to be some rounding error.

Other information in this report includes the density for the different columns that comprise the index, as well as the key that marks the start of each step. SQL Server statistics are computed in steps, and each step has approximately the same number of rows. There are 2,155 rows in this table, and 270 steps. Therefore, each step represents about 8 rows. If we look at the first few OrderIDs in the Order Details table, we find the following values.

OrderID	Count of Rows
10248	3
10249	2
10250	3
10251	3
10252	3
10253	3
10254	3
10255	4

Step 1 includes the rows for OrderIDs 10248, 10249, and 10250 (exactly 8 rows). Step 2 includes the rows for OrderIDs 10251 and 10252 (6 rows), and Step 3 includes orders 10253, 10254, and 10255 (10 rows). There is a maximum of 300 steps, regardless of how many rows there are in the table. This is the information that the Optimizer uses to determine how many rows are returned as a result of a query.

Managing Statistics with DMO

DMO provides methods for updating statistics on a table, index, or column, and for viewing the statistics. I cannot find a way to define column statistics in DMO.

Table and Index objects have an UpdateStatistics method. Invoking these methods produces the default behavior of the Transact-SQL UPDATE STATISTICS command. Table, Index, and Column objects also have a method named UpdateStatisticsWith that enables you to vary the way the statistics are computed.

The `UpdateStatisticsWith` method of the Table object has four arguments, as shown here.

Argument	Description
`AffectType`	Specifies whether all statistics, column statistics, or index statistics should be updated. Values for this property must be taken from the list of `AffectType` constants (see the `AffectType` Constants table).
`ScanType`	Specifies whether a full or sample scan should be performed. Values for this property must be take from the list of `ScanType` constants (see the `ScanType` Constants table).
`ScanNumber`	Specifies the number or rows or percentage to be scanned. It is used only when you specify a row or percentage scan. This argument is optional.
`NORECOMPUTE`	True to leave automatic statistics updating unchanged; false to disable automatic updating in the future. This argument is optional and is true by default.

The tables in the following sections list the constants mentioned in the preceding table.

AffectType *Constants*

Constant	Description
`SQLDMOStatistic_AffectAll`	Updates all statistics.
`SQLDMOStatistic_AffectColumn`	Updates column statistics only.
`SQLDMOStatistic_AffectIndex`	Default. Updates index statistics only.

ScanType Constants

Constant	Description
`SQLDMOStatistic_FULLSCAN`	Performs a full scan of the index(es) or column(s) to determine statistics values.
`SQLDMOStatistic_Percent`	Performs a sampled scan using a percentage value. When specified, use the `ScanNumber` value to indicate percentage. Specify percentage using a whole number (for example, 55 specifies 55%).
`SQLDMOStatistic_Rows`	Performs a sampled scan using a number of rows. When specified, use the `ScanNumber` argument to indicate number of rows.
`SQLDMOStatistic_Sample`	Performs a percentage-sampled scan using a system-defined percentage.

The `UpdateStatisticsWith` method of the Column and Index objects is very similar to that for the Table object. However, there is no `AffectType` argument. The other three arguments are the same and use the same constants as the `UpdateStatisticsWith` method for the Table object.

The Index object and the Table object have an EnumStatistics method. It takes no arguments and returns a QueryResult object containing the same information shown earlier for DBCC SHOW_STATISTICS. There's no way to view column statistics in DMO.

Managing Statistics with Enterprise Manager

There is no way to manage statistics with Enterprise Manager.

Analyzing Performance

SQL Server 7.0 provides several tools for studying the performance of Transact-SQL statements. To determine why performance problems exist, you need to study the execution plan and look at the I/O statistics. The following sections discuss both of these.

Studying the Execution Plan

The execution plan is the plan the Query Optimizer developed for retrieving the data. You can view a graphic representation of the plan in Query Analyzer, or you can get a textual representation of the plan by using the SET SHOWPLAN_TEXT or SET SHOWPLAN_ALL options before you issue the query. The query is not actually executed when you use these options. This can be extremely useful if you are analyzing a query plan for a query that takes a very long time to run.

To see the graphic representation of the plan, type the query in Query Analyzer. Then select Display Estimated Execution Plan from the Query menu. A display similar to that shown in Figure 10.1 appears.

Figure 10.1   Query and Estimated Execution Plan screen.

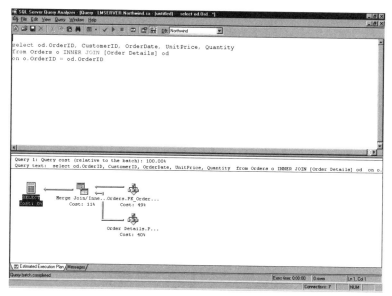

Notice that Figure 10.1 shows that the Optimizer has decided to use a merge join strategy for the query. The two inputs to the join are obtained from a clustered index scan. There are many icons (also called logical and physical operators) for the various Optimizer steps; there's complete documentation for each icon in the Books OnLine. When you pass your mouse over an icon, you get additional information about that part of the plan (see Figure 10.2).

Figure 10.2   Details about an Execution Plan step.

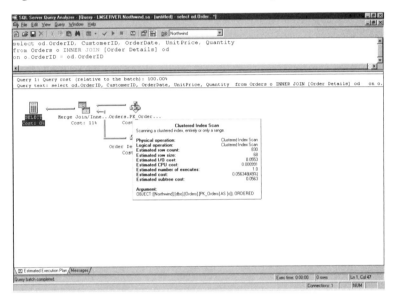

If you pass your mouse over one of the arrows on the plan, you get information about the data moving along that arrow (see Figure 10.3).

If the query plan contains potential problem areas, such as a table scan, the icon is red. Whether or not the icon is red, you can right-click it and see the menu shown in Figure 10.4.

This menu enables you to create, delete, or update indexes. It also enables you to manage statistics. If there are columns that might benefit from statistics, you have the option to create these statistics. This option is disabled in Figure 10.4 because there aren't any columns that don't already have statistics.

 General Tip

You can see the plan for a stored procedure without actually executing it. To see the plan for triggers, however, you must execute the query. To execute the query and see the execution plan, choose Show Execution Plan from the Query menu before you run the query. The query results are on the first tab. The second tab, the Execution Plan tab, shows you the plan.

Figure 10.3   Details about data.

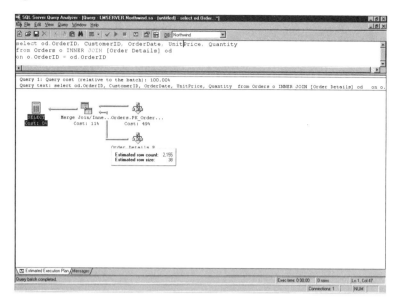

Figure 10.4   Execution Plan menu.

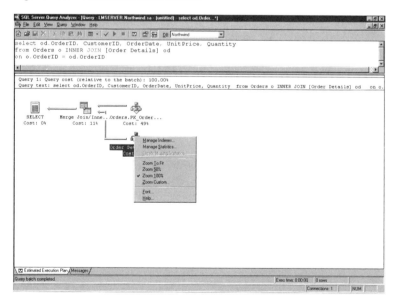

You can also see the execution plan in a textual format. To do this, you must issue the SET SHOWPLAN_TEXT or SET SHOWPLAN_ALL statement before you run the query. You must issue these commands on the connection that you are going to run the query on. SHOWPLAN_TEXT gives you less output than SHOWPLAN_ALL.

SHOWPLAN_TEXT

To get a limited-text execution plan, you issue commands similar to the following:

```
set showplan_text on
go
select od.OrderID, CustomerID, OrderDate, UnitPrice, Quantity
from Orders o INNER JOIN [Order Details] od
on o.OrderID = od.OrderID
```

In the results window, a report similar to the one shown here appears:

```
StmtText
-------------------------------------------------
 ¦--Merge Join(Inner Join,
MERGE:([o].[OrderID])=([od].[OrderID]),
RESIDUAL:([od].[OrderID]=[o].[OrderID]))
       ¦--Clustered Index Scan
(OBJECT:([Northwind].[dbo].[Orders].
[PK_Orders] AS [o]), ORDERED)
          ¦--Clustered Index Scan
(OBJECT:([Northwind].[dbo].
[Order Details].[PK_Order_Details]
AS [od]), ORDERED)
```

This shows the same information as that shown graphically in Figure 10.1.

SHOWPLAN_ALL

To see all the information that you get when you pass your mouse over an icon or an arrow in the graphic plan, use SHOWPLAN_ALL as shown here:

```
set showplan_all on
go
select od.OrderID, CustomerID, OrderDate, UnitPrice, Quantity
from Orders o INNER JOIN [Order Details] od
on o.OrderID = od.OrderID
```

The output is quite wide; you will probably find it easiest to put Query Analyzer in grid format. I have not included sample output here because it is too voluminous. For your information, however, the output is reflected in the following table.

Item	Description
StmtText	Either the Transact-SQL statement or the physical or logical operator and its description.
StmtId	Number of the statement in the current batch.
NodeId	ID of the node in the current query.
Parent	Node ID of the parent step.
PhysicalOp	Physical implementation algorithm for the node.
LogicalOp	Relational algebraic operator this node represents.
Argument	Provides supplemental information about the operation being performed. The contents of this column depend on the physical operator.
DefinedValues	Contains a comma-separated list of values introduced by this operator.

Item	Description
EstimateRows	Estimated number of rows output by this operator. For rows of type PLAN_ROWS only.
EstimateIO	Estimated I/O cost for this operator. For rows of type PLAN_ROWS only.
EstimateCPU	Estimated CPU cost for this operator. For rows of type PLAN_ROWS only.
AvgRowSize	Estimated average row size (in bytes) of the row being passed through this operator.
TotalSubtreeCost	Estimated (cumulative) cost of this operation and all child operations.
OutputList	Contains a comma-separated list of columns being output by the current operation.
Warnings	Contains a comma-separated list of warning messages relating to the current operation.
Type	Node type. For the parent node of each query, this is the Transact-SQL statement type (for example, SELECT, INSERT, EXECUTE, and so on). For subnodes representing execution plans, the type is PLAN_ROW.
Parallel	0 = Operator is not running in parallel. 1 = Operator is running in parallel.
EstimateExecutions	Estimated number of times this operator will be executed while running the current query.

If you want a textual description of the query plan and want to execute the query, use the following command:

```
set statistics profile on
go
```

The output from the query comes first in the Results window. After the query results is the output you would get from SHOWPLAN_ALL. You may want to combine this with the I/O statistics discussed in the following section.

Studying Statistics

SQL Server can report information about the I/O and time required for a query. This often helps to determine why a particular query is taking a long time to run. To see these statistics, you use the SET STATISTICS command.

 General Tip

The statistics I am talking about here are totally unrelated to the distribution statistics discussed earlier in this chapter.

To turn on I/O statistics, use the following command:

```
SET STATISTICS IO ON
```

To turn on time statistics, use the following command:

```
SET STATISTICS TIME ON
```

You can use both commands. I personally find IO more useful than time because many things can influence how long it takes the query to run—how many users there are, how much concurrent demand for the records required for the query, and so on. The same amount of I/O has to be done regardless. You must execute the query to get either of these statistics. Let's look at the result of the following statements:

```
set statistics io on
set statistics time on
go
select od.OrderID, CustomerID, OrderDate, UnitPrice, Quantity
from Orders o INNER JOIN [Order Details] od
on o.OrderID = od.OrderID
```

After the data has been returned, SQL Server gives the following information:

```
(2155 row(s) affected)Table 'Order Details'. Scan count 1, logical
reads 10,
 physical reads 0, read-ahead reads 0.
Table 'Orders'. Scan count 1, logical reads 27,
physical reads 0, read-ahead reads 0.

SQL Server Execution Times:
   CPU time = 210 ms,  elapsed time = 814 ms.
text
```

Scan count tells you the number of times the table was scanned. (This may not be an actual table scan.) The most important piece of information is the number of logical reads. A logical read is a read that must be performed regardless of whether the data is in cache. In the worst case, logical reads are equal to physical reads. Any reduction in logical reads generally means an improvement in performance. The preceding report contains no physical reads. But that's because I have been playing with this query and running it over and over while I have been writing this section, so all the necessary data was already in memory. For some queries, SQL Server can use read-ahead to put pages into the data cache before they are needed.

 General Tip

Although logical I/O is generally a better predictor of a query's performance than physical I/O, it is possible to clear out the buffers after running a query so that you see the physical I/O each time. To do this, use the following command:

```
DBCC DROPCLEANBUFFERS
```

SQL Profiler

The SQL Profiler is an incredibly useful tool. Unlike the SQL Trace utility of previous versions, which only captured messages sent to SQL Server, the Profiler interacts with the SQL Server Engine and has the capability to monitor and capture many different events, including the following:

- Login connects, failures, and disconnects
- *Remote Procedure Calls* (RPC)
- Starting or ending of a stored procedure
- Starting or ending of statements within stored procedures
- Start or end of a Transact-SQL batch
- Start or end of a Transact-SQL statement
- Errors written to the error log
- Locks, as they are applied and released
- Cursors, as they are opened and closed

For each of these events, SQL Profiler can capture the following:

- The type (class) of event
- The name of the client computer
- The ID of the object (such as a table) affected by the event
- The SQL Server name of the user
- The text of the Transact-SQL statement or stored procedure being executed
- The time the event started and ended

The Profiler includes a powerful set of filters that enable you to capture only the information you need. The information captured by the Profiler can be saved as a trace that you can subsequently replay, in its entirety or in a step-by-step Debugging mode. Traces created by the Profiler can also be used as input to the Index Tuning Wizard. It is also possible to save Profiler-captured information in a SQL file or store it in a table in a database.

You will find Profiler useful for performing the following tasks:

- Monitoring the performance of SQL Server
- Debugging Transact-SQL statements and stored procedures
- Identifying slow queries
- Testing SQL statements and stored procedures in the development phase of a project by single-stepping through statements to confirm that the code works as expected
- Troubleshooting problems in SQL Server

General Tip

You can use Profiler to capture a series of events on your production server and then replay the trace on a test server. This enables you to analyze problems without interfering with a production server.

 General Tip

Profiler can be particularly helpful when you are experiencing performance problems and do not have direct access to the SQL statements an application is issuing. This often happens when you have third-party applications or applications that generate SQL on-the-fly. Profiler can capture the actual SQL sent to the server. After you have the SQL, you can study execution plans and perform index analysis.

All the facilities of SQL Profiler are also available to you as extended stored procedures. This enables you to build your own monitoring tools if the Profiler does not provide exactly what you need, or if it provides more than you need. The names of these procedures all start with xp_trace, and there's a special section for them in Books OnLine. (Look in "System Stored Procedures: SQL Profiler Extended Stored Procedures" to find complete documentation.)

Trace definitions are stored in the Registry. There are two types of traces: private and shared. Private traces can only be used by the NT login that created them; shared traces can be used by anyone who can log in to the computer on which the trace was defined. Shared traces are stored under the following key:

```
HKEY_LOCAL_MACHINE\Software\Microsoft\MSSQLServer\SQLServerProfiler\
Client\Queues
```

Private traces are stored under the following key:

```
HKEY_CURRENT_USER\Software\Microsoft\MSSQLServer\SQLServerProfiler\
Client\Queues
```

 Warning

Be careful with shared traces. They may include password information that you would not want to be visible. I recommend that you create private traces.

 General Tip

You do not need to create traces on the server computer. In fact, you can create traces on a machine that is not even running SQL Server so long as you have SQL Profiler installed.

The Profiler is a complex tool to understand, but Microsoft has provided a Create Trace Wizard as well as some sample traces that will help you get started. I recommend using these until you become familiar with Profiler.

IMO

I'm not generally big on wizards. However, the Create Trace Wizard isn't just a pretty face on some SQL statements. Rather, it gives you some predefined traces that are all set up for the things you are most likely to want to monitor, and enables you to specify your own parameters for such things as query duration.

The Create Trace Wizard is accessible through Enterprise Manager. From the Tools menu, select Wizards. Expand the Management Wizards section and choose Create Trace Wizard. This wizard gives you a choice of six common problems:

1 Find the worst performing queries

2 Identify scans of large tables

3 Identify the cause of a deadlock

4 Profile the performance of a stored procedure

5 Trace Transact-SQL activity by application

6 Trace Transact-SQL activity by user

As you step through the Wizard's screens, you have the opportunity to do the following:

- Specify the database or databases you want to monitor

- Provide filters, such as the duration you consider "bad" for queries

- Include or exclude specific applications

 General Tip

Unless you are specifically interested in SQL Agent, I recommend excluding it. When it is running, it interacts continuously with SQL Server and generates a lot of entries in the trace that aren't of interest.

When you complete the wizard, SQL Profiler starts. You can further customize the trace in the Profiler if you want.

 General Tip

If your Enterprise Manager Server registration is set to Prompt for Password, SQL Profiler will not work regardless of whether the Wizard in Enterprise Manager starts it or you start it yourself from the Start menu. You must specify the password in the Enterprise Manager registration for Profiler to work.

 Warning

Profiler does not seem to work when the client's default network library is TCP/IP. It seems to want named pipes or Multiprotocol.

To create a trace definition without using the wizard, just start Profiler. If you want to use one of the sample traces, choose File, Open, Trace Definition, and select the sample trace from the drop-down list. There are six sample traces:

- **Sample 1—TSQL.** This trace captures connects, disconnects, existing connections, as well as the start of RPC and Transact-SQL batches. The trace displays the event class, the SQL text, and the start time. The Profiler application is excluded from tracing. This trace has the information you need for the Index Tuning Wizard.

- **Sample 2—TSQL—grouped.** This trace captures the same information as Sample 1. However, it displays the application name, Windows NT username, SQL Server username, connection ID, and spid, in addition to the fields displayed by Sample 1. It groups the display by application name, NT username, SQL Server username, and connection ID. Grouped results can be easier to read. The SQL Profiler application is excluded.

- **Sample 3—Stored Procedures counts.** This trace captures the Stored Procedure Starting event, and displays the event class, server name, database ID, and object ID. The SQL Profiler application is excluded.

ᏨᏨ   IMO

Sample 3 doesn't seem very useful to me. It would be much more useful if it showed the text of the stored procedure or the number of reads and writes or something like that.

- **Sample 4—TSQL and Stored Procedures.** This trace captures connects, disconnects, existing connections, stored procedure starts, stored procedure ends, stored procedure statement starts, RPC starts, and Transact-SQL batch starts. The display shows the event class, the server name, the database ID, the object ID, the SQL text, the start time, and something called *binary data* that contains the internal representation of the connection ID. The SQL Profiler application is excluded.

- **Sample 5—TSQL by duration.** This trace captures the RPC completed and SQL Batch Completed events. The display includes the event class, the duration, and the SQL text. The SQL Profiler application is excluded and the duration is filtered on a minimum of 1 millisecond, so queries that take less than a millisecond do not show in the output.

- **Sample 6—TSQL for replay.** This trace is designed to capture information you need when you plan to replay the trace on the same server or on a different server. It captures Cursor Execute, Cursor Open, Cursor Prepare, Exec Prepared, SQL Prepare, Connect, Disconnect, Existing Connections, RPC Starting, and SQL Batch Starting events. It displays event class, event subclass, application name, SQL text, SQL username, database ID, connection ID, server name, host name, binary data, and start time. The SQL Profiler application is excluded.

All the sample traces are private.

General Tip

If you modify one of the sample traces, I recommend saving the trace under a different name. This leaves the sample unchanged in case you want to refer to it in the future. The option to save the trace under a new name is on the General tab of the Create trace dialog box.

To create a trace from scratch, choose File, New. By default, SQL Profiler shows only the more commonly used events and data columns. To see the full set of events, choose Options from the Tools menu and select All Events. To see the full set of data columns, select All Columns.

 General Tip

Before you create a trace from scratch, I recommend that you study the excellent documentation on the Events and Data columns in Books OnLine.

When you create a trace, it starts when you click the OK button.

When you want to run a trace that you previously created, choose File, Run Traces and select the trace you want to use.

To save the trace results, choose File, Save As, and select Trace File, Trace Table, or SQL File. If you are planning to use the saved results with the Index Tuning Wizard, you can save either a trace file or a SQL file.

Index Analysis and Index Tuning Wizard

SQL Server 7.0 provides two tools for determining what indexes might improve the performance of problem queries: index analysis and the Index Tuning Wizard. The index analysis function is built in to Query Analyzer, which makes it real handy for doing an analysis after you have looked at the execution plan. The Index Tuning Wizard enables you to use a workload file of many queries as input. Both of these tools can be a bit slow, so you must be patient with them.

Index Analysis

To perform an index analysis in Query Analyzer, choose Perform Index Analysis from the Query menu. If there are indexes that might be useful, the dialog box that shows the indexes gives you the option of building them immediately or saving a script so that they can be built later.

 General Tip

The index analysis never recommends a clustered index. The Index Tuning Wizard recommends one or more clustered indexes.

Sometimes the index analysis does not find any useful indexes. This happens when the tables are small (fewer than 10 pages), when appropriate indexes already exist, or when the only useful index would be a clustered index.

Index Tuning Wizard

The Index Tuning Wizard can analyze a workload that contains up to 32,767 different queries. Be prepared for a long wait if you give it that many!

The Index Tuning Wizard can be started from Enterprise Manager. It is in the Management group of wizards. The wizard can work with a SQL file containing query text or a trace file or trace table created by SQL Profiler. The wizard enables you to say whether you want to keep all existing indexes. If you choose this option, existing indexes are unchanged. If you don't choose this, existing indexes may be dropped or modified. Keep existing indexes is the default.

 General Tip

If you have already tuned a set of queries, you probably want to keep those indexes. Changes to them might impair the performance of other queries at the expense of those currently being analyzed.

You also have the option of requesting a thorough analysis. This takes longer, but gives you better results. In most cases, you should do a thorough analysis. If the wizard is failing to complete because of the size of the workload, however, you can turn this option off.

You must choose a single database for the wizard to work on. It does not recommend indexes for tables in another database, even though your workload may reference these tables.

You can restrict the amount of space you want to use for the indexes as well as telling it the maximum number of columns you want to allow in the indexes. By default, it uses as much space as is available and allows 16 columns per index. (Sixteen is the maximum number of columns in an index regardless of whether you create it yourself or the Index Tuning Wizard creates it.)

By default, the wizard analyzes all tables in the database. You can request that it work on specific tables. The only tables that it makes recommendations for are the ones in the queries in the workload, in any case.

After the wizard completes its analysis of the workload, it presets its recommendations. It shows you the indexes that it proposes should be created, and gives you a estimate of the amount of performance improvement to expect. If you click the Analysis button on the recommendations display, the wizard tells you how many (in percentages) of the queries in your workload will benefit from each of the indexes it proposes. You can save this analysis to a tab-delimited file for later reference.

You can apply the changes immediately, schedule them for later application, or save a script file. If you save a script file, you can change the names of indexes and make any other changes you want. You will also have a script that you can use if you need to make the changes on another server.

The wizard does not propose indexes for primary key and unique constraints, because indexes are already in place for these. If you say that you want to drop existing indexes, the indexes that implement constraints will not be dropped.

SQL Performance Monitor

SQL Performance Monitor is just a set of objects and counters added to Windows NT's Performance Monitor. You can use Performance Monitor (also called Perfmon) to study the following:

- Disk activity
- CPU activity
- Memory utilization

Performance Monitor enables you to study SQL Server–related elements together with other operating system elements. Appendix B, "Performance Condition Alert Objects," contains a complete list of the SQL Server Performance Monitor objects and counters. This section discusses the most important ones for monitoring the three areas in the preceding listed.

General Tip

Performance Monitor does enable you to monitor things such as locks, but you will not find this tool as useful as some of the tools I mentioned in Chapter 5, "Transaction Management." Perfmon shows you serverwide statistics, and knowing the total number of blocking locks is not nearly as useful as knowing what process is holding them and what resources are locked.

General Tip

It is possible to define threshold alerts in Perfmon that can notify you when something exceeds or falls below a certain value. In earlier versions of SQL Server, it was possible to use a program called SQLALTR to tie these threshold alerts to SQL Server's alerting system. With SQL Server 7.0, SQL Server alerts can be defined for most of the important performance conditions (see Chapter 8, "Jobs and Alerts") and the old mechanism is no longer available.

When you are using Perfmon, it is important that spikes or sudden drops in the value of a counter don't mislead you. You want to make sure that the counter value is stable before you worry about it.

Monitoring Disk Activity

SQL Server uses underlying Windows NT facilities to read from and write to the database files. Disk activities are often a source of bottlenecks in database systems, and Perfmon can help you study them. When you monitor disk activity, you need to look at how the I/O subsystem is behaving and watch for excessive paging.

To monitor overall disk I/O, use the Physical Disk: % Disk Time and the Physical Disk: Avg. Queue Length counters. The % Disk Time counter describes the amount of time that the system is busy performing I/O activities. If this counter is steadily over 90%, you need to investigate the Avg. Queue Length counter. This counter shows you the number of outstanding requests for disk access. If this counter is consistently more than 1.5 to 2 times the number of spindles, you probably need additional or faster disk resources. (Most disks have one spindle, although RAID devices often have more than one.)

 General Tip

When you use software RAID, you may see that % Disk Time exceeds 100%. In this case, you should depend on the Avg. Queue Length counter to determine whether the device is saturated.

When you look at Avg. Queue Length, you may find that one database disk has a long queue and another has a short queue. This may indicate that using file groups and moving some data from one drive to the other could solve the bottleneck. You should also look at Avg. Queue Length in terms of the SQL Server max async io configuration option (see max async io later in the chapter). If Avg. Queue Length is consistently less than the value of max async io, you have unused disk resources and could increase the max async io value. Conversely, if Avg. Queue Length is consistently greater than max async io, you may need to lower the value for max async io.

 General Tip

Because monitoring disk I/O places its own demands on the system, the disk counters are not installed with Perfmon by default. If you want to use these counters, you must issue the DISKPERF -Y (or DISKPERF -YE) commands in the command shell, and then shut down and restart the computer.

To monitor SQL Server–specific disk activity, study the SQL Server: Buffer Manager Page Reads/sec and SQL Server Buffer Manager Page Writes/sec counters. If either of these is approaching the capacity of the disk hardware, you should do one or both of the following:

- Attempt to tune the application so that fewer I/O operations are required. For example, perhaps I/O would be reduced if there were appropriate indexes or if the database design were denormalized.

- If the applications cannot be tuned, you need to acquire disk devices with more I/O capacity.

To monitor paging, you need to look at the Memory: Pages/sec. This could be the cause of excessive I/O because the page file is also kept on disk. If your system has sufficient memory, the number of page faults should be low. If it is not, see the discussion of page faults in the section "Monitoring Memory Utilization" later in this chapter.

Monitoring CPU Activity

Database activities tend to be more I/O intensive than CPU intensive. But if SQL Server is doing operations such as computing aggregates with all of the data in memory, it can use all the CPU resources. It is important to monitor CPU utilization so that you can be sure you have enough CPU resources. The most important counter to watch is Processor: %Processor Time. If this counter is consistently showing values of 80% to 90%, you may need additional CPUs or a faster CPU. This counter measures the sum of all processors. If you have multiple processors, you can find the per-processor average in the System: % Total Processor Time counter.

You also want to watch the Processor: % Privileged Time counter. If this is consistently high and the Physical Disk counters described in the preceding section are also high, it is likely that SQL Server is I/O bound. Tuning the application and/or improving the disk subsystem may reduce CPU utilization.

Monitoring Memory Utilization

Available memory and a good disk subsystem are critical for a high-performance SQL Server. You want to monitor some important memory counters to make sure that SQL Server has sufficient resources.

One of the most important things to watch is the SQL Server: Buffer Manager Buffer Cache Hit Ratio counter. It should consistently be 90% or higher. If it is not at that level, you should add more memory until it reaches the 90% level. Another indicator of a low memory condition for SQL Server is the SQL Server: Buffer Manager: Free Buffers counter. If this is consistently low, you should add memory. A final check on memory is the SQL Server Memory Manager: Total Server Memory counter. If this is consistently high relative to the amount of physical memory in the machine, you need to add memory.

You should monitor the Process: Working Set counter. If this is consistently less than the amount of memory available to SQL Server (as specified by the `min server memory` and `max server memory` configuration options), you can either configure SQL Server so that it uses less memory or increase the size of SQL Server's working set by changing the configuration option `set working set size`.

Two counters tell you about memory on the machine. These are not specific to SQL Server. If Memory: Available Bytes is low, the machine is starved for memory. If Memory: Page Faults/sec is high, more memory is also needed. If the number of Page Faults count is high, you can determine whether SQL Server is causing the page faults by looking at the Process: Pages/sec counter.

Performance-Related Configuration Options

Chapter 3, "Managing Client Connectivity," describes setting configuration options. The tools I described there are used to set performance-related options as well. Configuration options are classified on two different dimensions:

- **Standard versus advanced.** Standard options are the most commonly changed, whereas advanced options are infrequently changed.
- **Static versus dynamic.** Static options do not take effect until the server is restarted, whereas the dynamic options take effect immediately.

In the following descriptions of the performance-related options, I place one of the following in parentheses after the discussion of the option:

- **(S, S).** Standard option, requires restart
- **(S, D).** Standard option, takes effect immediately
- **(A, S).** Advanced option, requires restart
- **(A, D).** Advanced option, takes effect immediately

Use these category descriptions to understand when options take effect and when you are required to restart SQL for them to take effect.

Some of the configuration options related to performance apply to any machine; others are meaningful only for multiprocessor computers.

Remember that configuration options apply to the SQL Server as a whole. Changing them can affect everything running on the SQL Server.

 General Tip

When you are considering tweaking configuration options to improve performance, it is important to do the following:

1 Measure performance before changing the option.

2 Change only one option at a time.

3 Measure performance after changing the option and determine whether there has been an improvement.

General Performance-Related Options

Options described in this section may be useful in single or multiprocessor machines:

- `cursor threshold`   This option specifies the number of rows at which the keysets for cursors should be generated asynchronously, enabling users to retrieve data from the cursor while it is still being populated. In other words, if `cursor threshold` is set to 5000, any cursors with more than 5000 rows will be populated asynchronously. If `cursor threshold` is −1 (the default), all keysets are generated synchronously. This is beneficial when most cursors involve a small number of rows. If `cursor threshold` is 0, all cursors are populated asynchronously. Do not set this value too low, because it is faster to populate small cursors synchronously. (A, D)

- `index create memory` (KB)   This option specifies how much memory should be used for sorts that may be required when creating indexes. This option is self-configuring, and in most cases you can leave it set that way. Creation of large indexes is not a common activity in production databases and is likely to be done during off-peak hours. If you are building large indexes when few users are online, you may want to experiment with setting this option. Make sure that you keep `min memory per query` set to a lower number so that the create index runs even if the amount of memory requested by the `index create memory` option is not available. (A, D)

- `max async io`   This option specifies the number of asynchronous I/O requests the server can issue against a file. By default, `max async io` is set to 32. If you have a sophisticated I/O subsystem with many disks and controllers, you can configure it to 64 or higher. Try multiplying the number of disks by 2 or 3 to arrive at an initial number. Use Performance Monitor to watch disk activity, and lower the value of `max async io` if you experience a lot of disk queuing. If I/O activity is low, increase `max async io`. If you have many files, you will find a lower value for `max async io` is better. (A, S)

- `max worker threads`   This option specifies the number of internal threads used by connected users to get SQL Server resources. By default, `max worker threads` is 255, which works reasonably well for many systems. If you expect to have fewer than 255 concurrent user connections, you can lower the number of worker threads to the number of concurrent connections, thus freeing the memory and other resources required by a thread for other uses. If there are fewer threads than concurrent users, SQL Server uses thread pooling, and share threads that are inactive. (A, D)

- `min memory per query` (KB)   This option specifies the minimum amount of memory that must be available for a query to run. In general, increasing this value benefits queries that use hashing or sorting operations, particularly if you have lots of memory and few concurrent queries. If you set this value too high, queries wait until the required memory is available (see the `query wait` option). This can cause performance degradation on busy systems. (A, D)

- `query governor cost limit`   This option enables you to prevent long-running queries from ever getting started. The limit is specified in terms of the cost determined by the Optimizer, not seconds as stated in the documentation. If the Optimizer determines that the query costs more than the limit specified in the `query governor cost limit` configuration option, the query does not run at all. (A, D)

 General Tip

There's also a SET option that can specify a `query governor cost limit` for a specific connection, as shown here:

   SET QUERY_GOVERNOR_COST_LIMIT *value*

 General Tip

I don't know any way to determine the cost of a query without looking at the estimated execution plan.

- `query wait (s)`   Memory-intensive queries wait until resources are available to process them. By default, a query waits for 25 times its estimated execution cost. You can specify a wait time between 0 and 2,147,483,647 seconds for this option. To reset the option to its default behavior, set it to −1. (A, D)

- `time slice (ms)`   This option controls the amount of time that a process is allowed to spend before scheduling itself out and waiting for another chance. The SQL Server kernel is not preemptive and depends on processes to release the CPU for others. By default, the time slice is 100 milliseconds. If you set it too low, the system slows down because there will be a lot of overhead as processes continually schedule themselves in and out of the CPU. If you set it too high, it delays response time for others because one process can monopolize the CPU. There is rarely a need to change this option. (A, S)

Performance-Related Options That Apply Only to Multiprocessor Machines

Options described in this section apply only to machines with more than one processor:

- `affinity mask`   This option enables you to specify which processor(s) SQL Server threads should run on. It is only useful on machines with more than four processors, or on an SQL Server running on a machine with another application that uses a lot of CPU. If you use this option, you can dedicate some processors to SQL Server and others to NT or other applications running on the machine. By default, `affinity mask` is 0, and NT determines which processor a SQL Server thread runs on.

`affinity mask` is a integer, with one bit corresponding to each of the processors. If you want SQL Server threads to run on processors 0, 1, 2, 3, and 4, for example, you would specify a value of 31, which corresponds to the following bit mask (A, S):

```
00011111
```

- `cost threshold for parallelism`   This option controls when SQL Server develops a parallel query plan. It computes a serial plan, and, if the cost of the serial plan is greater than the cost threshold, the Optimizer than develops a parallel plan. Parallel plans are of most benefit for longer queries. Values for cost threshold for parallelism can range from 0 to 32,767. The default is 5. If you have set `affinity mask` so that SQL Server runs on only one processor, or if you have set `max degree of parallelism` to 1, this threshold is ignored. (A, D)

- `lightweight pooling`   In multiprocessor systems, overhead is often associated with the context switches needed when a thread that had been running on one processor is scheduled to run on another. If you are experiencing this overhead (watch the Context Switches/sec counter in Perfmon), you will benefit from using lightweight pooling. This option can also be useful when you have a high-volume, OLTP application because it can reduce overall CPU utilization. SQL Server uses fibers rather than threads when this option is set to 1. By default, this option is turned off (0). (A, S)

- `max degree of parallelism`   This option limits the number of threads to be used in processing a single query in parallel. By default, the number of processors available to SQL Server sets the maximum number of threads. Set this option to 1 if you do not want any queries processed in parallel. There is rarely a need to change this option. (A, D)

- `priority boost`   This option changes SQL Server's scheduling priority in NT and allows SQL Server to run at a higher priority than other processes on the machine. By default, SQL Server's priority is 7 on a single processor computer and 15 on a multiprocessor computer. If you set priority boost to 1, SQL Server runs at priority 15 on a single processor machine and 25 on a multiprocessor machine. You should change priority boost only on multiprocessor computers that are dedicated to SQL Server. (A, S)

 General Tip

`priority boost` can cause Error 17824, `Unable to write to ListenOn` `connection messages`. Normally, this message indicates network problems. If this message is occurring frequently, however, check priority boost. If it has been set to 1, set it back to the default and the messages will go away.

- `spin counter`   This option specifies the number of attempts a process can make to acquire a resource. On single-processor machines, there is no possibility of contention and this option is always 0. On multiprocessor machines, this option defaults to 100 and can be as high as 10000. (A, D)

I said at the beginning of the chapter that the most significant factor in the performance of any SQL Server database is the design of the database itself. I have tried to show you some of the tools available to analyze performance problems. Keep in mind, however, that if the database design is flawed, or queries are badly written, there are no magic buttons you can push. Performance monitoring and troubleshooting is not easy. Here's a quote from Dennis Sasha's book, *Database Tuning, A Principled Approach*, which sums up the process well:

"…troubleshooters agree on three facts:

1 Troubleshooting requires tuning queries, indexes, lock contention and logging.

2 It requires balancing the load between the client and the server.

3 It is challenging, exasperating and fun.

May Murphy be absent. Good luck!"

A
Bibliography

SQL Server–Specific Books

Many, many SQL Server books are on the market. In this section, I've tried to list only those that I've actually used or read and that are particularly useful. Any book published before 1999 was probably written on Beta 3 and is likely to have several errors, because many things have changed between Beta 3 and the actual release of SQL Server 7.0.

Baird, Sean, Chris Miller, Michael Hotek. *SQL Server System Administration*. Indianapolis, IN: New Riders Publishing, 1999. ISBN: 1-5620-5955-6

> This is a thin (in number of pages), but highly useful, book. It covers most of the basic administrative tasks. The authors of this book have brought years of SQL Server experience to bear on SQL Server 7.0.

Delaney, Kalen, and Ron Soukup. *Inside Microsoft SQL Server 7.0*. Redmond, WA: Microsoft Press, 1999. ISBN: 0-7356-0517-3

> Delaney picked up Soukup's mantle and rewrote *Inside SQL Server 6.5* for this edition. The book is rich in details regarding SQL Server 7.0's internals, and it has a lot of best practices. It's oriented to the designer-developer, but there's plenty of useful stuff for the administrator as well.

Gunderloy, Mike, and Mary Chipman. *SQL Server 7 in Record Time*. San Francisco: Sybex, 1999. ISBN: 0-7821-2155-1

> This book covers a wide variety of tasks, both administrative and development. Mike and Mary bring their extensive experience as consultants to this book. It jumps around from topic to topic, but given the range of topics, it has a lot of useful information for the administrator and the developer.

Kline, Kevin, Lee Gould, and Andrew Zanevsky. *Transact-SQL Programming*. Sebastopol, CA: O'Reilly & Associates, Inc., 1999. ISBN: 1-56592-401-0

> This book provides in-depth coverage of Transact-SQL programming. You will gain a full command of the language if you work through this book. The authors are all SQL Server developers with a huge number of years of experience behind them. The book focuses on the SQL Server 6.5 and Sybase 11.5 level of Transact-SQL. The core language is still relevant for 7.0, and a long appendix covers what's new in SQL Server 7.0, including information about the query optimizer.

Petkovic, Dusan. *SQL Server 7: A Beginner's Guide*. Berkeley, CA: Osborne/McGraw-Hill, 1999. ISBN: 0-07-211891-1

> This is a very useful book if you're new to SQL Server and to databases in general. The book covers primarily developer aspects, but there is some treatment of administrative topics as well. Petkovic also provides information about Microsoft Decision Support Services (OLAP).

Talmage, Ronald R. *Microsoft SQL Server 7 Administrator's Guide*. Indianapolis, IN: Prima Publishing, 1999. ISBN: 1-5620-5955-6

> Talmage is another denizen of the SWYNK list. He's also replaced Kalen Delaney as the "SQL Essentials" columnist for *SQL Server Professional* magazine. This is a comprehensive guide for administrators, particularly those who are new to SQL Server because of its extensive coverage of Transact-SQL.

Wynkoop, Steven. *Special Edition Using Microsoft SQL Server 7.0*. Indianapolis, IN: Que Publishing, 1999. ISBN: 0-7897-1523-6

> This is a comprehensive reference for both developers and administrators. It tackles SQL Mail and ADO, and has a reasonable amount of information about setting up replication. Wynkoop has been running SWYNK.COM (see other resources listed in this appendix) for several years and he founded an international online SQL Server user group. He uses SQL Server to support the very active site.

General Database Books

Celko, Joe. *Joe Celko's SQL Puzzles and Answers*. San Francisco: Morgan Kaufmann Publishers, Inc., 1997. ISBN: 1-5586-0453-7

> For many years, Joe published a column in the *Database Programming and Design* magazine. He'd list a puzzle for readers to solve. The following month, he'd publish solutions and a new puzzle. Later, he was a columnist at *DBMS* magazine, and had a similar column. This book collects the puzzles and the answers, all of which are applicable to business problems that are often difficult to solve in SQL. It's a fun read, as well as a valuable resource.

Celko, Joe. *Instant SQL Programming*. Birmingham, UK: WROX Press, 1995. ISBN: 1-8744-1650-8

> This book gives a comprehensive treatment of SQL, including features of the 92 standard. An appendix has instructions for converting the many examples to Sybase/Microsoft Transact-SQL. It also includes a runtime version of WATCOM SQL.

Celko, Joe. *SQL For Smarties: Advanced SQL Programming*. San Francisco: Morgan Kaufmann Publishers, Inc., 1999. ISBN 1-5586-0323-9

> This book gives an expert explanation of ANSI SQL constructs, and it provides solutions to many different SQL problems. It belongs in the library of anyone who is writing serious Transact-SQL.

Date, C. J. *An Introduction to Database Systems, Sixth Edition*. Reading, MA: Addison-Wesley, 1995. ISBN: 0-201-54329-X

> Now in its seventh edition, this "bible" contains a comprehensive review of relational theory and is a must for serious database professionals.

Fleming, Candace, and Barbara Von Halle. *Handbook of Relational Database Design*. Reading, MA: Addison-Wesley, 1989. ISBN: 0-2011-1434-8

> This book gives a comprehensive treatment of the design process. It uses a case study to provide a step-by-step cookbook for both logical and physical design.

Gray, Jim, and Andreas Reuter. *Transaction Processing: Concepts and Techniques*. San Mateo, CA: Morgan Kaufmann Publishers, Inc., 1993. ISBN: 1-5586-0190-2

> This book is a definitive work on transaction processing by the architect of Microsoft's distributed transaction strategies. It's heavy going, but well worth it!

Hackathorn, Richard D. *Enterprise Database Connectivity: The Key to Enterprise Applications on the Desktop*. New York: John Wiley and Sons, Inc., 1993. ISBN: 0-4715-7802-9

> This is a leading reference for distributed computing. It provides both theoretical and practical approaches to distributing data and process throughout the enterprise.

Shasha, Dennis. *Database Tuning: A Principled Approach*. Englewood Cliffs, NJ: Prentice-Hall, 1992. ISBN: 0-1320-5246-6

> This book shows you how to apply general tuning principles to solve specific performance problems. Some Sybase/Microsoft-specific (System 10/SQL Server 6.0) material is included in it.

Periodicals

Microsoft Developer Network Library. Microsoft Corporation. 1 Microsoft Way, Redmond, WA 98052.

> This quarterly CD-ROM publication is aimed at the application developer. It is filled with useful articles and great code samples. Four subscription levels provide different materials. The Library edition gives you only the technical references. The Enterprise and Universal subscriptions include developer editions (limited number of users) of all BackOffice products. An online subscription also gives you Internet access to the technical references. A powerful search engine makes finding information easy.

Microsoft TechNet. Microsoft Corporation. 1 Microsoft Way, Redmond, WA 98052.

> This monthly CD-ROM publication is aimed at technical support professionals and MSCEs. Its powerful search engine makes finding information easy. It has the best troubleshooting information available

for SQL Server, and it includes service packs when available and a near-current version of the Knowledge Base.

SQL Server Magazine. Duke Communications, Inc. Loveland, CO.

This is a very useful magazine. It covers a wide range of topics every month, and the topics run the gamut from ADO to hard-core internals. The series it has been running on DTS has had the best information available on that topic. It is well worth the $49.95 per year. A companion Web site, www.sqlmag.com, has discussion forums as well as additional articles and downloadable code.

SQL Server Professional. Pinnacle Publishing, Inc. 18000 72nd Ave. South, Suite 217, Kent, WA 98032.

This newsletter has excellent coverage of SQL Server including a lot of tips and techniques. It focuses more on administrative topics than *SQL Server Magazine* does. To me, it's well worth the fairly expensive annual subscription fee. Code is available to subscribers at www.pinpub.com.

Other Resources

Professional Organization for SQL Server (PASS): www.sqlpass.org

This organization is relatively new. There are some discussion forums, and more is forthcoming on this site. A lot of discounts are available to members. Web membership is free. Voting memberships are available for corporations and individuals. PASS sponsors monthly online chats in conjunction with TechNet and has recently opened its knowledge portal, which serves as a repository of "everything SQL Server."

MSDN Online Newsgroups: msnews.Microsoft.com

Microsoft newsgroups offer extensive discussions on SQL Server. This is the place to get your questions answered by knowledgeable users, many of whom have been named "Most Valuable Professional" by Microsoft. Microsoft also responds to questions posted on this news server.

Microsoft Developer Network SQL Server: msdn.Microsoft.com\SQLServer

This site has recently become extremely useful; there are lots of white papers. It's part of the larger Microsoft Developer Network site, but focused on SQL Server. Online "experts" (other users) are available to answer questions on occasion, and online chats are scheduled on a periodic basis.

Steve Wynkoop's Web site: www.swynk.com

Sign up here for SQL Server 6.5 and 7.0, and other BackOffice product, mailing lists. This site has a lot of people posting interesting questions and getting answers from knowledgeable folks. There is no flaming, just the occasional religious discussion on the best way to do something. Several articles by guest columnists are available on the site, as well as a huge library of SQL Server scripts. I think it is the best BackOffice resource there is.

B

Performance Condition Alert Objects

When you're setting up performance condition alerts in DMO or Transact-SQL, you need to know the proper names of the various objects and counters. This table provides a list of each object, counter, and the instances that are available, if any, for each the counter.

Object Name	Counter Name	Instance Name
SQLServer:Buffer Manager	Buffer Cache Hit Ratio	
SQLServer:Buffer Manager	Buffer Cache Hit Ratio Base	
SQLServer:Buffer Manager	Page Requests/sec	
SQLServer:Buffer Manager	ExtendedMem Requests/sec	
SQLServer:Buffer Manager	ExtendedMem Cache Hit Ratio	
SQLServer:Buffer Manager	ExtendedMem Cache Hit Ratio Base	
SQLServer:Buffer Manager	ExtendedMem Cache Migrations/sec	
SQLServer:Buffer Manager	Free Buffers	
SQLServer:Buffer Manager	Committed Pages	
SQLServer:Buffer Manager	Reserved Page Count	
SQLServer:Buffer Manager	Stolen Page Count	
SQLServer:Buffer Manager	Lazy Writes/sec	
SQLServer:Buffer Manager	Readahead Pages/sec	
SQLServer:Buffer Manager	Cache Size (pages)	
SQLServer:Buffer Manager	Page Reads/sec	
SQLServer:Buffer Manager	Page Writes/sec	
SQLServer:Buffer Manager	Checkpoint Writes/sec	
SQLServer:Buffer Manager	Lazy Writer Buffers/sec	
SQLServer:General Statistics	Logins/sec	
SQLServer:General Statistics	Logouts/sec	
SQLServer:General Statistics	User Connections	

continues ▶

Object Name	Counter Name	Instance Name
SQLServer:Locks	Lock Requests/sec	Extent
SQLServer:Locks	Lock Timeouts/sec	Extent
SQLServer:Locks	Number of Deadlocks/sec	Extent
SQLServer:Locks	Lock Waits/sec	Extent
SQLServer:Locks	Lock Wait Time (ms)	Extent
SQLServer:Locks	Average Wait Time (ms)	Extent
SQLServer:Locks	Average Wait Time Base	Extent
SQLServer:Locks	Lock Requests/sec	Key
SQLServer:Locks	Lock Timeouts/sec	Key
SQLServer:Locks	Number of Deadlocks/sec	Key
SQLServer:Locks	Lock Waits/sec	Key
SQLServer:Locks	Lock Wait Time (ms)	Key
SQLServer:Locks	Average Wait Time (ms)	Key
SQLServer:Locks	Average Wait Time Base	Key
SQLServer:Locks	Lock Requests/sec	Page
SQLServer:Locks	Lock Timeouts/sec	Page
SQLServer:Locks	Number of Deadlocks/sec	Page
SQLServer:Locks	Lock Waits/sec	Page
SQLServer:Locks	Lock Wait Time (ms)	Page
SQLServer:Locks	Average Wait Time (ms)	Page
SQLServer:Locks	Average Wait Time Base	Page
SQLServer:Locks	Lock Requests/sec	Table
SQLServer:Locks	Lock Timeouts/sec	Table
SQLServer:Locks	Number of Deadlocks/sec	Table
SQLServer:Locks	Lock Waits/sec	Table
SQLServer:Locks	Lock Wait Time (ms)	Table
SQLServer:Locks	Average Wait Time (ms)	Table
SQLServer:Locks	Average Wait Time Base	Table
SQLServer:Locks	Lock Requests/sec	RID
SQLServer:Locks	Lock Timeouts/sec	RID
SQLServer:Locks	Number of Deadlocks/sec	RID

Object Name	Counter Name	Instance Name
SQLServer:Locks	Lock Waits/sec	RID
SQLServer:Locks	Lock Wait Time (ms)	RID
SQLServer:Locks	Average Wait Time (ms)	RID
SQLServer:Locks	Average Wait Time Base	RID
SQLServer:Locks	Lock Requests/sec	Database
SQLServer:Locks	Lock Timeouts/sec	Database
SQLServer:Locks	Number of Deadlocks/sec	Database
SQLServer:Locks	Lock Waits/sec	Database
SQLServer:Locks	Lock Wait Time (ms)	Database
SQLServer:Locks	Average Wait Time (ms)	Database
SQLServer:Locks	Average Wait Time Base	Database
SQLServer:Databases	Data File(s) Size (KB)	Northwind
SQLServer:Databases	Log File(s) Size (KB)	Northwind
SQLServer:Databases	Percent Log Used	Northwind
SQLServer:Databases	Active Transactions	Northwind
SQLServer:Databases	Transactions/sec	Northwind
SQLServer:Databases	Repl. Pending Xacts	Northwind
SQLServer:Databases	Repl. Trans. Rate	Northwind
SQLServer:Databases	Log Cache Reads/sec	Northwind
SQLServer:Databases	Log Cache Hit Ratio	Northwind
SQLServer:Databases	Log Cache Hit Ratio Base	Northwind
SQLServer:Databases	Bulk Copy Rows/sec	Northwind
SQLServer:Databases	Bulk Copy Throughput/sec	Northwind
SQLServer:Databases	Backup/Restore Throughput/sec	Northwind
SQLServer:Databases	DBCC Logical Scan Bytes/sec	Northwind
SQLServer:Databases	Shrink Data Movement Bytes/sec	Northwind
SQLServer:Databases	Log Flushes/sec	Northwind
SQLServer:Databases	Log Bytes Per Flush	Northwind
SQLServer:Databases	Log Flush Waits/sec	Northwind

continues ▶

Object Name	Counter Name	Instance Name
SQLServer:Databases	Log Flush Wait Time	Northwind
SQLServer:Databases	Log Truncations	Northwind
SQLServer:Databases	Log Growths	Northwind
SQLServer:Databases	Log Shrinks	Northwind
SQLServer:Databases	Data File(s) Size (KB)	backuptest
SQLServer:Databases	Log File(s) Size (KB)	backuptest
SQLServer:Databases	Percent Log Used	backuptest
SQLServer:Databases	Active Transactions	backuptest
SQLServer:Databases	Transactions/sec	backuptest
SQLServer:Databases	Repl. Pending Xacts	backuptest
SQLServer:Databases	Repl. Trans. Rate	backuptest
SQLServer:Databases	Log Cache Reads/sec	backuptest
SQLServer:Databases	Log Cache Hit Ratio	backuptest
SQLServer:Databases	Log Cache Hit Ratio Base	backuptest
SQLServer:Databases	Bulk Copy Rows/sec	backuptest
SQLServer:Databases	Bulk Copy Throughput/sec	backuptest
SQLServer:Databases	Backup/Restore Throughput/sec	backuptest
SQLServer:Databases	DBCC Logical Scan Bytes/sec	backuptest
SQLServer:Databases	Shrink Data Movement Bytes/sec	backuptest
SQLServer:Databases	Log Flushes/sec	backuptest
SQLServer:Databases	Log Bytes Per Flush	backuptest
SQLServer:Databases	Log Flush Waits/sec	backuptest
SQLServer:Databases	Log Flush Wait Time	backuptest
SQLServer:Databases	Log Truncations	backuptest
SQLServer:Databases	Log Growths	backuptest
SQLServer:Databases	Log Shrinks	backuptest
SQLServer:Databases	Data File(s) Size (KB)	ReachConversion
SQLServer:Databases	Log File(s) Size (KB)	ReachConversion
SQLServer:Databases	Percent Log Used	ReachConversion
SQLServer:Databases	Active Transactions	ReachConversion
SQLServer:Databases	Transactions/sec	ReachConversion
SQLServer:Databases	Repl. Pending Xacts	ReachConversion
SQLServer:Databases	Repl. Trans. Rate	ReachConversion

Object Name	Counter Name	Instance Name
SQLServer:Databases	Log Cache Reads/sec	ReachConversion
SQLServer:Databases	Log Cache Hit Ratio	ReachConversion
SQLServer:Databases	Log Cache Hit Ratio Base	ReachConversion
SQLServer:Databases	Bulk Copy Rows/sec	ReachConversion
SQLServer:Databases	Bulk Copy Throughput/sec	ReachConversion
SQLServer:Databases	Backup/Restore Throughput/sec	ReachConversion
SQLServer:Databases	DBCC Logical Scan Bytes/sec	ReachConversion
SQLServer:Databases	Shrink Data Movement Bytes/sec	ReachConversion
SQLServer:Databases	Log Flushes/sec	ReachConversion
SQLServer:Databases	Log Bytes Per Flush	ReachConversion
SQLServer:Databases	Log Flush Waits/sec	ReachConversion
SQLServer:Databases	Log Flush Wait Time	ReachConversion
SQLServer:Databases	Log Truncations	ReachConversion
SQLServer:Databases	Log Growths	ReachConversion
SQLServer:Databases	Log Shrinks	ReachConversion
SQLServer:Databases	Data File(s) Size (KB)	ReachConversionOld
SQLServer:Databases	Log File(s) Size (KB)	ReachConversionOld
SQLServer:Databases	Percent Log Used	ReachConversionOld
SQLServer:Databases	Active Transactions	ReachConversionOld
SQLServer:Databases	Transactions/sec	ReachConversionOld
SQLServer:Databases	Repl. Pending Xacts	ReachConversionOld
SQLServer:Databases	Repl. Trans. Rate	ReachConversionOld
SQLServer:Databases	Log Cache Reads/sec	ReachConversionOld
SQLServer:Databases	Log Cache Hit Ratio	ReachConversionOld
SQLServer:Databases	Log Cache Hit Ratio Base	ReachConversionOld
SQLServer:Databases	Bulk Copy Rows/sec	ReachConversionOld
SQLServer:Databases	Bulk Copy Throughput/sec	ReachConversionOld
SQLServer:Databases	Backup/Restore Throughput/sec	ReachConversionOld

continues ▶

Object Name	Counter Name	Instance Name
SQLServer:Databases	DBCC Logical Scan Bytes/sec	ReachConversionOld
SQLServer:Databases	Shrink Data Movement Bytes/sec	ReachConversionOld
SQLServer:Databases	Log Flushes/sec	ReachConversionOld
SQLServer:Databases	Log Bytes Per Flush	ReachConversionOld
SQLServer:Databases	Log Flush Waits/sec	ReachConversionOld
SQLServer:Databases	Log Flush Wait Time	ReachConversionOld
SQLServer:Databases	Log Truncations	ReachConversionOld
SQLServer:Databases	Log Growths	ReachConversionOld
SQLServer:Databases	Log Shrinks	ReachConversionOld
SQLServer:Databases	Data File(s) Size (KB)	REACH
SQLServer:Databases	Log File(s) Size (KB)	REACH
SQLServer:Databases	Percent Log Used	REACH
SQLServer:Databases	Active Transactions	REACH
SQLServer:Databases	Transactions/sec	REACH
SQLServer:Databases	Repl. Pending Xacts	REACH
SQLServer:Databases	Repl. Trans. Rate	REACH
SQLServer:Databases	Log Cache Reads/sec	REACH
SQLServer:Databases	Log Cache Hit Ratio	REACH
SQLServer:Databases	Log Cache Hit Ratio Base	REACH
SQLServer:Databases	Bulk Copy Rows/sec	REACH
SQLServer:Databases	Bulk Copy Throughput/sec	REACH
SQLServer:Databases	Backup/Restore Throughput/sec	REACH
SQLServer:Databases	DBCC Logical Scan Bytes/sec	REACH
SQLServer:Databases	Shrink Data Movement Bytes/sec	REACH
SQLServer:Databases	Log Flushes/sec	REACH
SQLServer:Databases	Log Bytes Per Flush	REACH
SQLServer:Databases	Log Flush Waits/sec	REACH
SQLServer:Databases	Log Flush Wait Time	REACH
SQLServer:Databases	Log Truncations	REACH

Object Name	Counter Name	Instance Name
SQLServer:Databases	Log Growths	REACH
SQLServer:Databases	Log Shrinks	REACH
SQLServer:Databases	Data File(s) Size (KB)	REACHjoe
SQLServer:Databases	Log File(s) Size (KB)	REACHjoe
SQLServer:Databases	Percent Log Used	REACHjoe
SQLServer:Databases	Active Transactions	REACHjoe
SQLServer:Databases	Transactions/sec	REACHjoe
SQLServer:Databases	Repl. Pending Xacts	REACHjoe
SQLServer:Databases	Repl. Trans. Rate	REACHjoe
SQLServer:Databases	Log Cache Reads/sec	REACHjoe
SQLServer:Databases	Log Cache Hit Ratio	REACHjoe
SQLServer:Databases	Log Cache Hit Ratio Base	REACHjoe
SQLServer:Databases	Bulk Copy Rows/sec	REACHjoe
SQLServer:Databases	Bulk Copy Throughput/sec	REACHjoe
SQLServer:Databases	Backup/Restore Throughput/sec	REACHjoe
SQLServer:Databases	DBCC Logical Scan Bytes/sec	REACHjoe
SQLServer:Databases	Shrink Data Movement Bytes/sec	REACHjoe
SQLServer:Databases	Log Flushes/sec	REACHjoe
SQLServer:Databases	Log Bytes Per Flush	REACHjoe
SQLServer:Databases	Log Flush Waits/sec	REACHjoe
SQLServer:Databases	Log Flush Wait Time	REACHjoe
SQLServer:Databases	Log Truncations	REACHjoe
SQLServer:Databases	Log Growths	REACHjoe
SQLServer:Databases	Log Shrinks	REACHjoe
SQLServer:Databases	Data File(s) Size (KB)	CodeTableWork
SQLServer:Databases	Log File(s) Size (KB)	CodeTableWork
SQLServer:Databases	Percent Log Used	CodeTableWork
SQLServer:Databases	Active Transactions	CodeTableWork
SQLServer:Databases	Transactions/sec	CodeTableWork
SQLServer:Databases	Repl. Pending Xacts	CodeTableWork
SQLServer:Databases	Repl. Trans. Rate	CodeTableWork
SQLServer:Databases	Log Cache Reads/sec	CodeTableWork

continues ▶

Object Name	Counter Name	Instance Name
SQLServer:Databases	Log Cache Hit Ratio	CodeTableWork
SQLServer:Databases	Log Cache Hit Ratio Base	CodeTableWork
SQLServer:Databases	Bulk Copy Rows/sec	CodeTableWork
SQLServer:Databases	Bulk Copy Throughput/sec	CodeTableWork
SQLServer:Databases	Backup/Restore Throughput/sec	CodeTableWork
SQLServer:Databases	DBCC Logical Scan Bytes/sec	CodeTableWork
SQLServer:Databases	Shrink Data Movement Bytes/sec	CodeTableWork
SQLServer:Databases	Log Flushes/sec	CodeTableWork
SQLServer:Databases	Log Bytes Per Flush	CodeTableWork
SQLServer:Databases	Log Flush Waits/sec	CodeTableWork
SQLServer:Databases	Log Flush Wait Time	CodeTableWork
SQLServer:Databases	Log Truncations	CodeTableWork
SQLServer:Databases	Log Growths	CodeTableWork
SQLServer:Databases	Log Shrinks	CodeTableWork
SQLServer:Databases	Data File(s) Size (KB)	REACHsfd
SQLServer:Databases	Log File(s) Size (KB)	REACHsfd
SQLServer:Databases	Percent Log Used	REACHsfd
SQLServer:Databases	Active Transactions	REACHsfd
SQLServer:Databases	Transactions/sec	REACHsfd
SQLServer:Databases	Repl. Pending Xacts	REACHsfd
SQLServer:Databases	Repl. Trans. Rate	REACHsfd
SQLServer:Databases	Log Cache Reads/sec	REACHsfd
SQLServer:Databases	Log Cache Hit Ratio	REACHsfd
SQLServer:Databases	Log Cache Hit Ratio Base	REACHsfd
SQLServer:Databases	Bulk Copy Rows/sec	REACHsfd
SQLServer:Databases	Bulk Copy Throughput/sec	REACHsfd
SQLServer:Databases	Backup/Restore Throughput/sec	REACHsfd
SQLServer:Databases	DBCC Logical Scan Bytes/sec	REACHsfd
SQLServer:Databases	Shrink Data Movement Bytes/sec	REACHsfd
SQLServer:Databases	Log Flushes/sec	REACHsfd

Object Name	Counter Name	Instance Name
SQLServer:Databases	Log Bytes Per Flush	REACHsfd
SQLServer:Databases	Log Flush Waits/sec	REACHsfd
SQLServer:Databases	Log Flush Wait Time	REACHsfd
SQLServer:Databases	Log Truncations	REACHsfd
SQLServer:Databases	Log Growths	REACHsfd
SQLServer:Databases	Log Shrinks	REACHsfd
SQLServer:Databases	Data File(s) Size (KB)	msdb
SQLServer:Databases	Log File(s) Size (KB)	msdb
SQLServer:Databases	Percent Log Used	msdb
SQLServer:Databases	Active Transactions	msdb
SQLServer:Databases	Transactions/sec	msdb
SQLServer:Databases	Repl. Pending Xacts	msdb
SQLServer:Databases	Repl. Trans. Rate	msdb
SQLServer:Databases	Log Cache Reads/sec	msdb
SQLServer:Databases	Log Cache Hit Ratio	msdb
SQLServer:Databases	Log Cache Hit Ratio Base	msdb
SQLServer:Databases	Bulk Copy Rows/sec	msdb
SQLServer:Databases	Bulk Copy Throughput/sec	v
SQLServer:Databases	Backup/Restore Throughput/sec	msdb
SQLServer:Databases	DBCC Logical Scan Bytes/sec	msdb
SQLServer:Databases	Shrink Data Movement Bytes/sec	msdb
SQLServer:Databases	Log Flushes/sec	msdb
SQLServer:Databases	Log Bytes Per Flush	msdb
SQLServer:Databases	Log Flush Waits/sec	msdb
SQLServer:Databases	Log Flush Wait Time	msdb
SQLServer:Databases	Log Truncations	msdb
SQLServer:Databases	Log Growths	msdb
SQLServer:Databases	Log Shrinks	msdb
SQLServer:Databases	Data File(s) Size (KB)	pubs
SQLServer:Databases	Log File(s) Size (KB)	pubs
SQLServer:Databases	Percent Log Used	pubs
SQLServer:Databases	Active Transactions	pubs

continues ▶

Object Name	Counter Name	Instance Name
SQLServer:Databases	Transactions/sec	pubs
SQLServer:Databases	Repl. Pending Xacts	pubs
SQLServer:Databases	Repl. Trans. Rate	pubs
SQLServer:Databases	Log Cache Reads/sec	pubs
SQLServer:Databases	Log Cache Hit Ratio	pubs
SQLServer:Databases	Log Cache Hit Ratio Base	pubs
SQLServer:Databases	Bulk Copy Rows/sec	pubs
SQLServer:Databases	Bulk Copy Throughput/sec	pubs
SQLServer:Databases	Backup/Restore Throughput/sec	pubs
SQLServer:Databases	DBCC Logical Scan Bytes/sec	pubs
SQLServer:Databases	Shrink Data Movement Bytes/sec	pubs
SQLServer:Databases	Log Flushes/sec	pubs
SQLServer:Databases	Log Bytes Per Flush	pubs
SQLServer:Databases	Log Flush Waits/sec	pubs
SQLServer:Databases	Log Flush Wait Time	pubs
SQLServer:Databases	Log Truncations	pubs
SQLServer:Databases	Log Growths	pubs
SQLServer:Databases	Log Shrinks	pubs
SQLServer:Databases	Data File(s) Size (KB)	tempdb
SQLServer:Databases	Log File(s) Size (KB)	tempdb
SQLServer:Databases	Percent Log Used	tempdb
SQLServer:Databases	Active Transactions	tempdb
SQLServer:Databases	Transactions/sec	tempdb
SQLServer:Databases	Repl. Pending Xacts	tempdb
SQLServer:Databases	Repl. Trans. Rate	tempdb
SQLServer:Databases	Log Cache Reads/sec	tempdb
SQLServer:Databases	Log Cache Hit Ratio	tempdb
SQLServer:Databases	Log Cache Hit Ratio Base	tempdb
SQLServer:Databases	Bulk Copy Rows/sec	tempdb
SQLServer:Databases	Bulk Copy Throughput/sec	tempdb
SQLServer:Databases	Backup/Restore Throughput/sec	tempdb

Object Name	Counter Name	Instance Name
SQLServer:Databases	DBCC Logical Scan Bytes/sec	tempdb
SQLServer:Databases	Shrink Data Movement Bytes/sec	tempdb
SQLServer:Databases	Log Flushes/sec	tempdb
SQLServer:Databases	Log Bytes Per Flush	tempdb
SQLServer:Databases	Log Flush Waits/sec	tempdb
SQLServer:Databases	Log Flush Wait Time	tempdb
SQLServer:Databases	Log Truncations	tempdb
SQLServer:Databases	Log Growths	tempdb
SQLServer:Databases	Log Shrinks	tempdb
SQLServer:Databases	Data File(s) Size (KB)	model
SQLServer:Databases	Log File(s) Size (KB)	model
SQLServer:Databases	Percent Log Used	model
SQLServer:Databases	Active Transactions	model
SQLServer:Databases	Transactions/sec	model
SQLServer:Databases	Repl. Pending Xacts	model
SQLServer:Databases	Repl. Trans. Rate	model
SQLServer:Databases	Log Cache Reads/sec	model
SQLServer:Databases	Log Cache Hit Ratio	model
SQLServer:Databases	Log Cache Hit Ratio Base	model
SQLServer:Databases	Bulk Copy Rows/sec	model
SQLServer:Databases	Bulk Copy Throughput/sec	model
SQLServer:Databases	Backup/Restore Throughput/sec	model
SQLServer:Databases	DBCC Logical Scan Bytes/sec	model
SQLServer:Databases	Shrink Data Movement Bytes/sec	model
SQLServer:Databases	Log Flushes/sec	model
SQLServer:Databases	Log Bytes Per Flush	model
SQLServer:Databases	Log Flush Waits/sec	model
SQLServer:Databases	Log Flush Wait Time	model
SQLServer:Databases	Log Truncations	model
SQLServer:Databases	Log Growths	model
SQLServer:Databases	Log Shrinks	model

continues ▶

Object Name	Counter Name	Instance Name
SQLServer:Databases	Data File(s) Size (KB)	master
SQLServer:Databases	Log File(s) Size (KB)	master
SQLServer:Databases	Percent Log Used	master
SQLServer:Databases	Active Transactions	master
SQLServer:Databases	Transactions/sec	master
SQLServer:Databases	Repl. Pending Xacts	master
SQLServer:Databases	Repl. Trans. Rate	master
SQLServer:Databases	Log Cache Reads/sec	master
SQLServer:Databases	Log Cache Hit Ratio	master
SQLServer:Databases	Log Cache Hit Ratio Base	master
SQLServer:Databases	Bulk Copy Rows/sec	master
SQLServer:Databases	Bulk Copy Throughput/sec	master
SQLServer:Databases	Backup/Restore Throughput/sec	master
SQLServer:Databases	DBCC Logical Scan Bytes/sec	master
SQLServer:Databases	Shrink Data Movement Bytes/sec	master
SQLServer:Databases	Log Flushes/sec	master
SQLServer:Databases	Log Bytes Per Flush	master
SQLServer:Databases	Log Flush Waits/sec	master
SQLServer:Databases	Log Flush Wait Time	master
SQLServer:Databases	Log Truncations	master
SQLServer:Databases	Log Growths	master
SQLServer:Databases	Log Shrinks	master
SQLServer:Latches	Latch Waits/sec	
SQLServer:Latches	Average Latch Wait Time (ms)	
SQLServer:Latches	Average Latch Wait Time Base	
SQLServer:Latches	Total Latch Wait Time (ms)	
SQLServer:Access Methods	Full Scans/sec	
SQLServer:Access Methods	Range Scans/sec	
SQLServer:Access Methods	Probe Scans/sec	
SQLServer:Access Methods	Scan Point Revalidations/sec	

Object Name	Counter Name	Instance Name
SQLServer:Access Methods	Workfiles Created/sec	
SQLServer:Access Methods	Worktables Created/sec	
SQLServer:Access Methods	Worktables From Cache Ratio	
SQLServer:Access Methods	Worktables From Cache Base	
SQLServer:Access Methods	Forwarded Records/sec	
SQLServer:Access Methods	Skipped Ghosted Records/sec	
SQLServer:Access Methods	Index Searches/sec	
SQLServer:Access Methods	FreeSpace Scans/sec	
SQLServer:Access Methods	FreeSpace Page Fetches/sec	
SQLServer:Access Methods	Pages Allocated/sec	
SQLServer:Access Methods	Extents Allocated/sec	
SQLServer:Access Methods	Mixed Page Allocations/sec	
SQLServer:Access Methods	Extent Deallocations/sec	
SQLServer:Access Methods	Page Deallocations/sec	
SQLServer:Access Methods	Page Splits/sec	
SQLServer:Access Methods	Table Lock Escalations/sec	
SQLServer:SQL Statistics	Batch Requests/sec	
SQLServer:SQL Statistics	Auto-Param Attempts/sec	
SQLServer:SQL Statistics	Failed Auto-Params/sec	
SQLServer:SQL Statistics	Safe Auto-Params/sec	
SQLServer:SQL Statistics	Unsafe Auto-Params/sec	
SQLServer:SQL Statistics	SQL Compilations/sec	
SQLServer:SQL Statistics	SQL Re-Compilations/sec	
SQLServer:Cache Manager	Cache Hit Ratio	Misc. Normalized Trees
SQLServer:Cache Manager	Cache Hit Ratio Base	Misc. Normalized Trees
SQLServer:Cache Manager	Cache Pages	Misc. Normalized Trees

continues ▶

Object Name	Counter Name	Instance Name
SQLServer:Cache Manager	Cache Object Counts	Misc. Normalized Trees
SQLServer:Cache Manager	Cache Use Counts/sec	Misc. Normalized Trees
SQLServer:Cache Manager	Cache Hit Ratio	Trigger Plans
SQLServer:Cache Manager	Cache Hit Ratio Base	Trigger Plans
SQLServer:Cache Manager	Cache Pages	Trigger Plans
SQLServer:Cache Manager	Cache Object Counts	Trigger Plans
SQLServer:Cache Manager	Cache Use Counts/sec	Trigger Plans
SQLServer:Cache Manager	Cache Hit Ratio	Replication Procedure Plans
SQLServer:Cache Manager	Cache Hit Ratio Base	Replication Procedure Plans
SQLServer:Cache Manager	Cache Pages	Replication Procedure Plans
SQLServer:Cache Manager	Cache Object Counts	Replication Procedure Plans
SQLServer:Cache Manager	Cache Use Counts/sec	Replication Procedure Plans
SQLServer:Cache Manager	Cache Hit Ratio	Adhoc Sql Plans
SQLServer:Cache Manager	Cache Hit Ratio Base	Adhoc Sql Plans
SQLServer:Cache Manager	Cache Pages	Adhoc Sql Plans
SQLServer:Cache Manager	Cache Object Counts	Adhoc Sql Plans
SQLServer:Cache Manager	Cache Use Counts/sec	Adhoc Sql Plans
SQLServer:Cache Manager	Cache Hit Ratio	Prepared Sql Plans
SQLServer:Cache Manager	Cache Hit Ratio Base	Prepared Sql Plans
SQLServer:Cache Manager	Cache Pages	Prepared Sql Plans
SQLServer:Cache Manager	Cache Object Counts	Prepared Sql Plans
SQLServer:Cache Manager	Cache Use Counts/sec	Prepared Sql Plans
SQLServer:Cache Manager	Cache Hit Ratio	Procedure Plans
SQLServer:Cache Manager	Cache Hit Ratio Base	Procedure Plans
SQLServer:Cache Manager	Cache Pages	Procedure Plans
SQLServer:Cache Manager	Cache Object Counts	Procedure Plans
SQLServer:Cache Manager	Cache Use Counts/sec	Procedure Plans
SQLServer:Memory Manager	Connection Memory (KB)	

Object Name	Counter Name	Instance Name
SQLServer:Memory Manager	Granted Workspace Memory (KB)	
SQLServer:Memory Manager	Lock Memory (KB)	
SQLServer:Memory Manager	Lock Blocks Allocated	
SQLServer:Memory Manager	Lock Owner Blocks Allocated	
SQLServer:Memory Manager	Lock Blocks	
SQLServer:Memory Manager	Lock Owner Blocks	
SQLServer:Memory Manager	Maximum Workspace Memory (KB)	
SQLServer:Memory Manager	Memory Grants Outstanding	
SQLServer:Memory Manager	Memory Grants Pending	
SQLServer:Memory Manager	Optimizer Memory (KB)	
SQLServer:Memory Manager	SQL Cache Memory (KB)	
SQLServer:Memory Manager	Target Server Memory(KB)	
SQLServer:Memory Manager	Total Server Memory (KB)	
SQLServer:User Settable	Query	User counter 10
SQLServer:User Settable	Query	User counter 9
SQLServer:User Settable	Query	User counter 8
SQLServer:User Settable	Query	User counter 7
SQLServer:User Settable	Query	User counter 6
SQLServer:User Settable	Query	User counter 5
SQLServer:User Settable	Query	User counter 4
SQLServer:User Settable	Query	User counter 3
SQLServer:User Settable	Query	User counter 2
SQLServer:User Settable	Query	User counter 1

C

Glossary

You should find the following terms useful to your study of SQL Server.

alerts   Alerts notify you when something happens, and they can execute jobs, perhaps to take corrective action. Alerts are triggered by a SQL Server error message recorded in the Windows NT Application event log or a performance condition.

cascading deletions   Deletions (and primary key updates) are said to cascade when deleting a parent also deletes any children of that parent. For example, a cascaded delete on the Department table would also delete any Employee records for that department. With a NULLIFY rule, if the parent is deleted or the parent primary key is changed, the foreign key reference in the child will be set to null.

check constraints   Check constraints are used to limit the values in a column to a specific set of values.

checkpoint   The checkpoint thread is responsible for the following: writing changed data pages to the database; recording a list of active transactions in the log; recording a list of dirty (changed) pages in the log; and, marking where recovery should begin when the server is restarted.

clustered indexes, see indexes.

constraints   Constraints (also called *Declarative Referential Integrity*, or (DRI) were introduced in SQL Server 6.0. Constraints are used to make sure that data in a database is correct. There are various types of constraints, including primary key constraints, unique, and foreign key.

datatypes   A datatype defines the type of values that can be placed in a column. For example, columns of datatype char can hold character strings, whereas columns of datatype int (integer) can hold only whole numbers.

default constraints   Default constraints specify a value that will be used if the value isn't provided when a row is added to a database.

file groups   These are named collections of files.

foreign key constraints   Foreign key constraints are used to enforce relationships between tables. Assume, for example, that we have a Department table and an Employee table. The Employee table contains the department number for each employee. A foreign key constraint would require that every department number in the Employee table match a department number in the Department table. SQL Server implements only a subset of the ANSI standard for foreign key constraints. It supports a RESTRICT rule for delete and update, but does not support CASCADE or NULLIFY.

indexes   Indexes are used to enforce uniqueness. (Both primary key and unique constraints automatically create indexes.) But the major purpose for indexes is to allow data to be retrieved quickly. SQL Server has two types of indexes. Clustered indexes sort the data in order on the clustering key. Non-clustered indexes sort the keys in order on the key, but the data is not in the same order as the index. A table may have only one clustered index; it can have many non-clustered indexes.

jobs   A job is a step or set of steps that runs on a schedule. A job may consist of several steps, and you can define conditional execution of the steps.

Log Sequence Number (LSN)   Each record in the transaction log is identified with a number called the Log Sequence Number.

master database   The master database contains tables that describe all other databases on the server, logins, running process and configuration settings. It is the most important database; SQL Server will not start if master is damaged or destroyed.

model database   The model database acts as a source for all new databases that are created. It contains tables common to every database.

msdb database   This database is used by the SQL Server Agent. It contains tables describing scheduled jobs, alerts, notifications, and replication setups. Backup and job histories are also stored here. If you store DTS packages in SQL Server, they are also stored in msdb.

non-clustered indexes   See *indexes*.

nullability   Nullability tells whether a column in a table allows NULL values. NULL is a special database value that means "missing" or "not known." It's not the same as an empty string, a blank, or a zero.

objects   A SQL Server database contains many *objects*. The term object doesn't have anything to do with object-oriented databases. Instead, it just means "stuff" in the database. There are a variety of objects in most SQL Server databases. Tables and datatypes are examples of objects found in databases.

primary key constraints   Primary key constraints define a column or set of columns that uniquely identify each row of a table. None of the columns of a primary key may allow nulls. A table can have only one primary key constraint.

scripts   A script is an ASCII file containing Transact-SQL statements. It can be run with Query Analyzer, isql, or osql.

stored procedures   A stored procedure is a program written in Transact-SQL. Procedures are reusable objects that are stored in SQL Server databases and execute on the server.

system tables   See *tables*.

tables   Tables are one type of object found in databases. A table is a named set of rows and columns. In SQL Server, there are two types of tables: system tables and user tables. User tables are the ones that support applications, such as an Employee table. System tables are used by SQL Server to manage its operations.

tempdb database   This is a scratch pad database used by everyone. For example, tempdb provides workspace for sorting data. Objects created in tempdb are transient; they die when the user who created them disconnects from SQL Server.

transaction   A logical unit of work, also called a *transaction*, is a set of related database modifications with the requirement that if one of them fails, none of the related changes will be made.

triggers   Triggers are a special kind of stored procedure. Triggers are tied to insert, update, and delete operations on tables. They happen as part of the operation without requiring the user to take any special action, or even be aware of their existence.

unique constraints   Unique constraints require that all the values in a column or set of columns be unique. There can be many unique constraints on a table.

user tables   See *tables*.

views   A view is a stored SQL SELECT statement that serves as a virtual table. It can be used just about anywhere that a table can be used. It is possible to update data through some views. Only the definition of a view is stored in a database. The data is retrieved only when someone uses the view.

write-ahead log   SQL Server's transaction log is a write-ahead log. As data is read, it is kept in memory. When data is modified, information about the modifications is written to the log but not necessarily to the database itself.

Index

Windows 2000 Answers

This is the updated edition of New Riders' best-selling *Inside Windows NT Server 4*. New Riders proudly offers something unique for Windows 2000 administrators—an interesting and discriminating book on Windows 2000 Server, written by someone in the trenches who can anticipate your situation and provide answers you can trust.

INSIDE
Windows 2000
Server

ISBN: 1-56205-929-7

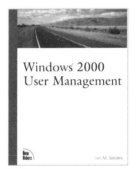

Windows 2000
User Management

ISBN: 0-56205-886-X

Managing the user and the user's desktop environment is a critical component in administering Windows 2000. *Windows 2000 User Management* provides you with the real-world tips and examples you need to get the job done.

Windows 2000 Active Directory is just one of several new Windows 2000 titles from New Riders' acclaimed *Landmark Series*. Perfect for network architects and administrators, this book describes the intricacies of Active Directory to help you plan, deploy, and manage Active Directory in an enterprise setting.

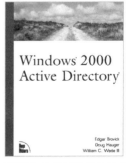

Windows 2000
Active Directory

ISBN: 0-7357-0870-3

Advanced Information on Networking Technologies

New Riders Books Offer Advice and Experience

LANDMARK
Rethinking Computer Books

We know how important it is to have access to detailed, solution-oriented information on core technologies. *Landmark Series* books contain the essential information you need to solve technical problems. Written by experts and subjected to rigorous peer and technical reviews, our *Landmark* books are hard-core resources for practitioners like you.

ESSENTIAL REFERENCE
Smart, Like You

The *Essential Reference* series from New Riders provides answers when you know what you want to do but need to know how to do it. Each title skips extraneous material and assumes a strong base of knowledge. These are indispensable books for the practitioner who wants to find specific features of a technology quickly. Avoiding fluff and basic material, these books present solutions in an innovative, clean format—and at a great value.

MCSE CERTIFICATION
Engineered for Test Success

New Riders offer a complete line of test preparation materials to help you achieve your certification. With books like the *MCSE Training Guide*, and software like the acclaimed *MCSE Complete* and the revolutionary *ExamGear*, New Riders offers comprehensive products built by experienced professionals who have passed the exams and instructed hundreds of candidates.

'her Titles of Interest from New Riders...

Windows 2000 Professional
By Jerry Honeycutt
1st Edition, April 2000
450 pages, $49.99
ISBN: 0-7357-0950-0

MCSE Training Guide: Windows 2000 Professional (70-210)
By Gordon Barker
1st Edition, June 2000
ISBN: 0-7357-0965-3

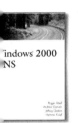

Windows 2000 DNS
By Roger Abell,
Herman Knief,
Andrew Daniels,
and Jeffrey A. Graham
2nd Edition
500 pages, $39.99
ISBN: 0-7357-0973-4

MCSE Training Guide: Windows 2000 Server (70-215)
By Dennis Maione
1st Edition, June 2000
ISBN: 0-7357-0968-8

Windows 2000 Deployment and Desktop Management
By Jeffrey Ferris
1st Edition
400 pages, $34.99
ISBN: 0-7357-0975-0

MCSE Training Guide: Windows 2000 Network Security Design (70-220)
By Roberta Bragg
1st Edition, July 2000
ISBN: 0-7257-0984-X

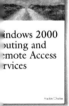

Windows 2000 Routing and Remote Access Service
By Kackie Charles
1st Edition
400 pages, $34.99
ISBN: 0-7357-0951-3

MCSE Training Guide: Windows 2000 Network Infrastructure Design (70-221)
By Dale Holmes and
Bill Matsoukas
1st Edition, July 2000
ISBN: 0-7357-0982-3

Windows 2000 Thin Client Solutions
By Todd Mathers
2nd Edition, June 2000
600 pages, $45.00
ISBN: 1-57870-239-9

MCSE Training Guide: Installing and Administering a Windows 2000 Directory (70-217)
By Damir Bersinic and
Rob Scrimger
1st Edition, July 2000
ISBN: 0-7357-0976-9